Pure Truth

from

God

TONY COOPER

FRONT COVER DESIGN

The front cover design was given to me by the Holy Spirit and it is representative of:

"And the light shineth in darkness, and the darkness comprehend it not".
The Yellow is representative of the all enveloping Yellow light that I experienced whilst in heaven.
The Shield is the Shield of Faith *"Wherewith ye shall be able to quench all the fiery darts of the wicked".*
Red is the blood of our Lord Jesus Christ shed for us.
The Sword is the *"Sword of the Spirit, which is the Word of God"*

Tony Cooper

PURETRUTHMINISTRY.COM

California U.S.A.

No part of this book may be reproduced or transmitted in any form or by any means, electronic or mechanical, including photocopying, recording, or by means of any information storage and retrieval system, without permission in writing from Tony Cooper or www.puretruthministry.com

CONTENTS

DEDICATIONS...5

FOREWORD...6

PREFACE...9

SIGNS AND WONDERS...17

WHAT AM I ?...26

WHY SHOULD I BELIEVE THE HOLY BIBLE ?......75

WHY AM I HERE ? WHAT IS THE REASON FOR
MY BEING ?...96

FIRST MAN - THE TRUTH.....................................147

SECOND MAN - THE TRUTH...............................180

THIRD MAN - THE TRUTH.....................................199

A SUMMARY OF CREATION................................225

GENESIS CHAPTERS 1 to 5 - A SLIGHTLY
DIFFERENT VERSION...241

THE MISSING LINK - A CHALLENGE FOR
HUMANKIND...259

END OF THE WORLD ?.......................................263

MY PERSONAL PRAYER.....................................280

REFERENCES...291

This book is dedicated to

My wife Marianne.
Without your love, belief and self-sacrifice this book may never have been written. You have been prepared to suffer financially to give me the greatest gift. That gift was to give me year upon year of time to spend with my Lord and Savior in prayer and in His word. I will be forever grateful and this book will stand as a testament to your sacrifice and your belief. A belief that was resolute despite a continual buffeting by the evil one.

Margaret Cooper.
Despite tremendous spiritual opposition you remained steadfast and led me to the Lord. The best advice I was ever given came from you. Never look to man, he will always let you down. Look only to the Lord Jesus, He will never let you down.

Alice Swan.
To the world you were a "person of no importance" who neither heard nor spoke. Praise be to the Lord God Almighty that He ALWAYS uses "persons of no importance".

Philip Lawton.
Rarely a day goes by that I don't remember the 27 June 1960. So very easily could I have worn your shoes on that day. God bless you my dear, dear friend. I look forward to the day when we will be together again to finish that game of soccer that we never even started.

Foreword

This book answers the most important question that has ever been asked by humankind, "Why should I believe in God as the Creator of all things, when His Holy Bible chronologically dates the creation of this earth and everything in it at only about six or seven thousand years ago?"

This is at the fundamental heart of Christianity and yet for almost two thousand years, we have not been able to answer this question.
Christians maintain that the Holy Bible is the inerrant, infallible and inspired word of God given to humankind for their salvation. Yet, from this Holy book and God's words, they have not been able to answer the question that is vital to the life and death of humankind.
If you want to live eternally, as you were originally created to do, then believe what you are about to read. These words are not those of my husband, he is merely the messenger. These are the **PURE TRUTH** words from God Himself.

When Tony asked me to write a brief foreword to this book, I sought the Lord for His guidance and His words. He immediately brought this passage to me as I was turning the pages of the New Testament and my eyes fell upon this verse:
Luke 10:21 *At that time Jesus, full of joy through the Holy Spirit said, " I praise you, Father, Lord of heaven and earth, because you have hidden these things from the wise and learned, and revealed them to little children. Yes, Father, for this was your good pleasure.*

This book contains the greatest revelations and understanding on creation, Christianity and our path to sanctification that only can come from our Heavenly Father through the Holy Spirit. You will read that creation (as written in Scripture), and science are more closely related than what is understood by both the church and the scientific community. I'm here to testify that this did not come from "man's" understanding, but came from the revelations and guidance of the Holy Spirit.

Also, as a special gift from the Holy Spirit, is what I refer to as the blueprint to Christianity. This book removes the shroud of misunderstanding that runs rampant in our church today. Very often, Christianity and religion are considered synonymous, but many are disappointed by what they see and hear as "religion." One requires submission to God's will and the other is usually run by man's will.

We will also be told the special role we have in God's purpose for us by answering the question, "Why are we here?" All of this has been written with such Truth, clarity and understanding that can only come from our Lord God because he has **NEVER** been the god of confusion or secrecy.

We know that our Heavenly Father, as the creator of all things, can move heaven and earth. So bringing the revelations in The **Pure Truth from God** to a man who only strives to be an obedient Christian should be no surprise. In fact, the key may lie in his obedience to our Heavenly Father! In turn, the Holy Spirit has given Tony an understanding of Scripture that transcends man's understanding. What you are about to read is not the result of man's intellectual attempts at understanding scripture. There are many books that try, but the results are always the same....man's will and not Gods! The **Pure Truth**

7

from God comes from *the Comforter, the Holy Spirit, whom the Father will send in my name, he shall teach you all things* (John 14:26). It comes from His knowledge, wisdom, understanding and most importantly it comes only from the will of God!

So, I end this foreword as I began with the same book and chapter, because this book is His gift to you:
Luke 10:23-24: *Then He turned to His disciples and said privately, "Blessed are the eyes that see what you see. For I tell you that many prophets and kings wanted to see what you see but did not see it, and to hear what you hear but did not here it".*

May God Bless and keep you through our Dear Lord and Savior Jesus Christ.

Marianne Cooper

Preface

If you are expecting a literary masterpiece then accept my apologies now. If you hope to read the **PURE TRUTH**, then you are in the right place. I am not a writer, I have merely written in the best way I could that which the Lord God shared with me.

C.L. Parker once wrote:- "The bible was written, not for great intellects, but for simple babes. Its' truths are so obvious that to deny them is the greatest crime, worthy of death, and impatient of any defense. "He that believeth not shall be damned" Mark 16:16, "that they all might be damned who believeth not the truth" 2nd Thessalonians 2:11/12. It is the things that worldly men believe, such as Mohammedanism or Evolution or Christian Science, that have to be believed against the evidence and the plain dictates of common sense, in which clever but wicked men have to think up every conceivable kind of argument that can serve to bolster up a bad case.
On the contrary the wisdom of God is so plain that John was able to write it in words of one syllable; while the wisdom of men invariably requires a particular sort of jargon that only the initiated can understand, correct thinking dresses itself in homespun; it is foolishness and muddle-headedness that requires verbal thrills and furbelows if it is to be acceptable. God is angry with men not just for evil living, but also for devious thinking wherewith to defend it, so that in the end their minds are permanently damaged and unable to think straight at all. "And even as they did not like to retain God in their knowledge, God gave them over to a reprobate mind". "The murder of the intelligence is as grave a crime as the

searing of the conscience, and truth is the seed plot of morality".

Almost every Christian religious sect very clearly states as one of their key Doctrines of Faith and Beliefs that, "The Holy Bible is the infallible and inerrant Word of God". In other words it is perfect, final and complete. It never is to be changed or altered in any way, it is to be believed as it is. I only pray that every Christian reading this book holds fast to that doctrine, regrettably God told me that it would be different. God told me that it wouldn't be non-believers who would question and try to debase that which is about to be written. Despite all of their proclamations, it would be Christians themselves.

In 1964, two years before he died in 1966, David J. Gibson, the great Old Testament scholar wrote in his book, "The Land of Eden Located":
"Chronology is the science of establishing the correct sequence of events and ascertaining the lapse of time from one event to another, in short, the setting of dates. The Bible is a unique book in that it is the only complete one preserved out of the past which gives a continuous, connected story from the first man down to the Greek era of history. Consequently, many have used the Bible as a basis upon which to construct a chronological system reaching back to set a date for the Advent of Man upon earth. However, the results have not been unanimous or conclusive. There are points of divergence of opinion, such as the duration of the Period of the Judges in Israel, and the length of sojourn of the Children of Israel in Egypt. But these divergences dwindle to insignificance when compared with the enormous difference between the date for the first appearance of man in biblically based chronologies, and the dates given by geologists. The date

for Adam is given by one as about 4,000 B.C.; or perhaps 5,000 or even 6,000 B.C. while the geologist puts the advent of man perhaps one million years ago. Is there any hope at all of this fantastic gulf of difference being satisfactorily bridged? In our present state of knowledge possibly, No; but we believe the difference will some day vanish. Let us be patient, for in time the **real truth** will be manifested"............................

This book rewrites centuries of Darwinian thoughts about the evolution of humankind. It also answers questions that the Christian church has been unable to answer concerning the creation of our human race as we know it. If you ever questioned where you came from and why you are here, this book will give you those answers. The answers will not come from myself, they will come from God Himself.

God told me,
"The vision is yet for an appointed time, but at the end it shall speak, and not lie: though it tarry, wait for it, because it will surely come, it will not tarry".
Habakkuk 2:3

And,
"In the third year of Cyrus king of Persia a thing was revealed unto Daniel, whose name was called Belteshazzar; and the thing was true, but the time appointed was long: and he understood the thing, and had understanding of the vision".
Daniel 10:1

And,
"For the prophesy came not in old time by the will of man: but holy men of God spake as they were moved by the Holy Ghost".

2nd Peter 1:21

Then God said to me,
"But the hour cometh and now is, when true worshipers shall worship the Father in spirit and in truth; for the Father seeketh such to worship Him. God is a Spirit: and they that worship Him must worship Him in spirit and in truth."
John 4:23/24

I have waited on God for years, but the appointed time has now come. Margaret Cooper (no relation) and my wife Marianne will both testify to this truth. I have wanted to share this truth with the world for year upon year, but God told me to wait. The time appointed was long, but the waiting is now over. The **PURE TRUTH** that God shared with me is here. I pray with all of my heart that at the end of this book, every reader will accept and acknowledge Jesus Christ to be the Son of God, and the Savior of humankind. One thing is certain, never again will there be any belief in a Big Bang theory or that humans evolved from Apes. Never again will anyone doubt, that Almighty God **IS THE CREATOR OF ALL THINGS.**

For centuries, the God of Abraham, Isaac and Jacob, has been ridiculed by people, evolutionists, archaeologists and scientists who said that He was not the creator of the universe and everything in it. They calculated that Adam only arrived on this earth about 6-7000 years ago, because chronologically that is how the bible dates him. Yet, we all know that fossils and artifacts have been discovered and carbon dated to confirm the existence of humankind for hundreds of thousands of years before this.
Since Darwin published his Theory of Evolution in 1859, even the Catholic Church in Rome has struggled to fully

support the truth of God being the creator of all things. Rather than battle to stand firm on God's word, numerous theologians have acquiesced and lessened the importance of the book of Genesis to better align themselves with the evolutionist view or the intelligent design view. In their own minds, a battle against the scientists was a battle they could not win. This conundrum made it very easy for Satan to persuade people not to believe in God as the creator of all things and to ridicule Christians. This book will convince even the most hardened Darwinian scientist or archaeologist to believe in God as **THE** creator of **ALL** things.

In addition, it will provide answers to very basic yet profound questions. Questions that have been asked by humankind for centuries yet never answered until now. On the 27 June 1960, I died and was taken into the presence of God. By God's grace He returned me into my earthly body and gave me life. This experience to any other person would have been enough to commit them to God for life. Regrettably, for me it changed nothing. Throughout the whole of my life the last thing I ever wanted to be was a Christian. Never ever did I want to associate with "churchy" type people. Thank God that He had other plans.

In the summer of 1987, and in total despair I cried out to God and He answered my cries. God then took me on a journey all over the world. A global journey that contained miraculous intervention after miraculous intervention. A global journey that culminated in a personal visitation by the Holy Spirit. A visit after which I would be spoken to by God. The results of these Godly communications I will try my best to share with you.

God always uses someone to "prepare the way," and I will be eternally grateful to God that in1999, He introduced me to Margaret Cooper who ministered to me continually. Despite my sinful nature, Margaret never once faltered or wavered in her determination to tell me the truth, which was very simply not to look at man, but to focus continually on Jesus Christ and Him alone. I knew God, but I didn't know Jesus Christ. To anyone who is reading this now and is in the same position, know that from my personal experience, your life will change dramatically and immediately once you invite Jesus Christ into your life. **THE ONLY WAY** to the **FATHER** is **THROUGH THE SON!**

John 14:6 *Jesus saith unto him, I am the way, the truth and the life: no man cometh unto the Father, but by Me.*

Margaret is living proof of the miraculous conversion that took place within me. From being an alcoholic, fornicator, nicotine addict, adulterer, blasphemer, viewer of pornography and worse, by God's grace and His grace alone, God changed me into a Christian. Margaret witnessed first hand all of my shortcomings and yet was resolute in her Christian love for me. Margaret gave herself up to be the vessel used by God, in which He would speak continually to me, to ensure that I set my face like flint on Jesus Christ and He alone. The **ONLY WAY** to the Father is **THROUGH THE SON**, and **THE ONLY WAY** to the **SON**, is through His Word, the Holy Bible.

God speaks His words of truth to the world through the Holy Bible, but He only allows the world to understand at a measured rate, so that our collective human brains can understand. I pray that this is God's perfect time for humankind to fully understand the **PURE TRUTH** revelations that they are about to read. I also pray that after reading this book, every Christian strives to empty themselves of themselves so that they may be filled with the Holy Spirit. Only when this happens, can Jesus communicate to the world the words which He wants the world to hear.

One night in 2007, I realized for the very first time that I was not in control of myself, but that God was. It was a terrifying thought and yet at the same time of immense comfort. To go from someone, who for such a long time had thought so much of himself and his achievements, to one who realized none of those things were due to my will or capability, made me question own sanity. That night I was overcome with fear and gratitude both in the same measure. I cried and cried, but also I realized that everything that had happened to me was none of my doing, and that which was about to happen would also be none of my doing. The whole of everything you are about to read, is not about my capability or incapability, it is about God's. I am merely the messenger and nothing else. I am not a historian, archaeologist or theologian. I have no special powers (other than those given to every believing Christian) and I am not a Middle East expert. I am not highly educated; I am also not an author. The only thing I am is a human being who for whatever reason God has chosen to speak to and to reveal the truth of His creation. So that the **PURE TRUTH** contained maybe understood by everyone, I will use the words that God gave to me and I will try to write them in the most simplistic way possible. In addition, I will support all of those words by quoting God's words given to humankind through scripture. All bible chapters and verses quoted are from the King James Bible. All bible chapters and verses are in Italics.
All Hebrew and Greek translation are taken from Strong's Exhaustive Concordance of the Bible.
Although it is hoped that Christians will fully understand the **PURE TRUTH** herein contained, I also pray that these words will be fully understood by the whole of humankind.

Never ever was it my intention to write this book.
Nothing herein is written that comes from my research.
Every word of supportive text comes from research that I
was led into by God.
To God be the power and the glory, forever and ever.
Amen.

Before you start reading this book, I ask the following.
Please believe these simple basic truths:
1, God is Love.
2, God created everything.
3, God gave every human, angel (demon), and even Satan
himself, a FREE WILL.
4, God's Words in the Holy Bible is the **PURE TRUTH**.
5, If you are not yet a Christian, please suspend your
disbelief until you have read and understood this book.

Signs and Wonders.

You can possess the most expensive, most powerful set of binoculars in the world, but if they are not focused correctly, you will see absolutely nothing at all! They don't have to be way out of focus, just a minute bit and it renders them of no use whatsoever.

On the 27 June 1960, I died, went to heaven, and then was brought back to earth and life. Such an experience should have been enough to persuade anyone to believe in and commit to God, regrettably I am not "anyone." It took another forty-four years and still further, a personal revelation by God Himself before I truly believed.

On the 23 May 2004, at 11.30am in the Hope Center church, God spoke to me and gave me the "vision" complete. If these things were not enough, on the 22 October 2005, in the early hours of a dark and damp autumn morning, the Holy Spirit appeared before me and opened my eyes. For the first time in my life I could "see." After years of reading the bible and nothing making any sense at all, now the whole book became as understandable as ABC! Now not only could I understand the bible, but I could see and fully understand my past, my present and much more important, my future and that of our world. Why should I say all of these things? Very simply, if you are a non-Christian reading this book, it is to help to set your mind. It is to help you to refocus ever so slightly those binoculars, so that you might "see" more clearly. It is to help you to understand.

Please don't think of me as anyone special; I am not. Apart from God I am nothing. The "sight" which I speak of is available to all who believe in Jesus Christ. What is more important is that it is so very close, as close as the Holy Spirit Who is omnipresent. That is why I refer to the binoculars, and the need to adjust the focus. Every revelation that I speak of is available to all. Literally, it's like tuning an old radio, just one slight tweak away, in other words, so very close. So close that everyone can tune in just by a very slight refocusing. It's also like watching a 3D movie. Put on the special glasses and everything will become real. Now try watching the same movie without the glasses, it will all be a blur. The Holy Spirit is just like those 3D specs, He will help you to see.

As a very young boy back in Stoke-on-Trent, I didn't own a wristwatch, very few people did. How then did I know what the time was? Very simply, I looked or listened for signs. I always knew when it was 8am, because the factory sirens would sound calling the men to work. In addition, I always knew when it was 5pm, because again those sirens would sound, but this time it would signal the end of the working day. I knew when it was 9am, because the school bell would ring and again at 10.30am for a 15 min break. The same bell at 12:00 noon would signal lunchtime for one hour and then after the 1pm bell, it would ring at 3pm for break time. Finally, the 4pm bell would signal the end of our school day. In between all of this, the local bus would stop outside the school every hour on the hour. From this and other signs I could always deduce what the time was.
The local public houses or bars would always open at 6pm (they were on every street corner) and the local churches would start their evening services at 7pm (they were also on every opposite street corner). In addition, the steel mills and coal mines always sounded sirens at 10pm, 6am and 2pm to signal the beginning or end of an eight-hour shift. I always knew when it was winter because the weather was cold and damp, and it went dark much earlier and became light much later. In exactly the same way I knew when

18

summer had arrived, the days were much longer, the nights much shorter and the temperature warmer.

Today I live in California, but nothing has changed, God was the same yesterday as He is today, as He will be forever. The signs that He promised are as visible today in California, as they were more than fifty years ago in Stoke-on-Trent.

As I write this book, I know that it's winter very simply because there are no leaves on the trees and it is cold. Some weeks ago I knew it was fall or autumn because all the leaves started to change color and "fall" off the trees. Prior to fall I knew it was summer because it was very hot and all the creeks were dry. In a few weeks I will know that spring has arrived because new growth will appear on the plants and trees and the weather will be warmer.

Being new to California, I couldn't understand why in early cold December, frogs would congregate in large numbers in the nature reserves and start croaking all night. In England, you never saw or heard frogs until late spring or early summer, but in England there was water all year round. After prayer God revealed to me why the frogs croaked. Following the coming together in the nature reserves of thousands of these frogs, the heavens opened and we received a deluge of the first winter rains. The creeks that were dry now flowed with water and lakes suddenly appeared in the middle of previously dry grassland. The croaking frogs heralded the coming of the winter rains and I presume that the new waters will provide them with the perfect habitat in which to breed and raise young before the forthcoming summer drought.

To most people these things today go totally unnoticed, but what does God teach us in the bible about all of these "signs and wonders?"

First, we know that God gave us signs.

Genesis 1:14 *And God said, Let there be lights in the firmament of the heaven to divide the day from the night; and let them be for signs, and for seasons, and for days, and years:*

And.

Psalm 104:19 to 24 *He appointed the moon for seasons: the sun knoweth his going down.*
20 Thou makest darkness, and it is night: wherein all the beasts of the forest do creep [forth].
21 The young lions roar after their prey, and seek their meat from God.
22 The sun ariseth, they gather themselves together, and lay them down in their dens.
23 Man goeth forth unto his work and to his labour until the evening.
24 O LORD, how manifold are thy works! in wisdom hast thou made them all: the earth is full of thy riches.

These "signs" from God give us our chronology. They not only give us time, but also they give us our seasons which in turn are vital to life through agriculture. They also allow us to know exactly where we are geographically on earth through positioning of the stars and moon at any given moment. They also provide many more things, but the purpose right now is only to alert the reader to the Almighty importance of them.

Interesting also, here in California a sure sign that winter is approaching is the ripening of oranges. Also, what's interesting is that they provide an excellent source of vitamin C. Is it coincidental that vitamin C is an excellent vitamin to help ward off colds and flu, both of which occur mainly during winter?

In addition, a sure sign that spring is approaching is the increased bird activity. Mating and nest building always appears to coincide with the onset of spring and early summer. Also, what's interesting is that when the young birds hatch there's always plenty of the exact type of correct food available for them. We have nesting Tree Swallows in our garden. Not only did they start laying eggs to coincide exactly with a rise in temperature, but the young flew the nest on exactly the day that the Dragonflies hatched! For six or seven days the skies were full of food for the young fledglings.

Of course, many people would say that these things are all mere coincidence. Some would also say that the birds know when spring and summer are coming and that's why they mate and nest. I would comment upon this by reinforcing what has already been said. God has even provided signs to the birds!

Again, my reasons for saying these things are to help you to prepare your mind for what is to come. It is to help you to refocus and to begin to see with spiritual eyes rather than your natural eyes.

Very often what we see with our carnal eyes blinds us to even attempt to open up our minds to things spiritual. Let me give you an example. It is impossible for any human to walk through a solid block of ice, yet we can all walk and swim through water. Ice and water have exactly the same constituents and yet both are totally different. Our understanding of their "oneness," will only come when we open our minds to see this simple truth.

We read in the bible that spirits, both good and evil, can be transferred through inanimate worldly objects. The Apostle Paul prayed and laid hands upon a handkerchief infusing it with the Holy Spirit. It was then sent out and the power therein of the Spirit healed the recipient!

Acts 19:11/12 *And God wrought special miracles by the hands of Paul:*

12 So that from his body were brought unto the sick handkerchiefs or aprons, and the diseases departed from them, and the evil spirits went out of them.

I'm sure non-believers will find this hard to believe, but again I mention it only to open up your minds. Remember, I spoke of both good and evil spirits and the importance of this cannot be overstated. Evil spirits are also transferred and again the Lord God warns about this:

Deuteronomy 7:25/26 *The graven images of their gods shall ye burn with fire: thou shalt not desire the silver or gold that is on them, nor take it unto thee, lest thou be snared therein: for it is an abomination to the LORD thy God.*

26Neither shalt thou bring an abomination into thine house, lest thou be a cursed thing like it: but thou shalt utterly detest it, and thou shalt utterly abhor it; for it is a cursed thing.

We all know about Ouija boards and crystal balls, but what about "good luck" charms, "lucky horseshoes", "wishbones" etc. All of these things have the potential to bring evil spirits into our home. Most Christians have never done a thorough cleansing of their homes, yet they wonder why their lives never seem to be joyous and peaceful. Quite possibly they might have unknowingly brought a "cursed" thing into their homes, and evil spirits are working through it!

To some my next statement might even seem questionable, but I make no apology simply because it's true. There is no more powerful object on earth for the transference of spirits than the Holy Bible.

Hebrews 4:12 *For the word of God is quick, and powerful, and sharper than any twoedged sword, piercing even to the dividing asunder of soul and spirit, and of the joints and marrow, and is a discerner of the thoughts and intents of the heart.*

The Holy Bible is the word of God. It is also a "discerner of the thoughts and intents of the heart". As we read the Holy Bible, it reads us! The Holy Bible is the Sword of the Spirit. No weapon has been or ever will be invented that is as powerful as the word of God, the Sword of the Spirit. The greatest power this earth will ever know is contained within the New Testament gospel of Jesus Christ.

Romans 1:16 *For I am not ashamed of the gospel of Christ: for it is **the power of God** unto salvation to every one that believeth; to the Jew first, and also to the Greek.* There is no greater Spiritual power than that of Almighty God through the Holy Spirit!

Again, let me refer to the block of ice. There is absolutely no way that I could get inside a solid block of ice, but if I was submerged in water and it froze, there I would be! In exactly the same way, we struggle to think of an inanimate object moving on its own, without contact by another. Yet, if this object happens to be metal and a powerful magnet gets close to it, it will move! We won't be able to see or touch the force that moved it, but nonetheless it was still there. We can't see, smell or touch the wind, yet it can be powerful enough to knock us off our feet! Another example is very simply electricity. We can't see it, yet this force will kill without even thinking! Again, these examples are only used to hopefully open your minds up to accommodating spiritual things and to help you better understand them.

In this chapter I'm not looking to convince you of anything. I merely want to open your eyes. If my words help you to see more clearly then your own intellect will do the rest. Your "free will" given to you by God can now be brought into action. You can choose to acknowledge and accept the truth, or you can choose to deny it, that choice is yours!

Old Moses, way back in the book of Deuteronomy offered the nation of Israel a choice. In chapter 28, Moses made known to the people all the blessings of God and all the curses. In chapter 30, verse 19, he implored them to choose life, and live.

Deuteronomy 30:19 *I call heaven and earth to record this day against you, that I have set before you life and death, blessing and cursing: therefore choose life, that both thou and thy seed may live*

A final thought to help you to focus your mind. Please do not approach this final thought with preconceived ideas. Do not allow Satanic or scientific influence to enter; just contemplate with your own totally free will and mind. Come to your conclusion with simplicity of thought.

Centuries before scientists were on this earth, or even before the word scientist had been invented, miraculous things happened. An acorn would fall from an oak tree into the ground. Out of the ground would then grow another oak tree. Out of the dust of the ground would be formed a complete oak tree, tens of feet high that would live for hundreds of years. No human had fertilized, tended to or even watered the acorn seed. Yet that seed formed itself into a mighty oak tree using only the dust of the ground. Man can take the pip or seed from an orange, place it into the ground and walk away. Without any care, without applying any fertilizer, without applying any water, that seed will grow into an orange tree full of fruit. All the man did was to place the seed into the ground, yet with nothing else but the dust of the ground, that orange seed formed itself into a large orange tree packed full of oranges! It is obvious to even the less well educated that the dust of the ground contained every thing necessary to give form to the seed. Of course, there is light (sunshine) and there is rain, but hopefully you will agree that everything else needed to form the complete tree comes out of the dust of the ground. Ever heard of the term "Mother Earth"? The earth that we inhabit gave "birth" to everything that is in existence. Every plane, space craft, nuclear bomb, and the most sophisticated computer ever developed, all came from the "dust of the ground". Out of the ground upon which we walk, came every material necessary to make every thing on our planet, including humankind. Is it not then fair and logical to assume that Almighty God Himself can "form humankind out of the dust of the ground?"

Genesis 2:7 *And the LORD God* **formed man of the dust of the ground**, *and breathed into his nostrils the breath of life; and man became a living soul.*

Sorry to be so obvious, but are not planets and stars, indeed our whole solar system born out of dust and gas? Scientists of today tell us these things because it is the truth and we believe them. Can we not then believe the writings of Moses which tells us exactly the same things?

If the whole of our galaxy and everything in it has been "formed" from dust, can we not then accept that man was "formed" from dust also?

We are all seekers after the truth, what you are reading is the truth, the **PURE TRUTH** from **GOD.**

What am I?

The answer to this question may at first seem too obvious.
Of course, we are all human beings, but where did we come
from and what exactly is a human being?
Today, we hear the sound bite that we are all "human
being's not human doings." We hear many famous
religious people make this statement and it's very catchy,
but what does God say? Does God say that we should just
"be?" Or does God say that we should "be" and "do" at the
same time?
Let us first look at what God said about human beings to
the prophet Isaiah.
Isaiah 43:7 *[Even] every one that is called by my name:
for I have created him for my glory, I have formed him;
yea, I have made him.*

We can see from this that there are three, clearly very
different processes. First, God says that He "created" us
for His glory. Second, God says that He "formed" us.
Third, God says that He "made" us. Evolutionists question
and ridicule the idea that God created the earth and
everything in it. They assumed as do all Christians that
Adam was the very first human. By this deduction, Adam
having existed only about six or seven thousand years ago
according to bible genealogy, could not possibly have been
the first human on earth. We know this because artifacts
have been found and carbon dated going back millions of
years. On this basis, Adam could not possibly have been the
first human and therefore God did not create us.

Why then did God say these things to Isaiah? What is more
important why did God say these things to Isaiah in exactly

the same way as he said them to Moses some 700 years before? We read in Genesis (the first book of the bible that was written by Moses) that God "created" us, that God "formed" us and that God "made" us.

The reason for this was revealed to me by God some years ago, and it is the main reason for this book.

Originally, man did not have a soul, he had only a body and a spirit, but his spirit did not become active until it had the means by which to achieve this activity.

This is the First Man whose remains can be dated back millions of years. This First Man I refer to is more commonly known by evolutionists as the "Hunter Gatherer."

The Second Man had a body, a spirit and a soul. This man, who I often refer to as the "farmer," was on this earth tens or even hundreds of thousands of years ago.

Finally, there came Third Man. This is you and I, humankind or human beings. We were given by God, a body, a soul and a spirit, but we also gained "knowledge" or as we know it better today, a "conscience."

We are a tripartite being in the same way as the Holy Trinity. We are body, soul and spirit. In the Holy Trinity we have Jesus, the body on earth, God in heaven, and the Holy Spirit, The Spirit that gives us our understanding or wisdom.

1st Thessalonians 5:23 *And the very God of peace sanctify you wholly; and [I pray God] your whole **spirit** and **soul** and **body** be preserved blameless unto the coming of our Lord Jesus Christ.*

Later in the book, I give all the evidence that God gave to me to support these statements, but for now let's just concentrate upon ourselves as human "beings."

Human beings were created by God, this we learn in the book of Genesis.

Genesis 1:26/27 *And God said, Let us make man in our image, after our likeness: and let them have dominion over the fish of the sea, and over the fowl of the air, and over the cattle, and over all the earth, and over every creeping thing that creepeth upon the earth.*
*So God **created** man in his [own] image, in the image of God **created** he him; male and female **created** he them.*
I don't think there can be any doubt, "First Man" was **created** by God.

"First Man," was created in the "image" of God and from scripture we know that God is Spirit. John 4:24 *God [is] a Spirit: and they that worship him must worship [him] in spirit and in truth.*
In other words, First Man was no more than a flesh and blood body that had a spirit. We will learn later from scripture that Second Man had a body, a spirit and a Soul. In addition, we will also learn from scripture that Third Man (you & me), had a body, a soul, a spirit and "knowledge" or conscience.

We know from the New Testament that if we believe in Jesus, we will be given a "glorified" body, a "sanctified" soul and a "justified" spirit. These three things will not only reconcile us to God, but they will enable us to move and live with Him in the Spirit world forever.
Let us look further at these three key components that make us who we are.

1. BODY.

Our body is the vehicle in which are carried the soul and spirit. Our body is born, it grows and then it eventually dies and goes back into the ground from whence it came. This is the same for everyone regardless of whether they are Christians. Most important, our body is that which connects us to our earthly environment and all the things in it. It is the vessel that contains the physical components that enable us to see, hear, touch, smell and taste all that we are physically surrounded by. It contains all of our physical senses. It also contains our heart, a vital component not just to our physical life on earth, but also to our actions. We know also that our body can act totally independently from our Soul and our Spirit. This is a vitally important fact when understanding about "First Man" or the Hunter Gatherer. When we are cold, we shiver and when we are hot we sweat. We don't think about these things. Our body does it totally independently of any thought. Never once have I told my heart to pump, also never once have I told my lungs to inhale or exhale. Praise be to God that since my birth in this body, both have functioned perfectly well without any interference from me!

Our bodies operate independently in numerous ways. We walk, eat, drink and relieve ourselves all automatically. No thought is given to any of these actions. Our bodies do these things and many more, totally automatically. Ever noticed how you can walk, eat, talk on the phone, sweat and be dribbling a soccer ball all at the same time? Yet your mind only gives instructions for the phone chat. Everything else, every other action, your body does without instruction.

The body enables us to regenerate our species through sexual reproduction and new birth.

The body does not exist forever, it starts to grow and then it starts to degenerate unto death and finally to decay into dust. Every human body goes back into the ground at death.

Believers in Jesus Christ will be given a "glorified" body which will house our "sanctified" soul, and our "justified" spirit. Our glorified body will be our eternal body which will live forever. We know this because God tells us:

1st Corinthian 15:49 to 52 *And as we have borne the image of the earthy, we shall also bear the image of the heavenly.*
50 Now this I say, brethren, that flesh and blood cannot inherit the kingdom of God; neither doth corruption inherit incorruption.
51 Behold, I shew you a mystery; We shall not all sleep, but we shall all be changed,
52 In a moment, in the twinkling of an eye, at the last trump: for the trumpet shall sound, and the dead shall be raised incorruptible, and we shall be changed.

1st Corinthian 15:24 *It is sown a natural body; it is raised a spiritual body. There is a natural body, and there is a spiritual body.*

Philippians 3:21 *Who shall change our vile body, that it may be fashioned like unto his glorious body, according to the working whereby he is able even to subdue all things unto himself.*

Finally, a few more specifics about our heart, the very core and center of our being.

Proverbs 4:23 *Keep thy heart with all diligence; for out of it are the issues of life.*

In other words guard your heart, because what comes out of it determines the course of your life!

What does Jesus say about our heart?

Matthew 15:16 to 19 *And Jesus said, Are ye also yet without understanding?*
17 Do not ye yet understand, that whatsoever entereth in at the mouth goeth into the belly, and is cast out into the draught?
18 But those things which proceed out of the mouth come forth from the heart; and they defile the man.

30

*19 For **out of the heart proceed evil thoughts, murders, adulteries, fornications, thefts, false witness, blasphemies:*** Interesting, we are taught to guard our heart and we then learn that words coming from our mouths originate in our hearts.

James 3:5 to 10 *Even so the tongue is a little member, and boasteth great things. Behold, how great a matter a little fire kindleth!*

6 And the tongue is a fire, a world of iniquity: so is the tongue among our members, that it defileth the whole body, and setteth on fire the course of nature; and it is set on fire of hell.

7 For every kind of beasts, and of birds, and of serpents, and of things in the sea, is tamed, and hath been tamed of mankind:

8 But the tongue can no man tame; it is an unruly evil, full of deadly poison.

9 Therewith bless we God, even the Father; and therewith curse we men, which are made after the similitude of God. 10 Out of the same mouth proceedeth blessing and cursing. My brethren, these things ought not so to be.

James tells us that thoughts from our hearts are then turned into words by our tongue and these words can basically destroy anything! What is more important, no man can tame the tongue! What hope do we have?

Proverbs 18:21 *Death and life are in the power of the tongue: and they that love it shall eat the fruit thereof.*

Life and death are both in the power of words that come out of our heart through our tongue! Let me ask you a question, has anything on this earth been created, formed or made, without someone talking about it first? The answer is no! Every thing that was created, formed or made, was spoken about first! Remember Genesis, "and God said" and there was! The words of Almighty God brought everything into being and it's no different today. The words that come from our mouths can mean life or death, such is there power.

So if man can't control his tongue and his words can mean life or death, what hope do we have?

Thank God we do have hope and the Apostle Paul tells us how to get it.

Ephesians 3:16 to 19 *That he would grant you, according to the riches of his glory, to be strengthened with might by his Spirit in the inner man;*
*17 That Christ may dwell in your hearts **by faith**; that ye, being rooted and grounded in love,*
18 May be able to comprehend with all saints what is the breadth, and length, and depth, and height;
19 And to know the love of Christ, which passeth knowledge, that ye might be filled with all the fulness of God.

We cannot purify our hearts alone, it is simply impossible. However good you believe you are, your heart is still full of impurity. The only way we can purify our hearts, is through the sanctification process provided by the Holy Spirit. How will this happen? Paul gives us the key, "By faith" in Jesus Christ as our Lord and Savior. Immediately we believe in Jesus, by the grace of God, we will be given a "justified" spirit. With help from the Holy Spirit our new "born again justified spirit" will start the "sanctification" process of our soul. The ultimate completion of the sanctification process being that Jesus Himself will dwell in our hearts. When Jesus is in control of your heart and tongue, you will be perfected.

I never believed the word "dwell" to be the best translation. A better translation is to "settle in". In other words Jesus will make His home within you and He will be as comfortable in your home as He is in His own.

Matthew 5:8 *Blessed are the pure in heart: for they shall see God.*

If you want to see God, follow Paul's advice, have faith in Jesus and do as He says!

2. SOUL.

The word soul comes from the Greek "psuche" (from where we get the word "Psyche or Psychology) and the Hebrew "nephesh," both refer to breath, wind, air & life. Remember, God breathed into man and he became a "living soul." It is the life-giving force which "animates" the body. Animates leads me onto the Latin words "anima" and "animus."

These two words perfectly describe the two sides to our soul.

Anima means air, breath, and life inherent in the body. It has more of a physical aspect to it and as we read in Deuteronomy this "life inherent in our body," relates also to our blood.

Deuteronomy 12:23/24 *Only be sure that thou eat not the blood: for the blood [is] the life; and thou mayest not eat the life with the flesh.*

24 Thou shalt not eat it; thou shalt pour it upon the earth as water.

The word "life" in the Hebrew translation is "nephesh." In other words our blood makes up a part of our soul.

The other Latin word is Animus. This Latin word for our soul means intellect, courage, sensibility, etc. In other words, it describes perfectly the other side of our soul which is the mind; the will and our emotions. This is described by God numerous times in the bible. Here are just three examples.

Job 30:25 *Did not I weep for him that was in trouble? was [not] my soul grieved for the poor?*

Jeremiah 31:25 *For I have satiated the weary soul, and I have replenished every sorrowful soul.*

Leviticus 26:11 *And I will set my tabernacle among you: and my soul shall not abhor you.*

Imagine first if you will, the soul being in the middle with the body to the left, and the spirit to the right. Our soul is what connects us to ourselves. This may seem like a stupid statement, but let me explain.

Our soul is what makes us who we are as individuals. It's what makes every person unique and different from any other person. Our soul is our mind, our emotions and our will, the free will that God gave to every human. Our soul is what makes us recognizable, not physically but intellectually. It's what gives us our unique characters and the intelligence that gives us an awareness of our surroundings and of our environment. God tells us that our soul enables us to sin, to believe, to prosper, and to love God.

We also are told by God that our soul possesses certain characteristics:

A) It leaves our body at death.

Genesis 35:18 *And it came to pass, as her soul was in departing, (for she died) that she called his name Benoni: but his father called him Benjamin.*

B) It belongs to God.

Ezekiel 18:3/4 *[As] I live, saith the Lord GOD, ye shall not have [occasion] any more to use this proverb in Israel. 4 Behold, all souls are mine; as the soul of the father, so also the soul of the son is mine: the soul that sinneth, it shall die.*

C) It possesses immorality.

Matthew 10:28 *And fear not them which kill the body, but are not able to kill the soul: but rather fear him which is able to destroy both soul and body in hell.*

34

D) It has enemies including, ignorance (Proverbs 8:36), lusts of the flesh (1st Peter 2:11), hell (Proverbs 23:14) and being in an evil environment (2nd Peter 2:8).

Proverbs 8:36 *But he that sinneth against me wrongeth his own soul: all they that hate me love death.*

1st Peter 2:11 *Dearly beloved, I beseech [you] as strangers and pilgrims, abstain from fleshly lusts, which war against the soul;*

Proverbs 23:14 *Thou shalt beat him with the rod, and shalt deliver his soul from hell.*

2nd Peter 2:8 *(For that righteous man dwelling among them, in seeing and hearing, vexed [his] righteous soul from day to day with [their] unlawful deeds;)*

E) It gives us our emotions, such as desire, feelings, affections.

2nd Samuel 5:8 *And David said on that day, Whosoever getteth up to the gutter, and smiteth the Jebusites, and the lame and the blind, that are hated of David's soul, he shall be chief and captain. Wherefore they said, The blind and the lame shall not come into the house.*

Psalm 84:2 *My soul longeth, yea, even fainteth for the courts of the LORD: my heart and my flesh crieth out for the living God.*

Isaiah 26:9 *With my soul have I desired thee in the night; yea, with my spirit within me will I seek thee early: for when thy judgments are in the earth, the inhabitants of the world will learn righteousness.*

Judges 10:16 *And they put away the strange gods from among them, and served the LORD: and his soul was grieved for the misery of Israel.*

Psalm 86:4 *Rejoice the soul of thy servant: for unto thee, O Lord, do I lift up my soul.*

1st Samuel 30:6 *And David was greatly distressed; for the people spake of stoning him, because the soul of all the people was grieved, every man for his sons and for his daughters: but David encouraged himself in the LORD his God.*

Most importantly, our soul gives us an awareness of God and that He exists. Our soul is the link or key not just to our social development, but also our spiritual. It's what links our bodies to our spirits and therefore gives us access, should we so choose, to God Himself. Remember that God gave every human being a free will and we all have a choice to know Him and choose eternal life, or to choose not to know Him and suffer eternal death.

One final yet very important point concerning our soul. We know that our soul gives us an awareness of God and an ability to believe in Him, but it is only through our spirit that we can communicate with God. I say this because even the greatest scientific brain on earth cannot communicate directly with God. In fact, at times a very high intellect may even be a hindrance when it comes to communicating with God. God is spirit, and the only way to communicate with God is through our spirit. If your mind (soul) is full of egotistical, worldly, selfish things, then it's impossible for it to be full of spiritual things.

How can I possibly say these things? I can't, but God can.

1st Corinthian 3:18 to 23 *Let no man deceive himself. If any man among you seemeth to be wise in this world, let him become a fool, that he may be wise.*

19For the wisdom of this world is foolishness with God. For it is written, He taketh the wise in their own craftiness.

20And again, The Lord knoweth the thoughts of the wise, that they are vain.

21Therefore let no man glory in men. For all things are yours;

22Whether Paul, or Apollos, or Cephas, or the world, or life, or death, or things present, or things to come; all are yours;

23And ye are Christ's; and Christ is God's.

If you want to become "spiritually" wise, then do as Jesus says.

Matthew 16:24 *Then said Jesus unto his disciples, If any man will come after me, let him deny himself, and take up his cross, and follow me.*

The greatest aid to communication with God, is to remove ourselves from ourselves. When we do this all that's left is our spirit and then automatically the communication channel is open, both to transmit and to receive. I used the analogy before of binoculars slightly out of focus. When you remove yourself, you automatically focus the binoculars perfectly and the hidden mysteries of God and the Holy Spirit will be shown to you. I give you my word, when you are able to remove yourself from yourself, you will see with spiritual eyes things that you never even dreamed of seeing. Much, much more important, Jesus Christ Himself will become manifest to you in ways that will enable you to see, smell, touch, hear and even taste Jesus Himself. I'm sure some of you reading this will find the last sentence hard to believe, but I am living proof of its authenticity.

1st Corinthian 2:9 to 12 *But as it is written, Eye hath not seen, nor ear heard, neither have entered into the heart of man, the things which God hath prepared for them that love him.*

10 But God hath revealed them unto us by his Spirit: for the Spirit searcheth all things, yea, the deep things of God.

11 For what man knoweth the things of a man, save the spirit of man which is in him? even so the things of God knoweth no man, but the Spirit of God.

12 Now we have received, not the spirit of the world, but the spirit which is of God; that we might know the things that are freely given to us of God.

3. SPIRIT. Now here comes the most important part of a human being. The spirit is who we are. Our spirit is immortal. We are a "spirit being" housed in an earthly, flesh and blood body. Our spirit is our means of communication with God; with other spirits be they Angelic or Demonic; and of course with Satan. Remember that originally, God created us in His own image.

Genesis 1:26/27 *And God said, Let us make man in our image, after our likeness: and let them have dominion over the fish of the sea, and over the fowl of the air, and over the cattle, and over all the earth, and over every creeping thing that creepeth upon the earth. 27 So God created man in his [own] image, in the image of God created he him; male and female created he them.*

We know that God is Spirit, that He is immortal, and that He possesses ALL wisdom. Nothing in the whole of our universe or earth is as valuable as a "spirit being." We know from the word of God that ALL things will pass away. Everything that God created, with the one exception of "spirit beings", will decay, die, become as the dust of the ground and eventually all will be burned up.

2nd Peter 3:10 *But the day of the Lord will come as a thief in the night; in the which the heavens shall pass away with a great noise, and the elements shall melt with fervent heat, the earth also and the works that are therein shall be burned up.*

All things change and will eventually pass away, but our spirits are immortal. They will never decay, become old or pass away, because they have been created by Almighty God in His image. Our spirit is eternal and at our physical death, it will eventually return to God Who gave it to us.

Ecclesiastes 12:7 *Then shall the dust return to the earth as it was: and the spirit shall return unto God who gave it.*

"Born Again" Christian "Justified" spirits will then spend
eternity with God. Non-believing spirits will then have to
give an account of themselves before the Great White
throne of God. The greatest gamble of their non-believing
earthly lives will now payout or not. If that gamble failed,
then eternity will be spent with Satan.

We know that God "created" (a causing to be out of
nothing) our spirit. We know that our spirit is who we
really are. We also know that at physical death, our spirit
goes back to God.

Let me now ask you a question. Is it coincidence or God-
incidence that two of the world's most famous quantum
physics experts believe that our "soul" (I believe this
should be "spirit") is contained inside a structure that
leaves our body at death. DR Stuart Hameroff, Professor
Emeritus at the University of Arizona together with British
Physicist, DR Roger Penrose, both believe that at death our
"soul" (see "spirit") leaves our nervous system and enters
the universe. They believe that "consciousness" is a
program for a quantum computer in the brain which can
persist in the universe after death. Has any reader yet
linked this to "eternal life"? Has any reader yet linked this
to "*spirit shall return unto God Who gave it*"?

These two experts base their belief on a quantum theory of
consciousness, which holds that the essence of our "soul",
is contained inside structures called microtubules within
brain cells.

They believe that our experience of consciousness is the
result of quantum gravity effects in these microtubules, a
theory they have dubbed "orchestrated objective
reduction". They believe that our "souls" (read spirit) are
more than the interaction of neurons in the brain. They
believe that they are constructed from the very fabric of the
universe and may have existed from the very beginning of
time.

Remember what God told us?

Daniel 12:1 to 7 *And at that time shall Michael stand up, the great prince which standeth for the children of thy people: and **there shall be a time of trouble, such as never was since there was a nation even to that same time**: and at that time thy people shall be delivered, every one that shall be found written in the book.*

*2 **And many of them that sleep in the dust of the earth shall awake, some to everlasting life**, and some to shame and everlasting contempt.*

3 And they that be wise shall shine as the brightness of the firmament; and they that turn many to righteousness as the stars for ever and ever.

*4 But thou, O Daniel, shut up the words, and seal the book, **even to the time of the end: many shall run to and fro, and knowledge shall be increased.***

5 Then I Daniel looked, and, behold, there stood other two, the one on this side of the bank of the river, and the other on that side of the bank of the river.

6 And one said to the man clothed in linen, which was upon the waters of the river, How long shall it be to the end of these wonders?

*7 And I heard the man clothed in linen, which was upon the waters of the river, when he held up his right hand and his left hand unto heaven, and sware by him that liveth for ever that it shall be for a time, times, and an half; and when he shall have accomplished to scatter the power of the holy people, **all these things shall be finished**.*

God bless these two quantum physics experts. They have established through "knowledge" what the Lord God told us through scripture two thousand years ago. I believe that they have simply used the word "soul", instead of "spirit". As you read earlier in this book, on the 27 June 1960, I died and went to heaven. Communication took place and I was returned to earth and back into my body. I completed more

40

than 200 pages of text concerning this experience and many others that have happened to myself, but God told me to completely remove myself from this book. This book is ALL about Almighty God and our Lord Jesus. It is NOT about me, but from personal experience I can confirm without doubt or question, what these two experts have established through quantum physics, is the truth as told by God. All we need to do is to substitute the word "spirit" for "soul".

I pray that as these two experts read this book, together with everyone else, they will "understand" more about the **PURE TRUTH** concerning, spirit, soul, consciousness, and understanding.

Again, let me remind everyone, the **ONLY WAY** to the Father, is through The Son. If you want to understand all of these "mysteries", and if you want eternal life, then believe in Jesus Christ.

Jesus confirms that our spirit gives us life and that He speaks to us through our spirit. Jesus confirmed to us also that this communication would come to us even after His death, it would come through the Holy Spirit, the Spirit of Truth.

John 6:63 *It is the spirit that quickeneth; the flesh profiteth nothing: the words that I speak unto you, [they] are spirit, and [they] are life.*

John 14:15 to 18 *If ye love me, keep my commandments.*
16 And I will pray the Father, and he shall give you another Comforter, that he may abide with you for ever;
17 [Even] the Spirit of truth; whom the world cannot receive, because it seeth him not, neither knoweth him: but ye know him; for he dwelleth with you, and shall be in you.
18 I will not leave you comfortless: I will come to you.

Can we trust Jesus? Can we really believe what He told us before He left this earth? The answer to that question is a great big YES! Don't just believe me, let's again look at the word of God for confirmation.

Acts 2:1 to 24 *And when the day of Pentecost was fully come, they were all with one accord in one place.*

2 And suddenly there came a sound from heaven as of a rushing mighty wind, and it filled all the house where they were sitting.

3 And there appeared unto them cloven tongues like as of fire, and it sat upon each of them.

4 And they were all filled with the Holy Ghost, and began to speak with other tongues, as the Spirit gave them utterance.

5 And there were dwelling at Jerusalem Jews, devout men, out of every nation under heaven.

6 Now when this was noised abroad, the multitude came together, and were confounded, because that every man heard them speak in his own language.

7 And they were all amazed and marvelled, saying one to another, Behold, are not all these which speak Galilaeans?

8 And how hear we every man in our own tongue, wherein we were born?

9 Parthians, and Medes, and Elamites, and the dwellers in Mesopotamia, and in Judaea, and Cappadocia, in Pontus, and Asia,

10 Phrygia, and Pamphylia, in Egypt, and in the parts of Libya about Cyrene, and strangers of Rome, Jews and proselytes,

11 Cretes and Arabians, we do hear them speak in our tongues the wonderful works of God.

12 And they were all amazed, and were in doubt, saying one to another, What meaneth this?

13 Others mocking said, These men are full of new wine.

14 But Peter, standing up with the eleven, lifted up his voice, and said unto them, Ye men of Judaea, and all [ye] that dwell at Jerusalem, be this known unto you, and hearken to my words:

15 For these are not drunken, as ye suppose, seeing it is [but] the third hour of the day.
16 But this is that which was spoken by the prophet Joel;
17 And it shall come to pass in the last days, saith God, I will pour out of my Spirit upon all flesh: and your sons and your daughters shall prophesy, and your young men shall see visions, and your old men shall dream dreams:
18 And on my servants and on my handmaidens I will pour out in those days of my Spirit; and they shall prophesy:
19 And I will shew wonders in heaven above, and signs in the earth beneath; blood, and fire, and vapour of smoke:
20 The sun shall be turned into darkness, and the moon into blood, before that great and notable day of the Lord come:
21 And it shall come to pass, [that] whosoever shall call on the name of the Lord shall be saved.
22 Ye men of Israel, hear these words; Jesus of Nazareth, a man approved of God among you by miracles and wonders and signs, which God did by him in the midst of you, as ye yourselves also know:
23 Him, being delivered by the determinate counsel and foreknowledge of God, ye have taken, and by wicked hands have crucified and slain:
24 Whom God hath raised up, having loosed the pains of death: because it was not possible that he should be holden of it.

Clear confirmation of the promise of our Lord being fulfilled. The Holy Spirit, the Spirit of Truth, came upon every believer on the day of Pentecost and they were all baptized in the Spirit. The Holy Spirit now gave them a greater "consciousness" (knowledge) of Jesus than they ever had whilst He was alive and still with them! They now had an "understanding" of the mysteries of the gospel message of truth which they never had, even whilst Jesus sat in their midst and preached it to them! At the very moment of their Holy Spirit baptism, they **UNDERSTOOD**. All the parables and countless other things Jesus had spoken of before, now became just like ABC. The Holy Spirit had given their spirit, **UNDERSTANDING**.

The Hebrew word for spirit comes from the root word RUWACH (ROO-AKH) and translated this is "wind, breath etc." It is also "to make of quick understanding." It is this definition of spirit that is vitally important when you come to understand exactly whom you are. In addition, it is vital if you are to have full understanding of the "creation" process, especially in relation the chapter THIRD MAN.

ALL KNOWLEDGE is within us, but
UNDERSTANDING of that knowledge can only come through our spirit.
How do I know that ALL knowledge is "within" us? God tells us so.
Genesis 3:4 to 7 *For God doth know that in the day ye eat thereof, then your eyes shall be opened, and ye shall be as gods, knowing good and evil.*
6 And when the woman saw that the tree was good for food, and that it was pleasant to the eyes, and a tree to be desired to make one wise, she took of the fruit thereof, and did eat, and gave also unto her husband with her; and he did eat.
7 And the eyes of them both were opened,

Satan told Eve "eat from the Tree of Knowledge and you shall be as gods, knowing good and evil". This knowledge would be passed down through Adam's seed, into every human being.
Adam and Eve now "knew" all things, but they didn't yet "understand".
Jesus confirmed this truth to us. Here Jesus refers to the evil "knowledge" that is within us.
Matthew 15:16 to *19 And Jesus said, Are ye also yet without understanding?*

44

17 Do not ye yet understand, that whatsoever entereth in at the mouth goeth into the belly, and is cast out into the draught?
18 But those things which proceed out of the mouth come forth from the heart; and they defile the man.
19 For out of the heart proceed evil thoughts, murders, adulteries, fornications, thefts, false witness, blasphemies:
Knowledge of the worst of the worst is within us.
Understanding of this type of knowledge comes spiritually through Satan. This is why Satan tempted Eve and Adam, because he could spiritually now influence all humankind. Satanic "understanding" is given for one purpose only, to kill, to steal and to destroy. How do we know this? Jesus tells us.
John 10:9 to 11 *I am the door: by me if any man enter in, he shall be saved, and shall go in and out, and find pasture.*
10 The thief cometh not, but for to steal, and to kill, and to destroy: I am come that they might have life, and that they might have it more abundantly.
11 I am the good shepherd: the good shepherd giveth his life for the sheep.

Praise be to God that there is also another type of understanding. This type is Godly, and if you pray to God, He will give it to you. It will be a heavenly understanding that will make you "see" things that before you could not even imagine existed.

Job confirms to us that understanding comes to us through our spirit.
Job 32:8 *But [there is] a spirit in man: and the inspiration of the Almighty giveth them understanding.*
Job is talking here about Godly understanding, but it is important to note that our spirit can also give us a "worldly" understanding.

Besides Godly and Satanic "understanding", the third means of understanding comes to our spirit through the world. This comes through teaching by another, reasoning, deduction or process of elimination. Worldly wisdom or "understanding" is confirmed to us by God.

James 3:13 to 15 *Who is a wise man and endued with knowledge among you? let him shew out of a good conversation his works with meekness of wisdom.*
14 But if ye have bitter envying and strife in your hearts, glory not, and lie not against the truth.
15 This wisdom descendeth not from above, but is earthly, sensual, devilish.

1st Corinthian 3:18 to 21 *Let no man deceive himself. If any man among you seemeth to be wise in this world, let him become a fool, that he may be wise.*
19 For the wisdom of this world is foolishness with God. For it is written, He taketh the wise in their own craftiness.
20 And again, The Lord knoweth the thoughts of the wise, that they are vain.
21 Therefore let no man glory in men.

As we can see, the wisdom or "understanding" that comes to us through the world, is considered foolishness by God. Why would God say that "worldly" understanding is foolishness? Let's go back to the book of Job to read the answer. God asks Job numerous questions that highlight just how insignificant "worldly" understanding is. Even the greatest of the great could never answer these simple questions unless the answers were given to them by God.

Job 38:1 to 36 *Then the LORD answered Job out of the whirlwind, and said,*
2 Who is this that darkeneth counsel by words without knowledge?
3 Gird up now thy loins like a man; for I will demand of thee, and answer thou me.
4 Where wast thou when I laid the foundations of the earth? declare, if thou hast understanding.

5 Who hath laid the measures thereof, if thou knowest? or who hath stretched the line upon it?

6 Whereupon are the foundations thereof fastened? or who laid the corner stone thereof;

7 When the morning stars sang together, and all the sons of God shouted for joy?

8 Or who shut up the sea with doors, when it brake forth, as if it had issued out of the womb?

9 When I made the cloud the garment thereof, and thick darkness a swaddlingband for it,

10 And brake up for it my decreed place, and set bars and doors,

11 And said, Hitherto shalt thou come, but no further: and here shall thy proud waves be stayed?

12 Hast thou commanded the morning since thy days; and caused the dayspring to know his place;

13 That it might take hold of the ends of the earth, that the wicked might be shaken out of it?

14 It is turned as clay to the seal; and they stand as a garment.

15 And from the wicked their light is withholden, and the high arm shall be broken.

16 Hast thou entered into the springs of the sea? or hast thou walked in the search of the depth?

17 Have the gates of death been opened unto thee? or hast thou seen the doors of the shadow of death?

18 Hast thou perceived the breadth of the earth? declare if thou knowest it all.

19 Where is the way where light dwelleth? and as for darkness, where is the place thereof,

20 That thou shouldest take it to the bound thereof, and that thou shouldest know the paths to the house thereof?

21 Knowest thou it, because thou wast then born? or because the number of thy days is great?

22 Hast thou entered into the treasures of the snow? or hast thou seen the treasures of the hail,

23 Which I have reserved against the time of trouble, against the day of battle and war?
24 By what way is the light parted, which scattereth the east wind upon the earth?
25 Who hath divided a watercourse for the overflowing of waters, or a way for the lightning of thunder;
26 To cause it to rain on the earth, where no man is; on the wilderness, wherein there is no man;
27 To satisfy the desolate and waste ground; and to cause the bud of the tender herb to spring forth?
28 Hath the rain a father? or who hath begotten the drops of dew?
29 Out of whose womb came the ice? and the hoary frost of heaven, who hath gendered it?
30 The waters are hid as with a stone, and the face of the deep is frozen.
31 Canst thou bind the sweet influences of Pleiades, or loose the bands of Orion?
32 Canst thou bring forth Mazzaroth in his season? or canst thou guide Arcturus with his sons?
33 Knowest thou the ordinances of heaven? canst thou set the dominion thereof in the earth?
34 Canst thou lift up thy voice to the clouds, that abundance of waters may cover thee?
35 Canst thou send lightnings, that they may go, and say unto thee, Here we are?
36 Who hath put wisdom in the inward parts? or who hath given understanding to the heart?

God continues with questions throughout this chapter and chapter 39. None are answered by Job. Then in chapter 40 God asks Job this question:
Job 40:2 *"Shall he that contendeth with the Almighty instruct him? he that reproveth God, let him answer it."*

It's a question that could be asked of every great man on earth. The answer which Job gave, should be mirrored by all:

Job 40:4 *Behold, I am vile; what shall I answer thee? I will lay mine hand upon my mouth.*

All those years ago Job realized just how insignificant he was. Today nothing has changed. We can present these simple questions to the greatest human brains on earth, and still their hands would cover their mouths.

These are the three ways by which "understanding" comes to us through our spirit. Let's read again more words from God which confirm this truth.

Proverbs 2:6 *For the LORD giveth wisdom: out of his mouth [cometh] knowledge and **UNDERSTANDING**.*
Proverbs 3:5 *Trust in the LORD with all thine heart; and lean not unto thine own **UNDERSTANDING**.* (Trust in heavenly understanding not worldly!)
Proverbs 16:22 ***UNDERSTANDING** [is] a wellspring of life unto him that hath it: but the instruction of fools [is] folly.*
Proverbs 20:5 *Counsel in the heart of man [is like] deep water; but a man of **UNDERSTANDING** will draw it out.*
Proverbs 24:3 *Through wisdom is an house builded; and by **UNDERSTANDING** it is established:*
Isaiah 11:2 *And the spirit of the LORD shall rest upon him, the spirit of wisdom and **UNDERSTANDING**, the spirit of counsel and might, the spirit of knowledge and of the fear of the LORD;*
Daniel 1:17 *As for these four children, God gave them knowledge and skill in all learning and wisdom: and Daniel had **UNDERSTANDING** in all visions and dreams.*
Daniel 5:12 *Forasmuch as an excellent spirit, and knowledge, and **UNDERSTANDING**, interpreting of dreams, and shewing of hard sentences, and dissolving of*

doubts, were found in the same Daniel, whom the king named Belteshazzar: now let Daniel be called, and he will shew the interpretation.

Daniel 5:14 *I have even heard of thee, that the spirit of the gods [is] in thee, and [that] light and **UNDERSTANDING** and excellent wisdom is found in thee.*

Daniel 9:22 *And he informed [me], and talked with me, and said, O Daniel, I am now come forth to give thee skill and **UNDERSTANDING**.*

Daniel 10:1 *In the third year of Cyrus king of Persia a thing was revealed unto Daniel, whose name was called Belteshazzar; and the thing [was] true, but the time appointed [was] long: and he understood the thing, and had **UNDERSTANDING** of the vision.*

Colossians 1:9 *For this cause we also, since the day we heard [it], do not cease to pray for you, and to desire that ye might be filled with the knowledge of his will in all wisdom and spiritual **UNDERSTANDING**;*

2nd Timothy 2:7 *Consider what I say; and the Lord give thee **UNDERSTANDING** in all things.*

1st John 5:20 *And we know that the Son of God is come, and hath given us an **UNDERSTANDING**, that we may know him that is true, and we are in him that is true, [even] in his Son Jesus Christ. This is the true God, and eternal life.*

Of all of these (and there are many more), I believe the most important to be the words spoken by our Lord Jesus which were recorded by Luke:

Luke 24:44/45 *And he said unto them, These [are] the words which I spake unto you, while I was yet with you, that all things must be fulfilled, which were written in the law of Moses, and [in] the prophets, and [in] the psalms, concerning me. 45 Then opened he their **UNDERSTANDING**, that they might **UNDERSTAND** the scriptures,*

Luke confirms the words of Jesus in relation to the two people who Jesus appeared to after His crucifixion and resurrection. On the road to Emmaus, Cleopas and his companion walked for mile upon mile in the presence of Jesus Who walked with them. They both "knew" that they walked with another man and they were "conscious" of His presence and His words. Nevertheless, despite seeing and hearing our Lord Jesus, they did not "understand" that it was Him until He opened their understanding.

The bible is littered with instances of people "knowing" and being "conscious" of, but lacking "understanding". The greatest and most well known must surely be of the Apostle Paul, previously known as Saul of Tarsus.

Saul was a Hellenistic Jew, a Pharisee and ringleader of a group that was determined to make Christianity extinct at any cost. Saul "knew" everything there was to know about Jesus and His disciples, but he did not "understand" them. On the road to Damascus, Saul had a miraculous conversion. Jesus appeared and spoke to him and Saul became blinded. Three days later in Damascus, Ananias who Jesus had spoken to in a vision, went to Saul and laid hands upon him. Immediately he was filled with the Holy Spirit and scales fell from his eyes. From that very moment, the man we would all come to know as the Apostle Paul, was able to see. Paul wasn't just given what we know to be normal sight, he was given "understanding". The Holy Spirit had given him "understanding". Paul now "understood" the truth about Jesus and from that moment he spent his life dedicated to preaching about that which previously he had tried to destroy.

It is important to realize that not every "see" or "seen" in the bible refers to our normal human eyesight. It can also refer to "understanding" which is given by the Holy Spirit. There are many examples in the bible of this special type of supernatural sight, this "understanding".

John 20:5 to 8 *And he stooping down, [and looking in],*
saw the linen clothes lying; yet went he not in.
6 Then cometh Simon Peter following him, and went into
the sepulchre, and seeth the linen clothes lie,
7 And the napkin, that was about his head, not lying with
the linen clothes, but wrapped together in a place by itself.
8 Then went in also that other disciple, which came first to
the sepulchre, and he saw, and believed.
In verse five, "Saw" comes from the Greek
"BLEPO" (BLEP-O) meaning to look at, behold, look on
or at.
In verse eight, "Saw" comes from the Greek "EIDO" (I-
DO) meaning to know, to "**understand**".
Interesting that in verse five the gospel writer John "looked
in" and simply "saw" (looked at or on) the clothes of Jesus
lying there. Yet in verse eight John "went in" and he
"saw" (**understood**), but what is more important, he
"believed". At that very moment, John was given
"understanding", and immediately he "believed".
I cannot overstate the importance of Godly
"understanding". Remember earlier we spoke about Saul
of Tarsus; the Apostle Paul. Saul wanted to destroy
Christianity by killing every Christian. Yet, what happened
to him after he was given "sight" or "understanding"?
Acts 9:17 to 22 *And Ananias went his way, and entered*
into the house; and putting his hands on him said, Brother
Saul, the Lord, even Jesus, that appeared unto thee in the
way as thou camest, hath sent me, that thou mightest
receive thy sight, and be filled with the Holy Ghost.
18 And immediately there fell from his eyes as it had been
*scales: and **he received sight** forthwith, and arose, and was*
baptized.
19 And when he had received meat, he was strengthened.
Then was Saul certain days with the disciples which were
at Damascus.

*20 And **straightway he preached Christ in the synagogues, that he is the Son of God.***
21 But all that heard him were amazed, and said; Is not this he that destroyed them which called on this name in Jerusalem, and came hither for that intent, that he might bring them bound unto the chief priests?
22 But Saul increased the more in strength, and confounded the Jews which dwelt at Damascus, proving that this is very Christ.
We can see very clearly that Paul immediately preached Christ as the Son of God. Paul was given "understanding" by the Holy Spirit, and immediately he then believed. There are countless other examples such as these in the Holy Bible. If you are reading this now and you do not have "understanding", please pray to God and He will give it to you.

We can see from the word of the Lord the importance of "understanding" and that this understanding comes through our spirit. We know that "knowledge" of everything is within us. How do we know this, what exactly is knowledge and how does it connect to our spirit?
We know from what we read previously that when Eve transgressed and ate of the fruit from the Tree of Knowledge, at that very moment human beings were given "knowledge," or a "conscience."
Genesis 3:5 *For God doth know that in the day ye eat thereof, then your eyes shall be opened, and ye shall be as gods, knowing good and evil.*
Genesis 3:22 *And the LORD God said, Behold, the man is become as one of us, to know good and evil: and now, lest he put forth his hand, and take also of the tree of life, and eat, and live for ever:*
Satan knew and told Eve that she could be as "gods" because both she and Adam would have "knowledge" or a "conscience."

It was at this very moment that human beings, as we know ourselves today, came into "being." From this moment on, all human beings would have an "inbuilt" knowledge of all things!

We know from both the Latin (Conscientia) and the original Greek (Suneidesis meaning "A knowing with") translations that our conscience is defined as "knowledge with."
We read that we would now know "good and evil", but how would this be? Even today ask yourself a question, "from where did I get to know the difference between right & wrong? Between Good & Evil?" How did I "understand" which was which?
Before we knew any laws of the land, before we could barely talk, we instinctively knew what was right, and what was wrong. Well, it could be argued that we got this from "knowledge" after our ancestor's Eve & Adam ate of the fruit of the Tree of Knowledge. It could be argued, but it would be wrong.
I once had an African Grey Parrot name "Georgie" If I so chose to teach Georgie, he could repeat every word from the bible. Would this make him a bible scholar? Would this make him a great theologian? Would this make him a TV Evangelist or a great man of God? The answer is that it would make him none of those things.
Knowledge without understanding, is totally useless.
We can "know" everything, but if we "understand" nothing, then there is nothing.
Certain people throughout the world today can quote the bible from back to front, but their spirit has been corrupted so badly that they have no understanding and even lie to themselves. Beware of these "religious" people.
1st Timothy 4:1/2 *Now the Spirit speaketh expressly, that in the latter times some shall depart from the faith, giving heed to seducing spirits, and doctrines of devils;*

2 Speaking lies in hypocrisy; having their conscience seared with a hot iron.

Hard to imagine but it's true, people even lie about their lies!

Imagine having a knife wound in your leg and a "hot iron" is placed upon it to stop the bleeding. The result will be a hard, crusty scab which unlike the wound, is now totally insensitive! Hopefully this little illustration will help you to understand the above.

Now let's just remind ourselves again that our "knowledge" or "conscience" is of both good and evil. Our spirit has a "free will" given by God, so it can choose to listen to Satan and "understand" evil. Or, it can listen to God, and "understand" good. It is important here to note that our spirit can choose to listen, not to act. The action comes in connection with our soul and body. This action can be a "good" Christian action, or a "bad" non-Christian action. God gave us this free will for a very good reason and this will be explained in the chapter, "Why are we here?" For now, lets concentrate upon our "knowledge" and "understanding".

We now have a "knowledge" of God and Satan, and most importantly we "understand" the difference.

Although our spirit has been corrupted (very early in our life we "understood" that something was "wrong", but we chose to do it anyway) by the influence of Satan through our worldly actions, it can still be "saved." This happens through the "Born Again" process when we repent of our sins and accept Jesus Christ as our Lord and Savior. As we read earlier, this is the giving by God to us of a "justified" spirit. A justified spirit is a brand new, uncorrupted, pure and clean spirit.

We read before that "wisdom" or "Godly understanding" can never come from Satan, it can only come from God.

Proverbs 9:10 *The fear of the LORD [is] the beginning of wisdom: and the knowledge of the holy [is] understanding.* We cannot fear the Lord unless our spirit is right and our free will responds accordingly, but when it does, we will receive wisdom from above, not from below!
James 3:13 to 18 *Who [is] a wise man and endued with knowledge among you? let him shew out of a good conversation his works with meekness of wisdom.*
14 But if ye have bitter envying and strife in your hearts, glory not, and lie not against the truth.
15 This wisdom descendeth not from above, but [is] earthly, sensual, devilish.
16 For where envying and strife [is], there [is] confusion and every evil work.
17 But the wisdom that is from above is first pure, then peaceable, gentle, [and] easy to be intreated, full of mercy and good fruits, without partiality, and without hypocrisy.
18 And the fruit of righteousness is sown in peace of them that make peace.

It is not God's intention for this book to be written in the most exhaustive, theological manner. It is Gods intention that His words are used and not mine, but not in every instance. God knows that there will be people reading this book who do not yet know the Lord Jesus. It is to those people, that the final few pages of this chapter are written in such a way that they are very easily understood.
God alerted me to one question that He believes many people will still have at this point, and so before ending, let me answer that question.

It was said earlier that our spirit has a free will to choose, or not to choose. People may well ask where does the soul come into this? The soul also has a free will. Let me try to give you a very simple example.

We desire or want to do something we know is wrong. We are at work and we realize that we need an elastic band or some paperclips at home. We put both of these items in our pocket and take them home. Our soul (mind, will, emotions) wanted us to take this action. At the same time as we decided to take this decision (our free will choice), we heard a small voice telling us that what we were doing was wrong because we were stealing from our employer. This was a "reprove" from the Holy Spirit giving our spirit "understanding", a "righteous" and Godly understanding. At the same time we hear another small voice saying it's OK, no one will notice. Many times we hear of the murderer who said they knew what they were doing was wrong, but a voice in their head told them to do it anyway. Our spirit chose to obey the other voice which was Satan giving us "understanding" of the wrong kind. Our corrupted spirit now chooses to agree with our soul and both have sinned.

All is not lost. Our spirit can be "cleansed" and made pure again through our belief in Jesus. When we truly believe in Jesus we will be given a "justified" spirit. This is where the battle begins. The next time our soul is tempted into doing wrong, our justified spirit will choose to say no, and attempt to persuade our soul to do likewise.

Remember both our soul and spirit were given a free will by God.   .

Now go back to what I said about the soul. Imagine it is in the middle, with the body on one side, and the spirit on the other. When we hear or read about the battle for our soul, this is where it starts. Our body (or in scriptural terms our flesh) lusts after the flesh. Our body lusts after "bodily" or "worldly" things. We read in scripture that we do not war in the flesh, but in the spirit. Our corrupted, sinful body, is tempted by Satan which in turn leads to the destruction of our soul and spirit. This is why we need to be saved, experience justification and salvation.

Ephesians 6:11 to 18 *Put on the whole armour of God, that ye may be able to stand against the wiles of the devil.*
12 For we wrestle not against flesh and blood, but against principalities, against powers, against the rulers of the darkness of this world, against spiritual wickedness in high [places].
13 Wherefore take unto you the whole armour of God, that ye may be able to withstand in the evil day, and having done all, to stand.
*14 Stand therefore, having your loins girt about with **truth**, and having on the breastplate of **righteousness**;*
*15 And your feet shod with the preparation of **the gospel** of peace;*
*16 Above all, taking the shield of **faith**, wherewith ye shall be able to quench all the fiery darts of the wicked.*
*17 And take the helmet of **salvation**, and the sword of the Spirit, which is **the word of God**:*
*18 **Praying always** with all prayer and supplication in the Spirit, and watching thereunto with all perseverance and supplication for all saints;*

Here the Apostle Paul uses the analogy of a Roman soldiers armor that was designed to withstand any attack from the enemy. Paul makes it easy for us to remember by associating a physical piece of armor, with spiritual armor necessary for our protection. Our spiritual armor is truth; righteousness; the gospel; faith and the word of God (the Holy Bible). In addition, the most important piece of our spiritual armor is communication with our Commander in Chief! In verse 18, Paul reminds us to pray always to Almighty God. Regrettably, people put on the armor but then fail to switch on their communication devices. They then wonder why they lose spiritual battles!

As Christians, we will undertake three key changes.

"Justification" of our **spirit** is instantaneous as we "Believe" in Jesus and become "Born Again."
The complete cleansing of our spirit is made possible through the death of Christ upon the cross. Our spirit is now justified through Christ.

"Sanctification" of our **soul** is a process of salvation. This is the ongoing cleansing of our soul helped by the Holy Spirit together with our own free will.

"Glorification" of our **body** (if we are Christians) will be instantaneous at the return of Jesus. Remember, at death our body goes back into the ground from whence it was taken. At the return of Jesus we will be given a "glorified" body that will enable us to leave earth and live forever with God.

Let's look at another example. A Christian man suddenly has an urge to look at pornography on his computer. Immediately, his "Born Again" spirit tells him NO. At the same time his soul (mind, etc) influenced by his "Born Again" spirit also tells him NO. His spirit has been "Justified" through the actions of Christ on the Cross and so it cannot sin anymore. His soul is going through the "sanctification" process of salvation and it heard his spirit very clearly, so it also took the "free will" decision not to access & view the pornography, and yet he still did it!
Why?
The Apostle Paul was the greatest Christian ever after Christ, and yet even he suffered the same thing. Not with the urge to view pornography, but with his spirit and soul wanting to do one thing and his body wanting to do another. How do we know this? Paul tells us very clearly:
Romans 7:14 to 25 *For we know that the law is spiritual: but I am carnal, sold under sin.*

15 For that which I do I allow not: for what I would, that do I not; but what I hate, that do I.

16 If then I do that which I would not, I consent unto the law that [it is] good.

17 Now then it is no more I that do it, but sin that dwelleth in me.

18 For I know that in me (that is, in my flesh,) dwelleth no good thing: for to will is present with me; but [how] to perform that which is good I find not.

19 For the good that I would I do not: but the evil which I would not, that I do.

20 Now if I do that I would not, it is no more I that do it, but sin that dwelleth in me.

21 I find then a law, that, when I would do good, evil is present with me.

22 For I delight in the law of God after the inward man:

23 But I see another law in my members, warring against the law of my mind, and bringing me into captivity to the law of sin which is in my members.

24 O wretched man that I am! who shall deliver me from the body of this death?

25 I thank God through Jesus Christ our Lord. So then with the mind I myself serve the law of God; but with the flesh the law of sin.

Let me translate this into simple language. Paul is saying what he wants to do he can't, and yet things that he does not ever want to do, he does! Paul blames his body because he knows that it contains sin!

Paul struggled with his body many times. He wanted to do one thing, but his body did completely the opposite! Have you ever wanted to go somewhere, but your body took you to the bathroom instead? More realistically have you ever wanted to refrain from chocolate, cigarettes or alcohol, but however hard you tried your body overcame you.

The Apostle Paul warned us of this ongoing battle.

Now you would think that when the spirit and soul of the Christian man both choose by the free will not to view pornography, that it would be impossible for the body to operate independently. Regrettably for all of us, on occasions it does. Why is this? We only have to remember Adam and Eve. These humans had perfect bodies and were in a perfect environment, but God had endowed their bodies with desires. Our bodies can, and at times do, act totally independently from our soul and spirit. At times our bodily instincts, especially when influenced by Satan, are so powerful that we cannot control them without help from God. Of course, the most powerful of these instincts is the sexual urge. How many times have highly intelligent men in positions of great authority been destroyed by an act of sexual indiscretion? They can be the most honest, caring men, but in a moment of "madness" they lose everything. Afterwards most say the same thing, "I have absolutely no idea why I did it!" It was the same for Adam and Eve, their bodies desired the fruit, and independently of their spirit, they rebelled against the command of God.

It is because of the knowledge of sin that is within us all (not sin but the knowledge of it) that the battle for our soul starts from a very early age. It is a battle that can be won. In fact, it's a battle that has already been won for humankind by Jesus Christ. Jesus took our place, He was punished for all of OUR sins on the cross at Calvary. We can be delivered from our sinful bodies, but only in and through our belief in Jesus Christ. Notice the key word, "Belief" in Jesus Christ.

John 6:28/29 *Then said they unto him, What shall we do, that we might work the works of God?*
*29Jesus answered and said unto them, This is the work of God, that **ye believe on him** whom he hath sent.*

The cynical men asked Jesus what God required of them? Jesus answered very simply, that "ye believe on Him whom He hath sent". I side with Greek scholars and replace the "on" with "into". In other words, anyone and even Satan believes all that was ever written on Jesus, but they don't believe "into" Him. To believe "into" Him, is to listen to everything that Jesus said and to "obey" Him.

It is at this moment that I must make one huge qualification lest anyone views any of the above as an easy "get out of jail free" card!
Hebrews 4:12 *For the word of God [is] quick, and powerful, and sharper than any twoedged sword, piercing even to the dividing asunder of soul and spirit, and of the joints and marrow, and [is] a discerner of the thoughts and intents of the heart.*
For me, this is the second most powerful verse in the bible and it is very often misread. It is "the word of God" that is a "discerner of the thoughts and intents of the heart." In other words, as a Christian reads his bible, his BIBLE will read him! Don't think you can trick God and use the excuse that "it was my body not me," if in your heart you really wanted to! Whether the action from the thought was "intentional" or not, God will know!
Our Born Again spirit might say no, but our soul decides to do it anyway! This is another scenario and it happens to most new Christians a lot, hence the term "battle for the soul."

God is a very forgiving God. Anyone can make a genuine mistake. David did so when he took Bathsheba, the wife of Uriah, and then arranged for Uriah to be killed. It doesn't get much worse than this, adultery and murder! Yet because David was genuinely remorseful, God forgave him and more important, the Holy Spirit remained with him.
2nd Samuel 11:2 to 17. *And it came to pass in an eveningtide, that David arose from off his bed, and walked upon the roof of the king's house: and from the roof he saw*

*a woman washing herself; and the woman [was] very
beautiful to look upon.*

*3 And David sent and enquired after the woman. And [one]
said, [Is] not this Bathsheba, the daughter of Eliam, the
wife of Uriah the Hittite?*

*4 And David sent messengers, and took her; and she came
in unto him, and he lay with her; for she was purified from
her uncleanness: and she returned unto her house.*

*5 And the woman conceived, and sent and told David, and
said, I [am] with child.*

*6 And David sent to Joab, [saying], Send me Uriah the
Hittite. And Joab sent Uriah to David.*

*7 And when Uriah was come unto him, David demanded
[of him] how Joab did, and how the people did, and how
the war prospered.*

*8 And David said to Uriah, Go down to thy house, and
wash thy feet. And Uriah departed out of the king's house,
and there followed him a mess [of meat] from the king.*

*9 But Uriah slept at the door of the king's house with all the
servants of his lord, and went not down to his house.*

*10 And when they had told David, saying, Uriah went not
down unto his house, David said unto Uriah, Camest thou
not from [thy] journey? why [then] didst thou not go down
unto thine house?*

*11 And Uriah said unto David, The ark, and Israel, and
Judah, abide in tents; and my lord Joab, and the servants of
my lord, are encamped in the open fields; shall I then go
into mine house, to eat and to drink, and to lie with my
wife? [as] thou livest, and [as] thy soul liveth, I will not do
this thing.*

*12 And David said to Uriah, Tarry here to day also, and to
morrow I will let thee depart. So Uriah abode in Jerusalem
that day, and the morrow.*

*13 And when David had called him, he did eat and drink
before him; and he made him drunk: and at even he went*

*out to lie on his bed with the servants of his lord, but went
not down to his house.*

*14 And it came to pass in the morning, that David wrote a
letter to Joab, and sent [it] by the hand of Uriah.*

*15 And he wrote in the letter, saying, Set ye Uriah in the
forefront of the hottest battle, and retire ye from him, that
he may be smitten, and die.*

*16 And it came to pass, when Joab observed the city, that
he assigned Uriah unto a place where he knew that valiant
men [were].*

*17 And the men of the city went out, and fought with Joab:
and there fell [some] of the people of the servants of David;
and Uriah the Hittite died also.*

How do we know that God forgave him? David (as will
every "Born Again" Christian) was brought to repentance
by the Holy Spirit and he immediately obeyed. This is the
absolute key. Do not repent and ask forgiveness if you are
not genuine, because the inner intent of your heart is known
to God. David was genuinely remorseful and he asked for
forgiveness. David immediately "yielded" to the Holy
Spirit. If we study closely Psalm 51, especially verses 1 to
14, we will read the process and sincerity of David's
request.

Psalm 51:1 to 14. *(To the chief Musician, A Psalm of
David, when Nathan the prophet came unto him, after he
had gone in to Bathsheba.) Have mercy upon me, O God,
according to thy lovingkindness: according unto the
multitude of thy tender mercies blot out my transgressions.*

*2 Wash me throughly from mine iniquity, and cleanse me
from my sin.*

*3 For I acknowledge my transgressions: and my sin [is]
ever before me.*

*4 Against thee, thee only, have I sinned, and done [this] evil
in thy sight: that thou mightest be justified when thou
speakest, [and] be clear when thou judgest.*

5 Behold, I was shapen in iniquity; and in sin did my mother conceive me.

6 Behold, thou desirest truth in the inward parts: and in the hidden [part] thou shalt make me to know wisdom.

7 Purge me with hyssop, and I shall be clean: wash me, and I shall be whiter than snow.

8 Make me to hear joy and gladness; [that] the bones [which] thou hast broken may rejoice.

9 Hide thy face from my sins, and blot out all mine iniquities.

10 Create in me a clean heart, O God; and renew a right spirit within me.

*11 Cast me not away from thy presence; **and take not thy holy spirit from me.***

12 Restore unto me the joy of thy salvation; and uphold me [with thy] free spirit.

13 [Then] will I teach transgressors thy ways; and sinners shall be converted unto thee.

14 Deliver me from bloodguiltiness, O God, thou God of my salvation: [and] my tongue shall sing aloud of thy righteousness.

Despite committing adultery and murder, the Holy Spirit did **NOT DEPART** from David. Quite a startling revelation I'm sure to some, but nonetheless the truth. David was honest, genuine and full of remorse, but more important, he did what the Holy Spirit told him to do; he repented.

Now I'm sure that one question still remains. What controls our bodies if it's not our soul or our spirit? To explain this as simply as possible, let me again give you three examples.

When we walk, do we need to think about and control every step that we take? Or can we talk as we walk, sing as we walk, think and read as we walk. Well, we can do all of these things because our bodies walk independently of our conscious, free will thought. We decide that we will walk to the store, and without any help from us, our bodies walk. I love to eat and I choose with my free will and "knowledge" exactly what I will eat. However, the action of my eating requires no thought or consciousness whatsoever on my part. In fact, I can watch TV and talk and eat all at the same time! My body eats the food entirely independently of me. In addition, my body tells me when it's hungry!

Finally, the most powerful of these "independent" bodily actions is the sexual urge. God "created" First Man and we know that First Man did not have a soul or knowledge. How then could First Man do as God commanded him? Genesis 1:27/28 *So God created man in his [own] image, in the image of God created he him; male and female created he them.*

28 And God blessed them, and God said unto them, Be fruitful, and multiply, and replenish the earth, and subdue it: and have dominion over the fish of the sea, and over the fowl of the air, and over every living thing that moveth upon the earth.

Be fruitful, and multiply said God. As with hunger, or walking, or thirst, our sexual urge can happen totally independently of our soul or spirit. We use the word's human nature and we use the term animal instinct. I cannot think of any better descriptions of how the body operates independently, and I pray that my examples will have answered your question.

The main reason for this chapter apart from the obvious, is to make you aware of the life and death choice that's in your hands. I am a spirit being and so are you. Spirits live forever and they do not die. This bodily life that we now enjoy is very short lived and we then go on to eternity. That eternity can be spent with God in His paradise, or it can be spent in hell with Satan. The "free will" choice is yours. I pray that you choose Christ and live.

I hope that this chapter, when read in conjunction with First, Second and Third man, will aid your understanding of the truth about whom we are.

Finally, there might be one other question remaining from non-believers who are reading this. A fair and valid question might be, "I don't believe in Jesus or God, or what is more important, the Holy Spirit. I am not a Christian and so how and why would the Holy Spirit give me understanding"? This is a very fair question and one that I could not answer, but I know a God Who can! Let's again look at the word of God.

John 16:7/8 *Nevertheless I tell you the truth; It is expedient for you that I go away: for if I go not away, the Comforter will not come unto you; but if I depart, I will send him unto you.*

8And when he is come, he will reprove the world of sin, and of righteousness, and of judgment:

Jesus was about to leave our earth after His crucifixion and resurrection. As Christians, we understand that at Pentecost the Holy Spirit came upon and baptized the disciples, but what about non-believers in either Jesus or God? Jesus gives us the answer, "He will reprove THE WORLD of sin, and of righteousness, and of judgement". Satan will give you "understanding" of evil knowledge, but immediately after, the Holy Spirit will reprove (convict, convince) whatever Satan said by telling you the TRUTH. This TRUTH will be the righteousness of God, it will be that which is right. Once again you can still exercise your free will to listen and act, or not.

It doesn't matter that you are a non-believer. Gone are the days when only the Hebrew Nation of Israel enjoyed the great privilege of salvation. Now we all have a choice to listen to God, believe in Jesus and live, or deny the truth of Jesus and die. Jesus gave Himself and the Holy Spirit to the WHOLE WORLD! There is so much more to say on just these two verses, but hopefully this will "convince" the non-believer that however much they disbelieve and ridicule God and our Lord Jesus Christ, God will still love them and want to bring them into communion with Himself. Every religion on this earth is all about man seeking God, Christianity is all about God seeking man!

A special additional note.

You read earlier that our spirit is "Justified" when we believe in Jesus Christ. It is by God's grace that after the Holy Spirit searches our hearts, God gives us a brand new cleansed spirit. This is because Jesus took upon Himself all of our sins and through faith in Him, we are "Justified". This is exactly the way it was explained to me before I became a Christian, but it always left me with questions. Regrettably, no human could answer my questions so I asked God. I wanted to understand from God the process and practical aspects of this "Justification". First, why was it necessary (that might seem obvious to most, but I wasn't "most")? Second, what would this physically do to me? I could have written pages on IMPUTATION and Justification by Faith in relation to Abraham and others, but this is how it was explained to me years ago and I simply didn't understand it. What is more important, I couldn't understand it's practical aspect and how it would affect me. So I asked God. This is what He told me, and I will share it with you in exactly the same way.

First, God is not careless or unclear.
1st Corinthian 14:33 *For God is not the author of confusion, but of peace, as in all churches of the saints.*

He always gives us very clear instructions about how we can go to Him. If we choose to ignore these instructions, the consequences can be fatal.

Ecclesiastes 5:1 *Keep thy foot when thou goest to the house of God, and be more ready to hear, than to give the sacrifice of fools: for they consider not that they do evil.*
In other words guard your steps, approach God with reverence, awe and humility, and listen to Him.

Leviticus 10:1/2 *And Nadab and Abihu, the sons of Aaron, took either of them his censer, and put fire therein, and put incense thereon, and offered strange fire before the LORD, which he commanded them not.*
2 And there went out fire from the LORD, and devoured them, and they died before the LORD.

Nadab and Abihu wanted to go before God, but they did not adhere to God's instructions and so God "devoured them by fire". God had told them not to offer up "strange fire". They chose to disobey and suffered the consequences.
Fire is a purifying force and incense was the sweet smelling aromatic smoke that would carry the prayers up to God in heaven. In other words, only the holy, pure and cleansed come before God in heaven. The fire and incense that Nadab and Abihu offered up to God was not holy, pure and cleansed. Of course, this was way back in the Old Testament and we are under the New Testament, so what about us?
We were also given very clear instructions by God.

John 14:6 *Jesus saith unto him, I am the way, the truth, and the life: no man cometh unto the Father, but by me.*
How can we get to Jesus? This is Jesus's answer to that question.

John 6:44/45 *No man can come to me, except the Father which hath sent me draw him: and I will raise him up at the last day.*

45 It is written in the prophets, And they shall be all taught of God. Every man therefore that hath heard, and hath learned of the Father, cometh unto me.

Two very important statements from Jesus.

Jesus tells us that we cannot go to Him directly, we must be "drawn" by God to Him. If this happens, Jesus promises to "raise him up at the last day". In other words, give us eternal life.

Second Jesus says that "all will be taught of God" and those that listen and act, will go to Him.

I'm sure the next question will be, "How will God draw me"? "What if I am a non-Christian and I know nothing of God or the Holy Bible?" "If after reading this book and I believe what is written in it, but I don't yet know God, what do I do?

As always God's answer is very simple; cry out to Him.

Psalm 107:6 *Then they cried unto the LORD in their trouble, and he delivered them out of their distresses.*

Throughout the Holy Bible and history, great men and women were in situations of desperate need and they "cried out" to God. What is the one common denominator of every great man or woman in the bible? They all "cried out" to God.

The Hebrew word for "cried" is TSA-AQ (TSAW-AK) and translated it is to shriek, to proclaim, to cry out. It is a loud, impassioned, emotional cry.

In 1987, I cried out to God, "Why me? "Why am I here if I cannot reproduce? "What is the point of my being?"

It was the only time in my life that I felt suicidal. I never wanted to be a Christian, but I did "cry out" to God. God answered my cries as He does with everyone. From that moment, a miraculous sequence of events took place that led me to where I am now.

Let me now make a bold statement. If you are a non-Christian reading this, let me suggest that you have already "cried out" to God, and that is why you have this book. God has "drawn" you to this book and right now the door to Jesus Christ is wide open for you to walk right through. When you confess your belief in Jesus Christ, your spirit will immediately be made holy, pure and cleansed. It will be "Justified" through faith in Jesus and what He did for you on the cross.

Romans 1:17 *For therein is the righteousness of God revealed from faith to faith: as it is written, The just shall live by faith.*

All of this is wonderful, but practically what will happen? 2nd Corinthian 5:21 *For he hath made him to be sin for us, **who knew no sin**; that we might be made the righteousness of God in him.*

Jesus took upon Himself the sin of the world for our sakes, but what else does it say?

"Who knew no sin that we might be made the righteousness of God in Him". Remember earlier I wrote about our "conscience" which is "knowledge with"? Remember I wrote that knowledge of EVERYTHING is within us, but only spiritually will we be given "understanding" of it? Remember I wrote that the knowledge within us is of both good and evil?

The next part is the most important, so please read carefully.

Hebrews 9:12 to 28 *Neither by the blood of goats and calves, but by his own blood **he entered in once into the holy place, having obtained eternal redemption for us.** 13 For if the blood of bulls and of goats, and the ashes of an heifer sprinkling the unclean, sanctifieth to the purifying of the flesh:*

14 How much more shall the blood of Christ, who through the eternal Spirit offered himself without spot to God,

purge your conscience from dead works *to serve the living God?*

15 And for this cause he is the mediator of the new testament, that by means of death, for the redemption of the transgressions that were under the first testament, they which are called might receive the promise of eternal inheritance.

16 For where a testament is, there must also of necessity be the death of the testator.

17 For a testament is of force after men are dead: *otherwise it is of no strength at all while the testator liveth.*

18 Whereupon neither the first testament was dedicated without blood.

19 For when Moses had spoken every precept to all the people according to the law, he took the blood of calves and of goats, with water, and scarlet wool, and hyssop, and sprinkled both the book, and all the people,

20 Saying, This is the blood of the testament which God hath enjoined unto you.

21 Moreover he sprinkled with blood both the tabernacle, and all the vessels of the ministry.

22 And almost all things are by the law purged with blood; and without shedding of blood is no remission.

23 It was therefore necessary that the patterns of things in the heavens should be purified with these; but the heavenly things themselves with better sacrifices than these.

24 For Christ is not entered into the holy places made with hands, which are the figures of the true; but into heaven itself, **now to appear in the presence of God for us:**

25 Nor yet that he should offer himself often, as the high priest entereth into the holy place every year with blood of others;

26 For then must he often have suffered since the foundation of the world: but now once in the end of the world hath he appeared to put away sin by the sacrifice of himself.
27 And as it is appointed unto men once to die, but after this the judgment:
28 So Christ was once offered to bear the sins of many; and unto them that look for him shall he appear the second time without sin unto salvation.

I have enlarged and highlighted the most important words, the rest I believe will now be easily understood.
"Purge your conscience from dead works". Remember the Greek word SUNEIDESIS, we read earlier that it means "conscience", which in turn means "knowledge with".
Our "Justified" spirit will have been cleansed of ALL evil, it will only contain knowledge of ALL good! The evil knowledge will have been "purged"!
Purge means to cleanse, to purify. All knowledge and understanding of any sinful act or works that would lead to our spiritual death have been removed from us. Another way of understanding justification is that it is a declaration by God that you are "not guilty". It is impossible for a conscience purged by the blood of Jesus Christ to be found guilty.
Our spirit will now be as originally "created" by God. God is Spirit and He "created" us in His image. Originally, we were pure, holy and cleansed spirit beings and through our faith in Jesus, we will be again!

I give thanks again to the Lord God Almighty. God never complicates, He always keeps it very, very simple. Christianity is not about knowing every word in the Holy Bible and being able to repeat them. Christianity is not about high intellect and exhaustive theology. Christianity is about belief in the Lord Jesus Christ, the message of

Salvation that He brought, and having an ongoing, living, experiential relationship with Him.

Why should I believe the Holy Bible?

Before continuing I feel led by the Lord to provide more help to non-believers. I give thanks to God if you are a non-believer and you have reached this far in the book. The next chapter that you are about to read will challenge you to believe like you have never believed before. Before you reach that point I want to offer words of support that will hopefully reinforce your will to go on to believe.
"Why should I believe in the Holy Bible?" Seems to me like a very fair question. It's certainly a question I asked myself many times years ago.
"Why should I believe the words of some men?" Again, years ago I asked the same question.

We hear from great men of God, Christians and of course our local church leaders, that "The Holy Bible is the inerrant (free from error or untruth, and infallible) and inspired Word of God." Look on any church website and this is what you will read. They go on to say that "it is the sole authoritative guide in all aspects of faith and practice." Surely that should be enough for us? If this is what great men and women of God say, then I should immediately believe it.
Regrettably you don't. Regrettably, you probably have zero faith or belief in the great men and women who preach these things. Regrettably, you have probably seen often these, so called, "Great men" of God behave in ways which are totally the opposite of what the bible teaches. They behave in ways which not only make you disbelieve, but make you positively hate anything to do with the fraudulent church.

It might surprise you to learn that I felt exactly the same way, and sometimes still do. I used to have an absolute hatred of "Christians" who were always asking for money, preaching the bible, and then getting caught out enjoying the most sinful things! Nothing but nothing made me want to stay away from the church more than the antics of these "great men." They developed in me a real hatred because they were liars, fraudsters, cheats and doing it all in the name of God.

I didn't necessarily disbelieve in God, but I didn't believe either. As a basically honest person, I wanted nothing whatsoever to do with what appeared to me to be a group of self righteous, pompous, hypocrites who preached one thing to me, yet did another thing themselves.

The best advice I was ever given was, "Never look to man, he will ALWAYS let you down. Look only to Jesus Who is the same yesterday, today and forever." Jesus will never let you down.

When you find a "perfect church" and walk through the door, it will immediately become imperfect! Regrettably, in all areas and aspects of our lives we will find imperfection and be let down by people. Men and women may let you down, but Jesus Christ never will.

I'm now hearing you say, "That's wonderful, but it still doesn't tell me why I should believe in the Holy Bible?"

I wrote this chapter, apart from other things, to let you know that you are not alone and you are not unique. I understand, because I was exactly the same. Never ever did I want to be a Christian, but by God's grace; I am.

So, let's get back to the question, "Why should I believe in the Holy Bible?"

First, let's keep it simple, what is the bible?

It's a book of two halves, the Old Testament and the New Testament.

The definition of "testament" is, "Something that serves as a sign, evidence or tangible proof of a specified fact, event or quality."

The Old Testament is a translation into English of the original Hebrew and Greek manuscripts, tablets of stone and scrolls written centuries before the birth of Jesus Christ. Very simply, writers of the time compiled evidence and tangible proof not only of the story of creation, but of God's relationship with humankind throughout this period. We are not talking about one book written by one man. We are talking about many manuscripts and writings by numerous people totally independent of one another. All confirming the "tangible proof of facts and events" concerning God and humankind from the beginning of creation. The important thing to note is that the Old Testament was written from approximately 1400 BC to approximately 400 BC. Why should this be considered important?

It should be considered important because more than 1000 years before the birth of Jesus Christ, it speaks of Jesus Christ on more than 350 occasions! One Thousand years before Jesus came, numerous people who had never met one another, and who lived at different times, wrote more than 350 prophesies concerning Jesus and what He would do!

I'm not a gambler, but try to imagine the odds of someone writing today about another person who is yet to be born. Try to imagine them writing about three or four things that person would do, and then 50, 100 or 1000 years later that person is born and does those three or four things. I think the odds would empty your pen of ink just writing the zero's! Now try to imagine the odds of Jesus fulfilling ALL the prophesies which were written about Himself, some 1000 or so years before He was born. I do not think there is a computer powerful enough to mathematically perform this calculation, or even large enough to display all the zero's! I might not be the brightest star in the sky, but even I am not silly enough to dismiss this as merely coincidental!

The New Testament bible speaks of Jesus as "the Word," as "the Word made flesh Who came and dwelt amongst us" and "the Word was with God."
John 1:1/2 *In the beginning was the Word, and the Word was with God, and the Word was God.*
2The same was in the beginning with God.
John 1:14 *And the Word was made flesh, and dwelt among us, (and we beheld his glory, the glory as of the only begotten of the Father,) full of grace and truth.*

Now you know why Jesus is known as "The Word." Jesus fulfilled every word that was ever written about Himself. After His crucifixion and resurrection, Jesus appeared to two men who walked on the road to Emmaus. As He walked with these two men, Jesus described every word concerning Himself that was written by Moses, the Prophets and the Psalmists.
Luke 24:13 to 48 *And, behold, two of them went that same day to a village called Emmaus, which was from Jerusalem [about] threescore furlongs.*
14 And they talked together of all these things which had happened.
15 And it came to pass, that, while they communed [together] and reasoned, Jesus himself drew near, and went with them.
16 But their eyes were holden that they should not know him.
17 And he said unto them, What manner of communications [are] these that ye have one to another, as ye walk, and are sad?

18 And the one of them, whose name was Cleopas, answering said unto him, Art thou only a stranger in Jerusalem, and hast not known the things which are come to pass there in these days?

19 And he said unto them, What things? And they said unto him, Concerning Jesus of Nazareth, which was a prophet mighty in deed and word before God and all the people:

20 And how the chief priests and our rulers delivered him to be condemned to death, and have crucified him.

21 But we trusted that it had been he which should have redeemed Israel: and beside all this, to day is the third day since these things were done.

22 Yea, and certain women also of our company made us astonished, which were early at the sepulchre;

23 And when they found not his body, they came, saying, that they had also seen a vision of angels, which said that he was alive.

24 And certain of them which were with us went to the sepulchre, and found [it] even so as the women had said: but him they saw not.

25 Then he said unto them, O fools, and slow of heart to believe all that the prophets have spoken:

26 Ought not Christ to have suffered these things, and to enter into his glory?

27 And beginning at Moses and all the prophets, he expounded unto them in all the scriptures the things concerning himself.

28 And they drew nigh unto the village, whither they went: and he made as though he would have gone further.

29 But they constrained him, saying, Abide with us: for it is toward evening, and the day is far spent. And he went in to tarry with them.

30 And it came to pass, as he sat at meat with them, he took bread, and blessed [it], and brake, and gave to them.

31 And their eyes were opened, and they knew him; and he vanished out of their sight.

32 And they said one to another, Did not our heart burn within us, while he talked with us by the way, and while he opened to us the scriptures?

33 And they rose up the same hour, and returned to Jerusalem, and found the eleven gathered together, and them that were with them,

34 Saying, The Lord is risen indeed, and hath appeared to Simon.

35 And they told what things [were done] in the way, and how he was known of them in breaking of bread.

36 And as they thus spake, Jesus himself stood in the midst of them, and saith unto them, Peace [be] unto you.

37 But they were terrified and affrighted, and supposed that they had seen a spirit.

38 And he said unto them, Why are ye troubled? and why do thoughts arise in your hearts?

39 Behold my hands and my feet, that it is I myself: handle me, and see; for a spirit hath not flesh and bones, as ye see me have.

40 And when he had thus spoken, he shewed them [his] hands and [his] feet.

41 And while they yet believed not for joy, and wondered, he said unto them, Have ye here any meat?

42 And they gave him a piece of a broiled fish, and of an honeycomb.

43 And he took [it], and did eat before them.

44 And he said unto them, These [are] the words which I spake unto you, while I was yet with you, that all things must be fulfilled, which were written in the law of Moses, and [in] the prophets, and [in] the psalms, concerning me.

45 Then opened he their understanding, that they might understand the scriptures,

46 And said unto them, Thus it is written, and thus it behoved Christ to suffer, and to rise from the dead the third day:

*47 And that repentance and remission of sins should be
preached in his name among all nations, beginning at
Jerusalem.*
48 And ye are witnesses of these things.

The two important verses are 27 and 44. Beginning at
Moses and all the Prophets, he expounded unto them in all
the scriptures the things concerning Himself. Jesus then
went on to say "these are the words which I spake unto
you, while I was yet with you, that all things must be
fulfilled, which were written in the Law of Moses, and in
the Prophets, and in the Psalms concerning Me."
Luke, the gospel writer, then goes on to tell us that "opened
He their **UNDERSTANDING**, that they might
UNDERSTAND the scriptures." Cleopas and his friend
had their eyes opened. From that moment, they both
believed in the Holy Bible and in Jesus Christ. I pray that
at the end of this book you will do the same.
I don't propose to list all the prophesies in the bible, they
can be found by accessing many websites. I will however
just list a few from sections of the Old Testament.

Exodus 12:5 *Your lamb shall be without blemish, a male of
the first year: ye shall take it out from the sheep, or from
the goats:*
"A lamb without blemish". This prophesy was fulfilled and
confirmed in the New Testament.
1st Peter 1:19 *But with the precious blood of Christ, as of a
lamb without blemish and without spot:*

Exodus 12:46 *In one house shall it be eaten; thou shalt not
carry forth ought of the flesh abroad out of the house;
neither shall ye break a bone thereof.*

"Neither shall ye break a bone thereof," referring to the Passover lamb. This prophesy was fulfilled and confirmed in the New Testament.

John 19:31 to 36 *The Jews therefore, because it was the preparation, that the bodies should not remain upon the cross on the sabbath day, (for that sabbath day was an high day,) besought Pilate that their legs might be broken, and that they might be taken away.*

32 Then came the soldiers, and brake the legs of the first, and of the other which was crucified with him.

33 But when they came to Jesus, and saw that he was dead already, they brake not his legs:

34 But one of the soldiers with a spear pierced his side, and forthwith came there out blood and water.

35 And he that saw it bare record, and his record is true: and he knoweth that he saith true, that ye might believe.

36 For these things were done, that the scripture should be fulfilled, A bone of him shall not be broken.

Leviticus 17:11 *For the life of the flesh is in the blood: and I have given it to you upon the altar to make an atonement for your souls: for it is the blood that maketh an atonement for the soul.*

"It is the blood that maketh an atonement for the soul." This prophesy was fulfilled and confirmed in the New Testament.

Hebrews 9:14 *How much more shall the blood of Christ, who through the eternal Spirit offered himself without spot to God, purge your conscience from dead works to serve the living God?*

Psalm 22:7 *All they that see me laugh me to scorn: they shoot out the lip, they shake the head, saying,*

"They shoot out the lip, they shake the head." This prophesy was fulfilled and confirmed in the New Testament.

Matthew 27:39 *And they that passed by reviled him, wagging their heads,*

Psalm 22:8 *He trusted on the LORD that he would deliver him: let him deliver him, seeing he delighted in him.*

"He trusted on the Lord that he would deliver him: let him deliver him." This prophesy was fulfilled and confirmed in the New Testament.

Matthew 27:43 *He trusted in God; let him deliver him now, if he will have him: for he said, I am the Son of God.*

Psalm 22:18 *They part my garments among them, and cast lots upon my vesture.*

"They part my garments among them, and cast lots." This prophesy was fulfilled and confirmed in the New Testament.

Luke 23:34 *Then said Jesus, Father, forgive them; for they know not what they do. And they parted his raiment, and cast lots.*

Before continuing to three examples from the Old Testament book of Prophets, it is worth noting that Psalm 22 virtually foretells the whole story of Jesus.

Isaiah 7:14 *Therefore the Lord himself shall give you a sign; Behold, a virgin shall conceive, and bear a son, and shall call his name Immanuel.*

"A virgin shall conceive, and bear a son, and shall call his name Immanuel." Immanuel meaning, "God with us." This prophesy was fulfilled and confirmed in the New Testament.

Luke 1:34/35 *Then said Mary unto the angel, How shall this be, seeing I know not a man?*
35 And the angel answered and said unto her, The Holy Ghost shall come upon thee, and the power of the Highest shall overshadow thee: therefore also that holy thing which shall be born of thee shall be called the Son of God.

Isaiah 53:3/4/5 *He is despised and rejected of men; a man of sorrows, and acquainted with grief: and we hid as it were our faces from him; he was despised, and we esteemed him not.*
4 Surely he hath borne our griefs, and carried our sorrows: yet we did esteem him stricken, smitten of God, and afflicted.
5 But he was wounded for our transgressions, he was bruised for our iniquities: the chastisement of our peace was upon him; and with his stripes we are healed.
These prophesies were fulfilled and confirmed in the New Testament.
Luke 4:28/29 *And all they in the synagogue, when they heard these things, were filled with wrath,*
29 And rose up, and thrust him out of the city, and led him unto the brow of the hill whereon their city was built, that they might cast him down headlong.
Matthew 27:21 to 23 *The governor answered and said unto them, Whether of the twain will ye that I release unto you? They said, Barabbas.*
22 Pilate saith unto them, What shall I do then with Jesus which is called Christ? They all say unto him, Let him be crucified.
23 And the governor said, Why, what evil hath he done? But they cried out the more, saying, Let him be crucified.
Luke 19:41/42 *And when he was come near, he beheld the city, and wept over it,*

42 Saying, If thou hadst known, even thou, at least in this thy day, the things which belong unto thy peace! but now they are hid from thine eyes.

Luke 23:33 *And when they were come to the place, which is called Calvary, there they crucified him, and the malefactors, one on the right hand, and the other on the left.*

Matthew 27:26 *Then released he Barabbas unto them: and when he had scourged Jesus, he delivered him to be crucified.*

Isaiah 53:7 *He was oppressed, and he was afflicted, yet he opened not his mouth: he is brought as a lamb to the slaughter, and as a sheep before her shearers is dumb, so he openeth not his mouth.*

"He was oppressed, and he was afflicted, yet he opened not his mouth: He is brought as a lamb to the slaughter." This prophesy was fulfilled and confirmed in the New Testament.

John 1:29 *The next day John seeth Jesus coming unto him, and saith, Behold the Lamb of God, which taketh away the sin of the world.*

Matthew 27:12 to 14 *And when he was accused of the chief priests and elders, he answered nothing.*

13 Then said Pilate unto him, Hearest thou not how many things they witness against thee?

14 And he answered him to never a word; insomuch that the governor marvelled greatly.

Matthew 27:27 to 31 *Then the soldiers of the governor took Jesus into the common hall, and gathered unto him the whole band of soldiers.*

28 And they stripped him, and put on him a scarlet robe.

29 And when they had platted a crown of thorns, they put it upon his head, and a reed in his right hand: and they

bowed the knee before him, and mocked him, saying, Hail,
King of the Jews!
30 And they spit upon him, and took the reed, and smote
him on the head.
31 And after that they had mocked him, they took the robe
off from him, and put his own raiment on him, and led him
away to crucify him.

The whole of Isaiah Chapter 53, prophesies the atonement of our Lord Jesus.

I said at the beginning of this chapter that numerous writers of the time, totally independently of one another, all wrote the same things. These writings are Testament or "tangible proof" of the truths that were written.
Someone once asked me if I believed in Julius Caesar, of course, I answered "yes." They then told me that there was vastly more documented evidence of Jesus Christ than there was of Julius Caesar, so why didn't I believe in Jesus?
It wasn't until I started to write this book that I found out just how much more evidence there was. There are almost 25,000 ancient manuscripts already archived relating to the New Testament. There are no other ancient writings of any kind that get even close in number to this. Of Julius Caesars the "Gallic Wars," only 10 manuscripts remain.
This is what Peter wrote about the authenticity of the New Testament. It isn't some fabricated story invented by men. Peter was there, he bears witness to the truth.
2nd Peter 1:15/16 *Moreover I will endeavour that ye may be able after my decease to have these things always in remembrance.*
16 For we have not followed cunningly devised fables, when we made known unto you the power and coming of our Lord Jesus Christ, but were eyewitnesses of his majesty.

Also consider this interesting fact. The Old Testament was written about 1400 years before the birth of Jesus Christ, and it was written by and about men, who were spoken to by God. The last book in the Old Testament is that of the Prophet Malachi who condemns the nation of Israel for their sins. For the next 400 years after the book of Malachi, God is TOTALLY SILENT. God does not speak to anyone on earth for 400 years. These are what became known as the "Silent Years". What is interesting is that before God's silence, He tells Malachi that He will send His messenger and this messenger shall prepare the way for Him. This we can read in Malachi 3:1 to 3 *Behold, I will send my messenger, and he shall prepare the way before me: and the Lord, whom ye seek, shall suddenly come to his temple, even the messenger of the covenant, whom ye delight in: behold, he shall come, saith the LORD of hosts.*
2 But who may abide the day of his coming? and who shall stand when he appeareth? for he [is] like a refiner's fire, and like fullers' soap:
3 And he shall sit [as] a refiner and purifier of silver: and he shall purify the sons of Levi, and purge them as gold and silver, that they may offer unto the LORD an offering in righteousness.

It's also interesting that God told others that He would send His messenger who would prepare the way for Him. One of these was the Prophet Isaiah as we read in Isaiah 40:3 to 5.
The voice of him that crieth in the wilderness, Prepare ye the way of the LORD, make straight in the desert a highway for our God.
4 Every valley shall be exalted, and every mountain and hill shall be made low: and the crooked shall be made straight, and the rough places plain:

5 And the glory of the LORD shall be revealed, and all flesh shall see [it] together: for the mouth of the LORD hath spoken [it].

Now, isn't it also interesting that after this 400 year silence, the New Testament begins with the coming of John the Baptist. Why is it interesting? Well, let's see what it says. In Matthew, Mark, Luke and John we read repeatedly about John the Baptist. All these gospel writers say exactly the same thing, but let's just look at one only.
Mark 1:1 to 9 *The beginning of the gospel of Jesus Christ, the Son of God;*
2 As it is written in the prophets, Behold, I send my messenger before thy face, which shall prepare thy way before thee.
3 The voice of one crying in the wilderness, Prepare ye the way of the Lord, make his paths straight.
4 John did baptize in the wilderness, and preach the baptism of repentance for the remission of sins.
5 And there went out unto him all the land of Judaea, and they of Jerusalem, and were all baptized of him in the river of Jordan, confessing their sins.
6 And John was clothed with camel's hair, and with a girdle of a skin about his loins; and he did eat locusts and wild honey;
7 And preached, saying, There cometh one mightier than I after me, the latchet of whose shoes I am not worthy to stoop down and unloose.
8 I indeed have baptized you with water: but he shall baptize you with the Holy Ghost.
9 And it came to pass in those days, that Jesus came from Nazareth of Galilee, and was baptized of John in Jordan.

Now of course people could understandably say it was mere coincidence that in a totally uncorroborated way the four Gospel writers would all write the same things. They could also say that after 400 years of silence, it was merely coincidental that this "messenger of God" could come out of the wilderness preaching about the fact that he was preparing the way for God. I know what I believe, you must decide for yourself.

I am not a great scholar or reader of the "Classics", and I feel somewhat inadequate in writing this next part, so let me use the words from Randall Niles, "All about the Journey". Randall starts with the words of F.F.Bruce. F. F. Bruce was one of the greats of the last Century, his first book, "New Testament Documents, Are They Reliable?", influenced the American Christian Evangelical movement more than any other. This is what he said concerning the Holy Bible:

"There is no body of ancient literature in the world which enjoys such a wealth of good textual attestation as the New Testament".

Randall then goes on to say:

"Homers Iliad, the most renowned book of ancient Greece, is the second best-preserved literary work of all antiquity, with 643 copies of manuscript support discovered to date. In those copies, there are 764 disputed lines of text, as compared to 40 lines in all the New Testament manuscripts. In fact, many people are unaware that there are no surviving manuscripts of any of William Shakespeare's 37 plays (written in the 1600s), and scholars have been forced to fill some gaps in his works. This pales in textual comparison with the over 5,600 copies and fragments of the New Testament in the original Greek that together, assure us that nothings been lost. All the New Testament except Eleven minor verses can be reconstructed outside the Bible from the writings of the early church leaders in the Second and Third Centuries, AD.

In real terms the New Testament is easily the best attested ancient writing for the sheer number of documents, the time span between the events and the document, and the variety of documents available to sustain or contradict it. There is nothing in ancient manuscript evidence to match such textual availability and integrity.

The academic discipline of textual criticism assures us that the Bible translations we have today are essentially the same as the ancient Bible manuscripts, with the exception of a few inconsequential discrepancies that have been introduced over time through copyist error. We must remember that the Bible was hand-copied for hundreds of years before the invention of the first printing press. Nevertheless, the text is exceedingly well preserved. Again I pondered this - of the approximate 20,000 lines that make up the entire New Testament, only 40 lines are in question. These 40 lines represent one quarter of one percent of the entire text and do not in any way affect the teaching and doctrine of the New Testament. I again compared this with Homers Iliad. Of the approximately 15,600 lines that make up Homer's classic, 764 lines are in question. These 764 lines represent over 5% of the entire text, and yet nobody seems to question the general integrity of that ancient work. To my real surprise, I discovered the Bible to be better preserved - by far - than any other ancient works I've read and accepted over the years such as Homer, Plato and Aristotle. As far as my "interpretation of an interpolation of an oral tradition" theory, I found that the Bible was not changed or interpreted from the ancient source texts. Simply, as the Bible was carried from country to country, it was translated into languages that don't necessarily mirror the original languages of Greek, Hebrew and Aramaic. However, other than some grammatical and cultural differences, the Bible manuscripts are absolutely true to their original form and content, and remarkably well-preserved in their various translations."

I hope that this chapter will help you to believe that the Holy Bible is the truth, but before ending this chapter let me just say a few more words.

The Lord God gave everyone a free will to choose. The Holy Bible is the truth. No other book on earth can be authenticated to be as factually true to it's origins as this one book. No other historical document on earth has anywhere near the supportive volume of text as this one book. Over the course of more than 2000 years numerous great works and peoples have come and gone. The Holy Bible and gospel of Jesus Christ is the only one that is still as powerful, up to date and popular as it was when originally written. Nothing on earth compares to this one book.

If you do not believe in the Holy Bible, I implore you to ask yourself why? It's a very simple question and I only ask that you be honest with yourself.

Throughout my whole life I have tried to keep things very simple. Whenever my faith and belief in Jesus Christ are questioned, nothing changes, I keep it very simple.

Does anyone with a brain on this materialistic planet, really and truly believe that any human would go through the most horrendous ridicule and torture? Then endure a lingering, painful death for absolutely no gain whatsoever? Even more, does anyone truly believe that Jesus, knowing years in advance what was going to happen to Him, and at any time could have easily backed out, would still choose to go ahead just to save someone like you or me? I think it fair to say, no one on this earth would do those things unless he was for real. Unless He truly was, Jesus Christ, Son of God.

I'll leave all non-believers with one final thought. If I am right in my belief in Jesus, I am guaranteed eternal life. If I am wrong in my belief in Jesus, I have lost absolutely nothing at all, I've just had a great life.

If you are wrong in your disbelief, then you have lost absolutely EVERYTHING.

Please, please, choose Jesus and live.

This chapter was completed, edited and ready to go into print, but God compelled me to write more and here it is. Genesis 1:1 *"In the beginning God"* This is the one true fact. Every other fact that was, that is, or that will be, are circumstantial in relation to this.

"I know God and I'm a very spiritual person so that's all I need. I don't need any of that Jesus, churchy rubbish." This is exactly what I used to say not so many years ago. By the very facts written in this book, and what I now understand to be the truth, I believe what I said years ago to be half right. Praise be to God that today I also believe what I said years ago to be half wrong!

I believe that knowledge of all things is within us and so I probably did "know" God. As a small child those great, first four words of the bible were read to me and almost certainly because of this, I came to "know" God, but I never understood Him!

Most of my life I believed that there must be some greater power than humankind. I believed that there was something else out there. I was comfortable with the word God, but if anybody mentioned Jesus, I did not want to go there. Never ever did I want to be a Christian. Just the thought of being around "churchy" type people horrified me! Despite countless "spiritual" experiences in my life, never ever did I want to link these to any human, and Jesus was a human.

This was my state in life, this was my "spiritual" condition, and Satan loved it!

The truth is, I was totally ignorant of God. I "knew" absolutely nothing about Him, and more important, I understood even less!

Throughout my whole life I've always kept things very simple, but I was blinded to the simplicity of my ignorance towards God.

Let's keep it very simple. How could I possibly "know" God?

I hardly ever read the bible. The only time I ever saw one was in church, at weddings or funerals. How then could I possibly "know" anything about God? More important, what or who was it that I was believing in and whom I called God?

Let me ask you a simple question. How can you "know" anyone who you have never read about, seen, touched or even heard about?

God gave us the Holy Bible so that through it we would come to "know" Him. I had never even read the bible, so who was it that I thought I "knew"? Pretty scary when I consider this question today, but nevertheless it was the truth.

Jesus came to earth to offer salvation to humankind, but equally as important, He came to give us a complete knowledge of God. More important still, Jesus came to give us an "understanding" of God.

Jesus not only is the Son of God, but through His life here on earth He explained God to us. If you want to know and understand the character and nature of God, then get to know Jesus.

This is what the gospel writer Luke said.

Luke 1:1 to 4 *Forasmuch as many have taken in hand to set forth in order a declaration of those things which are most surely believed among us.*

2 Even as they delivered them unto us, which from the beginning were eye witnesses, and ministers of the word;

3 It seemed good to me also, having had perfect understanding of all things from the very first, to write unto thee in order, most excellent The-oph-i-lus,
4 That thou mightest know the certainty of those things, wherein thou hast been instructed.

Luke is saying that like the other gospel writers, he witnessed first hand the ministry of Jesus here on earth. Luke is able to write about all of these things in exactly the same way as the others because he understood everything perfectly. He then confirms to Theophilus to be certain that all of this is the truth. Can we believe what Luke says? The gospel of Luke was written in the first century at a time when there was absolute violent hatred throughout the whole Roman empire concerning anything to do with Christianity. If Luke and the other gospel writers were lying about Jesus, does no one ever question why then did not the enemies of Christ simply expose the lies that were being written? I can assure you that if the gospels of Christ were incorrect even in the minutest detail, the Romans would have exposed the lies to the whole world. The only reason the Romans did not is because they are the truth!

Now, let me ask you one very simple final question. If the earth were about to end, but you have been given a huge spaceship that will take you to another planet that contains everything you need for life and happiness, who will you take with you?

Will it be people you have never met? Will it be people you know nothing about? Will you risk having your future life and happiness destroyed by taking people who live their lives in completely different ways to yours? If you are the most perfect family man or woman, would you invite murderers, rapists and child molesters onto your spaceship?

Let me suggest that you would invite none of these types of people. Let me suggest that you would choose very carefully those people who you know to be proven to be exactly like yourself. Let me suggest that you would choose only people who you knew very well. Let me suggest that you would not invite anyone whom you did not know.

Jesus is the way, the truth and the life. No one goes to the Father unless it's through Him. God does not want another rebellion. The ones invited to spend eternity with God, will have a knowledge and understanding of God which will be given to them through our knowledge and understanding of Jesus. Jesus lived the perfect life, so in and through your belief in Him, you will be perfected also. Your spirit will be "justified", your soul will be "sanctified" and your body will be "glorified"!
Again, I beseech you, do not be ignorant of God! Choose life through Jesus Christ.

Why am I here? What is the reason for my being?

One night in the early summer of 1987, after I had been told that I would never father a child, I cried out to God, "Why me"? "Why am I here"? "What is the point of my being if I cannot reproduce"? It was the lowest point in my life, so low that I even contemplated suicide.

Never in my wildest dreams did I really think that God would answer, but He did. That very night God spoke to me, and then He started to take me on a miraculous journey. A journey that would take me all over the world and culminate in every one of my questions being answered.

Remember, never ever did I want to be a Christian. From this pivotal moment in 1987, I battled against God for year upon year, but in the end I could fight Him no more. God gave me spiritual eyes that enabled me to see the truth and I could deny that truth no more. Part of that truth I will share with you now, and I pray that your eyes will be opened to enable you to see it.

"All the world's a stage, all the men and women merely players. They have their exits, and they have their entrances".

William Shakespeare wrote this in his play As You Like It, I don't think he realized just how truthful and powerful these words are.

Isaiah 43:7 *Even every one that is called by my name: for I have created him for my glory, I have formed him; yea, I have made him.*

You see, we were all created by God for His glory. This is the reason for our being. We will all glorify God by the ways in which we live our lives here on earth. As Shakespeare so well recorded, we enter the world's stage, we act on it, and then we exit.

Straight away I hear you say, "I am not a Christian and I don't believe in God, so I can't possibly glorify God." That would appear at first to be a valid statement, but let's look at the definition of "glorify".

Glorify - **To reveal or make clearer the glory of God by ones actions.**

By our actions, be they good or evil, we will demonstrate to the angels in heaven the glory of God. I will qualify this statement later.

The way you "act" on the world stage will make clearer or reveal the glory of God. Again, I hear cries from non-believers questioning how they can possibly make clearer or reveal the glory of God through their actions. What you are about to read will answer this question and many more, but before continuing I remind you again that God gave us all a free will. We can choose to believe and live, or we can choose to disbelieve and die. God is love, and so that this statement can be proven, no one is forced to do anything against their own free will.

Deuteronomy 30:19 *I call heaven and earth to record this day against you, that I have set before you life and death, blessing and cursing: therefore choose life, that both thou and thy seed may live:*

Again, I can hear some saying, "I'll carry on enjoying the goodies now and turn to Jesus later". The problem is, none of us know if we will have a "later"! Remember what God said:

Luke 12:16 to 20 *And he spake a parable unto them, saying, The ground of a certain rich man brought forth plentifully:*

17 And he thought within himself, saying, What shall I do, because I have no room where to bestow my fruits?
18 And he said, This will I do: I will pull down my barns, and build greater; and there will I bestow all my fruits and my goods.
19 And I will say to my soul, Soul, thou hast much goods laid up for many years; take thine ease, eat, drink, and be merry.
*20 But God said unto him, Thou fool, **this night thy soul shall be required of thee:** then whose shall those things be, which thou hast provided?*

At the beginning of this book I asked all non-believers to suspend your disbelief until the end. I ask again the same thing, but with an additional thought.

That thought comes not from me but from you. You say, "How can I possibly believe and have faith in something that I can't see or touch"? Let me ask you a question, have you ever ordered anything by phone or computer using your debit or credit card? You are able to have faith and belief in this so much that you even PAY for something that you have never seen or touched! God is asking for no money and He is offering to give you life!

Ever wonder why people pay hundreds or even thousands of dollars for a piece of crystal made by a man, just because he says it will help them to see into the future or cure an illness?

Ever wonder why the same people will pay money for metal, gold, silver, bronze, wooden, glass or clay objects that a man has made, just because he says they will bring them luck?

Ever wonder why people give huge amounts of money to men just because they say that they have some "special" power to heal or cure?

Ever wonder why none of these men can substantiate any claim they make or offer any guarantee of success?

Question yourselves about these things and then do no more than answer honestly.

In addition, "spiritualists" charge huge amounts of money for a "manifestation" or a "revelation" and people happily pay them. What they claim is accepted by almost everyone, yet are they able to prove or substantiate their claims? One thing I can confirm without doubt and through personal experience, the Lord Jesus will "manifest" or "reveal" Himself to all who believe and He will not charge you a cent for the privilege! Remember what I said earlier in this book. We can "know" every word in the bible, but if we don't have an "understanding" of and "communion" with the Person of whom the bible speaks, then we have nothing at all. Jesus is waiting and wanting to have a personal relationship with you. This will come through belief and prayer, it will save your life and cost you nothing.

Romans 1:16 *For I am not ashamed of the gospel of Christ: for it is the power of God unto salvation to every one that believeth; to the Jew first, and also to the Greek.* The "Supernatural" power of the creator of all things is available to everyone. Jesus is the gospel, believe and receive!

I don't offer any apology for the above; I want you to live! What you are about to read will challenge you to believe like never before. I pray that you do believe, because it is the truth, the **PURE TRUTH** from God.

You now have to do as I asked at the beginning of this book; open your minds to the "Supernatural." Accept what you have read and will read, because it is the truth, the **PURE TRUTH** from God.

Remember, God is love. God is also omniscient (all knowing of that which was, which is, and which is to come). God is omnipresent (present everywhere at the same time) and God is omnipotent (all powerful and able to do anything).

God's overwhelming purpose in His plan for all the heavenly host and humankind, is to prove that it is impossible to be permanently happy, contented and secure, unless we love God, His righteousness and each other. God will prove through pure love, that selfishness and disobedience to Him, will always result in destructive carnage, total misery and complete chaos. Remember what Jesus said:

Matthew 16:24 *Then said Jesus unto his disciples, If any man will come after me, let him deny himself, and take up his cross, and follow me.*

When man decides to promote himself, put down his cross, and refuse to follow Jesus, the resulting sin and selfishness is guaranteed to bring misery, destruction and death.

Back in time (I don't know how long ago), God knew that a rebellion would take place in heaven. This rebellion would be led by Lucifer, God's favorite created being. Lucifer wanted to take control and he wanted to take God's place. All the angels were told by Lucifer that his was a better way. His way was the complete opposite of love and innumerable heavenly angels believed him.

God had to act fast, but He had to act in such a way as to prove to the remaining angels that love and good were better than evil. Remember that the angels had never seen anything other than pure love, the love of God. Remember also that angels have a free will. Some people may question this last sentence, but Lucifer gives us confirmation of its truth.

God through pure love had to convince the remaining angels that His was a better way. To do this God had to allow them to witness first hand Lucifers pure evil. Of their own free will, the angels would then be able to decide to follow God or Lucifer.

A stage had to be set where this almighty play could be acted out. That stage would be planet earth, and all humankind throughout every age would be it's actors. The audience to this almighty play are (it's still ongoing) the remaining angels in heaven.

Lucifer, and his rebellious angels, would be cast down to our earth. What is more important, God would give Lucifer complete authority on our earth, Lucifer could do exactly as he pleased. The only way he could be defeated would be through the love of God.

God would speak the truth to the world through people such as Abraham, Moses, the Prophets the Psalmists and most important of all, Jesus Christ. The world would have a free will to choose to listen to God, or not. Regrettably, most of humankind would choose not to listen. Whilst all this was happening the most horrendous evils were taking place. Remember King Solomon saying "there is nothing new under the sun"? Of course, he was right. At this point let me go forward in time for one moment, to qualify the enormity of that statement and the sacrifice that Lord Jesus made.

Luke 22:41 to 44 *And he was withdrawn from them about a stone's cast, and kneeled down, and prayed,*
42 Saying, Father, if thou be willing, remove this cup from me: nevertheless not my will, but thine, be done.
43 And there appeared an angel unto him from heaven, strengthening him.
44 And being in an agony he prayed more earnestly: and his sweat was as it were great drops of blood falling down to the ground.

On the night before His capture and crucifixion, Jesus prayed to His Father God in heaven. Jesus asked that if it were at all possible, the "cup" be removed from Him. At that very moment every sin that had been committed, or ever would be committed on planet earth, were in that

"cup". It's hard to imagine the horror of the concoction that the only totally sin free man ever to walk this earth had to drink. Jesus had to take upon Himself at that moment, every sin that had or would ever be committed by humankind. No sin to come after this event would be a new sin. It would merely be old sins magnified and multiplied. There is "nothing new under the sun".
We also read that Jesus was in such agony that He sweat blood. There is a clinical name for this phenomenon, it is "Hematohidrosis". Under rare cases of extreme anxiety due to unbearable pressures, our blood vessels constrict and then dilate and rupture. Blood then gets into our sweat glands and mixes with our sweat so that we "sweat blood". This phenomenon is so rare that it only normally occurs in people who are facing death. The intensity of the agony of Jesus at that moment is almost impossible to imagine. He lived the perfect life, yet now He had to take upon Himself the most vile concoction this world will ever know. Again, can we believe this is true? The simple answer once more is "yes". You see, the man who was with Jesus and wrote of this was the gospel writer Luke and he was a physician!

Now, let's get back to a review of the chronological sequence of events:
God knew that there would be a rebellion in heaven and so He created the earth and everything in it. The rebellion happened, and Lucifer and his angels were cast down to earth (God never told me how long ago this was, it could be a million or billions of years ago, or it could be as little as tens of thousands of years ago) and authority was given to them by God. Lucifer has a free will, and so that the remaining angels in heaven can witness the evil and destructive nature of Lucifer (who we will now refer to as Satan), God implemented the first part of His plan.
What do we know about Satan? First we know that he was once God's favorite being:

Ezekiel 28:2 to 19 *Son of man, say unto the prince of Tyrus, Thus saith the Lord GOD; Because thine heart [is] lifted up, and thou hast said,* **I [am] a God, I sit [in] the seat of God**, *in the midst of the seas; yet thou [art] a man, and not God, though* **thou set thine heart as the heart of God***:*

3 Behold, thou [art] wiser than Daniel; there is no secret that they can hide from thee:

4 With thy wisdom and with thine understanding thou hast gotten thee riches, and hast gotten gold and silver into thy treasures:

5 By thy great wisdom [and] by thy traffick hast thou increased thy riches, and thine heart is lifted up because of thy riches:

6 Therefore thus saith the Lord GOD; Because thou hast set thine heart as the heart of God;

7 Behold, therefore I will bring strangers upon thee, the terrible of the nations: and they shall draw their swords against the beauty of thy wisdom, and they shall defile thy brightness.

8 They shall bring thee down to the pit, and thou shalt die the deaths of [them that are] slain in the midst of the seas.

9 Wilt thou yet say before him that slayeth thee, I [am] God? but thou [shalt be] a man, and no God, in the hand of him that slayeth thee.

10 Thou shalt die the deaths of the uncircumcised by the hand of strangers: for I have spoken [it], saith the Lord GOD.

11 Moreover the word of the LORD came unto me, saying,

12 Son of man, take up a lamentation upon the king of Tyrus, and say unto him, Thus saith the Lord GOD; Thou sealest up the sum, **full of wisdom**, *and* **perfect in beauty***.*

13 Thou hast been in **Eden the garden of God***; every precious stone [was] thy covering, the sardius, topaz, and the diamond, the beryl, the onyx, and the jasper, the sapphire, the emerald, and the carbuncle, and gold: the* *workmanship of thy tabrets and of thy pipes was prepared in thee in the day that thou wast **created**.*

*14 Thou [art] the **anointed cherub** (the archangel in charge) that covereth; and I have set thee [so]: thou **wast upon the holy mountain of God**; thou hast walked up and down in the midst of the stones of fire.*

*15 **Thou [wast] perfect** in thy ways from the day that **thou wast created**, till iniquity was found in thee.*

16 By the multitude of thy merchandise they have filled the midst of thee with violence, and thou hast sinned: therefore I will cast thee as profane out of the mountain of God: and I will destroy thee, O covering cherub, from the midst of the stones of fire.

17 Thine heart was lifted up because of thy beauty, thou hast corrupted thy wisdom by reason of thy brightness: I will cast thee to the ground, I will lay thee before kings, that they may behold thee.

18 Thou hast defiled thy sanctuaries by the multitude of thine iniquities, by the iniquity of thy traffick; therefore will I bring forth a fire from the midst of thee, it shall devour thee, and I will bring thee to ashes upon the earth in the sight of all them that behold thee.

*19 All they that know thee among the people shall be astonished at thee: thou shalt be a terror, **and never [shalt] thou [be] any more.***

Don't be confused by the prince or king of "Tyrus" reference by Ezekiel. God through the prophet Ezekiel is referring to Lucifer. We read here that Lucifer was "created", "perfect in beauty", "great wisdom", "an anointed cherub", "in the garden of Eden" and "wast upon the Holy Mountain of God". It doesn't get much better than that! Lucifer, as he was known at this time, was God's favorite created spirit being, and he had a knowledge of God like no other.

The problem was, Lucifer was too bright for his own good! *"Thou hast corrupted thy wisdom by reason of thy brightness"*.

Lucifer, like all the other created beings (including ourselves), was given a "free will". Regrettably, together with all of his wisdom given to him by God, he chose to rebel and wanted to be a god.

We read above where Lucifer said *"I [am] a God, I sit [in] the seat of God"*, and, " *thou set thine heart as the heart of God"*.

If we look at the book of Isaiah, we see further confirmation that the intention of Lucifer was to rebel and overthrow God.

Isaiah 14:12 to 14   *How art thou fallen from heaven, O Lucifer, son of the morning! [how] art thou cut down to the ground, which didst weaken the nations!*

13 For thou hast said in thine heart, I will ascend into heaven, I will exalt my throne above the stars of God: I will sit also upon the mount of the congregation, in the sides of the north:

14 I will ascend above the heights of the clouds; I will be like the most High.

These three verses contain what are known as the "i's" of Satan. Lucifer (Satan), demonstrates here his selfish nature by saying "I will do this and I will do that, etc".

Also, before continuing let me just add one important point about these three verses of scripture. Most people, including some "bible scholars", think that God through Isaiah is referring directly to Lucifer; he is not. God through Isaiah is referring to the King of Babylon, but He makes direct derisory reference to the same behavior by Lucifer.

Lucifer comes from the Hebrew word HEYLEL (HAY-LALE) meaning brightness or the morning star. Even more appropriate is the Greek translation of this word which is PHOSPHOROS meaning light bringer!

Devil comes from the Greek word DIABLOS meaning slanderer or accuser. In scripture, Lucifer, Satan and the Devil are also known as the "accuser of the brethren".

Revelation 12:10 *And I heard a loud voice saying in heaven, Now is come salvation, and strength, and the kingdom of our God, and the power of his Christ: for the **accuser of our brethren** is cast down, which accused them before our God day and night.*

Lucifer incited rebellion in heaven and innumerable angels followed him. This resulted in a war between Lucifer and his angel followers, and Michael and his angel followers. Lucifer was defeated, and together with his angels was cast down to earth.

Revelation 12:7 to 11 *And there was war in heaven: Michael and his angels fought against the dragon; and the dragon fought and his angels,*

8 And prevailed not; neither was their place found any more in heaven.

9 And the great dragon was cast out, that old serpent, called the Devil, and Satan, which deceiveth the whole world: he was cast out into the earth, and his angels were cast out with him.

10 And I heard a loud voice saying in heaven, Now is come salvation, and strength, and the kingdom of our God, and the power of his Christ: for the accuser of our brethren is cast down, which accused them before our God day and night.

11 And they overcame him by the blood of the Lamb, and by the word of their testimony; and they loved not their lives unto the death.

Jude 1:6 *And the angels which kept not their first estate, but left their own habitation, he hath reserved in everlasting chains under darkness unto the judgment of the great day.*

Lucifer and his angels are now allowed by God to rule with power on earth. In fact, Lucifer who now becomes known as Satan, is considered to be the "god of this world".

2nd Corinthian 4:4 *In whom the **god of this world** hath blinded the minds of them which believe not, lest the light of the glorious gospel of Christ, who is the image of God, should shine unto them.*

Satan is also the prince of the power of the air.

Ephesians 2:2 *Wherein in time past ye walked according to the course of this world, according to the prince of the power of the air, the spirit that now worketh in the children of disobedience:*

Satan is at this moment the ruler of our world.

John 12:31 *Now is the judgment of this world: now shall the prince of this world be cast out.*

God has allowed Satan power on earth. Satan has the freedom to do exactly as he wishes. It is only by allowing him this freedom that Satan's destructive power can be witnessed by the remaining angels in heaven. The full horrors of Satan can be clearly contrasted against the love of God, and every action is being watched.

At this point, it is important to note a few things:
First God is still sovereign. Although Satan has been allowed power, at certain times God exercises restraint over him.

2nd Thessalonians 2:6 to 8 *And now ye know what withholdeth that he might be revealed in his time.*
7 For the mystery of iniquity doth already work: only he who now letteth will let, until he be taken out of the way.
8 And then shall that Wicked be revealed, whom the Lord shall consume with the spirit of his mouth, and shall destroy with the brightness of his coming:

Job 2:3 to 6 *And the LORD said unto Satan, Hast thou considered my servant Job, that there is none like him in*

the earth, a perfect and an upright man, one that feareth
God, and escheweth evil? and still he holdeth fast his
integrity, although thou movedst me against him, to destroy
him without cause.
4 And Satan answered the LORD, and said, Skin for skin,
yea, all that a man hath will he give for his life.
5 But put forth thine hand now, and touch his bone and his
flesh, and he will curse thee to thy face.
6 And the LORD said unto Satan, Behold, he is in thine
hand; but save his life.

Basically, God allowed Satan to do whatever he wanted to
do with Job, but not to kill him. Regrettably, most of the
time God lifts this type of restraint from Satan so that the
full horrors of his actions be witnessed. Very often when
terrible tragedies happen, especially to very young people,
relatives will question Christians as to why? They will say,
"If God is so loving and great, why did He allow this to
happen"? In the past I have asked Vicars, Pastors, Priests
exactly the same question and the answer was always the
same, "If I knew the answer to that question, I would be
God, but I don't and I'm not". The answer, however
unpalatable to some, is as I stated above. God has to allow
Satan to reveal the full horrors of what subjection to his
rule would be like. The most important thing to remember
is that we are not the body in which we live. We are all
spirit beings. From personal experience of watching my
best friend die aged only eight, fifty or even one hundred
years is a mere millisecond in eternity. Why do I say this?
If you have experienced the tragic loss of a young child,
these next words are for you. Remember, we are all created
in the image of God with a pure, sin free spirit. We have all
knowledge, but understanding of that knowledge only
comes from God, Satan or the world. A young child is
either sin free or virtually sin free, and they will be judged
by God accordingly.

Luke 12:48 *But he that knew not, and did commit things worthy of stripes, shall be beaten with few stripes. For unto whomsoever much is given, of him shall be much required: and to whom men have committed much, of him they will ask the more.*

Jesus here is saying if you had no understanding of the truth then you will be judged upon that basis. It is highly unlikely that a young child will have understanding of good and evil as an adult and therefore they will be judged on that basis. Every human being will be judged by God as to their acceptance into heaven and eternal life. All Christians will be judged by Jesus at what is called the "Bema Seat" judgement.

2nd Corinthian 5:10 *For we must all appear before the judgment seat of Christ; that every one may receive the things done in his body, according to that he hath done, whether it be good or bad.*

What if the young child was not a Christian? Take great comfort. All non-Christians will be judged by God at what is known as the "Great White Throne" judgement.

Revelation 20:11 to 13 *And I saw a great white throne, and him that sat on it, from whose face the earth and the heaven fled away; and there was found no place for them.*

12 And I saw the dead, small and great, stand before God; and the books were opened: and another book was opened, which is the book of life: and the dead were judged out of those things which were written in the books, according to their works.

13 And the sea gave up the dead which were in it; and death and hell delivered up the dead which were in them: and they were judged every man according to their works.

Every non-Christian will be judged by God according to their works whilst alive on this earth. At death all will stand before God to give an account of themselves. Every second of everyone's life is recorded by God and it will be presented at this judgement. Can we believe this? From personal experience as an eight year old boy I give you my word that this is true. On the 27 June 1960, I died. At that exact moment I saw every second of my eight year life go before me. I don't mean random experiences, I mean every single second of my eight years. All of every action of those minutes, hours, days, weeks, months and years I saw in a millisecond. It will be exactly the same for all humankind. God doesn't count, He weighs. An innocent child with no or very little understanding will be judged by God, accepted into heaven and given eternal life. Remember, God is love, He is ever merciful, ever forgiving and full of grace. This earthly life that we now enjoy however long or short in years, is the equivalent of a "finger snap" in eternity. If you have suffered the loss of a small child, know that they are in an infinitely better place. Again, how can I say this? Very simply because I've been there. If you also want to spend eternity there, become a Christian now!

Furthermore, Satan only has dominion, rule or power over non-believing Christians. Partly because Christians are not bound by the world and worldly things, and partly because they have a weapon that is more powerful than any other.
1st John 2:15 to 17 *Love not the world, neither the things that are in the world. If any man love the world, the love of the Father is not in him.*
16 For all that is in the world, the lust of the flesh, and the lust of the eyes, and the pride of life, is not of the Father, but is of the world.
17 And the world passeth away, and the lust thereof: but he that doeth the will of God abideth for ever.
Ephesians 6:11 to 18 *Put on the whole armour of God, that ye may be able to stand against the wiles of the devil.*
12 For we wrestle not against flesh and blood, but against principalities, against powers, against the rulers of the

darkness of this world, against spiritual wickedness in high places.

13 Wherefore take unto you the whole armour of God, that ye may be able to withstand in the evil day, and having done all, to stand.

14 Stand therefore, having your loins girt about with truth, and having on the breastplate of righteousness;

15 And your feet shod with the preparation of the gospel of peace;

16 Above all, taking the shield of faith, wherewith ye shall be able to quench all the fiery darts of the wicked.

17 And take the helmet of salvation, and the sword of the Spirit, which is the word of God:

18 Praying always with all prayer and supplication in the Spirit, and watching thereunto with all perseverance and supplication for all saints;

Isaiah 54:17 *No weapon that is formed against thee shall prosper; and every tongue that shall rise against thee in judgment thou shalt condemn. This is the heritage of the servants of the LORD, and their righteousness is of me, saith the LORD.*

In simple language, Satan can only tempt with the things of this world and if you don't love them, then you cannot be tempted by them. In addition, Christians have access to the most powerful armor and more importantly, the greatest weapon which is, the Sword of the Spirit. The Sword of the Spirit, is the word of God, it is the Holy Bible. When Christians are fully "suited up" with the armor, and are in communication permanently with the Commander in Chief Almighty God, no weapon will be powerful enough to hurt them. This protection is pretty good, but what else does God say?

Romans 8:37 *Nay, in all these things we are **more than conquerors** through him that loved us.*

A conqueror is good, but it doesn't get any better than being "more than conquerors"!

Just in case all the above were not enough, God also provides additional Spiritual protection. Every Christian is guarded by a Spiritual barrier erected by God through His legal covenant decrees:

1st Peter 1:3 to 5 *Blessed be the God and Father of our Lord Jesus Christ, which according to his abundant mercy hath begotten us again unto a lively hope by the resurrection of Jesus Christ from the dead,*
4 To an inheritance incorruptible, and undefiled, and that fadeth not away, reserved in heaven for you,
5 Who are kept by the power of God through faith unto salvation ready to be revealed in the last time.

Identifying with Christ through our water baptism old self death and new self resurrection.

1st Peter 1:18 to 21 *Forasmuch as ye know that ye were not redeemed with corruptible things, as silver and gold, from your vain conversation received by tradition from your fathers;*
19 But with the precious blood of Christ, as of a lamb without blemish and without spot:
20 Who verily was foreordained before the foundation of the world, but was manifest in these last times for you,
21 Who by him do believe in God, that raised him up from the dead, and gave him glory; that your faith and hope might be in God.

Our belief in the redeeming and atoning blood of the Lamb of God, Jesus Christ.

John 17:22 to 24 *And the glory which thou gavest me I have given them; that they may be one, even as we are one:*
23 I in them, and thou in me, that they may be made perfect in one; and that the world may know that thou hast sent me, and hast loved them, as thou hast loved me.
24 Father, I will that they also, whom thou hast given me, be with me where I am; that they may behold my glory, which thou hast given me: for thou lovedst me before the foundation of the world.

Acknowledgment of our new birth and being adopted by God to become sons of God. Hard to imagine sometimes, but God loves a Christian equally as much as He loves His Son, Jesus Christ.

Remember that God is love and this love must be seen to overcome all. Although Satan has power on earth, his power is spiritual. As the Apostle Paul told us, *"we wrestle not against flesh and blood, but against principalities, against powers, against the rulers of the darkness of this world, against spiritual wickedness."*
Remember also that "understanding" or "wisdom" comes from three sources, God, Satan and the world through our spirit. Also remember that "understanding" is rendered useless if we don't have "knowledge" and vice versa. Although Satan and his angels had authority and power on earth, this was rendered impotent whilst humankind had no "knowledge".
God now took humankind into a paradise, a utopian protected area on earth, which we know as the Garden of Eden. Humankind could live for eternity in this paradise providing they obeyed God. God told humankind to eat of every tree in the garden including the Tree of Life. There is no discrimination with God and He always keeps things very simple, humankind had to obey two simple commandments. God also said "don't eat from the Tree of Knowledge".
Genesis 2:16/17 *And the LORD God commanded the man, saying, Of every tree of the garden thou mayest freely eat: 17 But of the tree of the knowledge of good and evil, thou shalt not eat of it: for in the day that thou eatest thereof thou shalt surely die.*

Let me anticipate your question. If humankind didn't have knowledge, how did they "know" which was the Tree of Knowledge?

Go back to the chapter, What am I. Remember that our bodies can and do act totally independently at certain times through basic "animal" instinct. Now picture this example: I tell my dog in a very authoritative way, "don't eat that cookie"! Later in the day my wife comes home, sees the cookie and offers it to our lovely dog. Guess what? Our dog is tempted and he eats it! I come home and see that the cookie is missing and my dog is very submissive and sheepish towards me. I love my dog dearly, but nevertheless, he still disobeyed my order.

Satan knows that his destructive power is useless unless he can tempt humankind into disobeying God and eating of the Tree of Knowledge.

Also, we know that there is "understanding" or "wisdom" that comes from the world. In relation to animals and humans this is described perfectly by the writer Jude:

Jude 1:10 *But these speak evil of those things which they know not: but what they know naturally, as brute beasts, in those things they corrupt themselves.*

Jude is warning about worldly "reasoning" or animal instincts. How important or valuable are these? Jude tells us:

Jude 1:12/13 *These are spots in your feasts of charity, when they feast with you, feeding themselves without fear: clouds they are without water, carried about of winds; trees whose fruit withereth, without fruit, twice dead, plucked up by the roots;*
13 Raging waves of the sea, foaming out their own shame; wandering stars, to whom is reserved the blackness of darkness for ever.

What value is there in a "cloud without water"? What good is a "fruitless dead tree"? How powerful is a "raging wave" that is all "foam"? Can you think of a good reason for a "wandering star" that cannot be seen because it doesn't shine? Jude then goes on to say:

114

Jude 1:16 *These are murmurers, complainers, walking after their own lusts; and their mouth speaketh great swelling words, having men's persons in admiration because of advantage.*

These people are and will be admired by men, but regrettably that will be their only reward. Jude goes on to remind believers to seek their "wisdom" or "understanding" from God through Jesus Christ. He reminds them that there is only one way to God and eternal life with Him. Jude tells them that only Jesus can "justify" our spirits so that we can be presented "faultless" before God and enjoy eternity with Him.

Jude 1:21 to 25 *Keep yourselves in the love of God, looking for the mercy of our Lord Jesus Christ unto eternal life.*

22 And of some have compassion, making a difference:
23 And others save with fear, pulling them out of the fire; hating even the garment spotted by the flesh.
24 Now unto him that is able to keep you from falling, and to present you faultless before the presence of his glory with exceeding joy,
25 To the only wise God our Saviour, be glory and majesty, dominion and power, both now and ever. Amen.

So, Satan and his rebellious angels are cast down to earth, and Satan's first action was to tempt humankind into disobeying God.

This was Act One for the angels in heaven to witness. They witness God's love and protection for humankind, and the first act of Satan which was designed to destroy it. From this moment on, all knowledge is within humankind and Satan goes all out to give humankind "understanding" of the most evil of that knowledge.

Now God punishes humankind for their disobedience. God removes any access to the Tree of Life so that humankind becomes mortal, and he "curses the ground" thereby returning the paradise Garden of Eden back into desert. Also, God removes humankind and takes them back from "whence they were taken".

Now comes Act Two for the angels in heaven. Starting with Cain, Satan now had power to destroy humankind by giving them understanding of the most sinful, evil actions. Genesis 6:5 to 7 *And GOD saw that the wickedness of man was great in the earth, and that every imagination of the thoughts of his heart was only evil continually.*

6 And it repented the LORD that he had made man on the earth, and it grieved him at his heart.

7 And the LORD said, I will destroy man whom I have created from the face of the earth; both man, and beast, and the creeping thing, and the fowls of the air; for it repenteth me that I have made them.

The angels in heaven were witness to it all, but God acted again to demonstrate His love. One man was not tempted by Satan, this man was Noah.

Genesis 6:8/9 *But Noah found grace in the eyes of the LORD.*

9 These are the generations of Noah: Noah was a just man and perfect in his generations, and Noah walked with God.

God told Noah to build an ark, because God was going to cause huge flooding across planet earth. God gave Noah strict instructions on how to construct this huge ship and which creatures to save.

God never spoke to me about this, but my own personal belief is to believe the word of God. I believe that a great tsunami like event happened and at this time humankind without knowledge, plus certain species of animals, were wiped out. To me it's just as simple as that.

Now comes Act Three for the angels in heaven. Again, Satan is given another chance to prove himself. Also, God again gives very simple rules to humankind. Increasingly, as this play is acted out, we will see the endless forgiveness, mercy, grace and love poured out onto humankind. We will also witness God giving chance upon chance to Satan to prove himself. Regrettably, Satan does just that, but in the most evil of ways.

So, the earth was flooded and every creature upon the earth died in the flood. Noah, his family and all the creatures in the ark were saved. Once all the flood waters had receded, Noah built an altar to God and worshiped Him offering sacrifices. God loved Noah and as with Adam and Eve, God made a covenant with him.

Genesis 9:1 *And God blessed Noah and his sons, and said unto them, Be fruitful, and multiply, and replenish the earth.*

Genesis 9:9 *And I, behold, I establish my covenant with you, and with your seed after you;*

God's covenant was again very simple, just obey God and you and your family will enjoy security, happiness, joy and be blessed mightily. Noah was blessed and his three sons went on to replenish most of the earth with their offspring. However, these offspring were tempted by Satan and again humankind sinned against God.

Genesis 11:4 to 9 *And they said, Go to, let us build us a city and a tower, whose top may reach unto heaven; and let us make us a name, lest we be scattered abroad upon the face of the whole earth.*

5 And the LORD came down to see the city and the tower, which the children of men builded.

6 And the LORD said, Behold, the people is one, and they have all one language; and this they begin to do: and now nothing will be restrained from them, which they have imagined to do.

7 Go to, let us go down, and there confound their language, that they may not understand one another's speech.

8 So the LORD scattered them abroad from thence upon the face of all the earth: and they left off to build the city.

9 Therefore is the name of it called Babel; because the LORD did there confound the language of all the earth: and from thence did the LORD scatter them abroad upon the face of all the earth.

It might to some seem difficult to identify the sin committed, but look closely. God told Noah and his sons in verse one to "replenish the earth", not to "build a city" and stay in one place. Furthermore, they wanted to "make us a name". Pride had entered into the people and the one thing that God abhors, is "pride".

James 4:6 to 8 *But he giveth more grace. Wherefore he saith, God resisteth the proud, but giveth grace unto the humble.*

7 Submit yourselves therefore to God. Resist the devil, and he will flee from you.

8 Draw nigh to God, and he will draw nigh to you. Cleanse your hands, ye sinners; and purify your hearts, ye double minded.

When we look to make a name for ourselves, we are looking to ourselves rather than looking to God. The more "self", the less God!

In addition, the people clearly understood that they should "be scattered abroad upon the face of the whole earth", because they were fearful that this is what God would do to them!

Again, God is merciful! God introduced different languages for them all and "scattered them abroad from thence upon the face of all the earth". It could have been a much more severe punishment, but God gives humankind another opportunity.

Now, comes the Fourth Act for the angels in heaven. Out of the scattered peoples comes Abraham, another man chosen by God. Again, God makes a covenant with humankind through Abraham.

Genesis 12:1 to 3 *Now the LORD had said unto Abram, Get thee out of thy country, and from thy kindred, and from thy father's house, unto a land that I will shew thee:*
2 And I will make of thee a great nation, and I will bless thee, and make thy name great; and thou shalt be a blessing:
3 And I will bless them that bless thee, and curse him that curseth thee: and in thee shall all families of the earth be blessed.
Genesis 17:1 to 9 *And when Abram was ninety years old and nine, the LORD appeared to Abram, and said unto him, I am the Almighty God; walk before me, and be thou perfect.*
2 And I will make my covenant between me and thee, and will multiply thee exceedingly.
3 And Abram fell on his face: and God talked with him, saying,
4 As for me, behold, my covenant is with thee, and thou shalt be a father of many nations.
5 Neither shall thy name any more be called Abram, but thy name shall be Abraham; for a father of many nations have I made thee.
6 And I will make thee exceeding fruitful, and I will make nations of thee, and kings shall come out of thee.
7 And I will establish my covenant between me and thee and thy seed after thee in their generations for an everlasting covenant, to be a God unto thee, and to thy seed after thee.
8 And I will give unto thee, and to thy seed after thee, the land wherein thou art a stranger, all the land of Canaan, for an everlasting possession; and I will be their God.
9 And God said unto Abraham, Thou shalt keep my covenant therefore, thou, and thy seed after thee in their generations.
At first reading it would appear that God is asking nothing of Abraham, but closer examination of the book of Genesis

would suggest otherwise. Most people believe that it was an "unconditional" covenant, I do not agree with that viewpoint.

Genesis 26:5 *Because that Abraham obeyed my voice, and kept my charge, my commandments, my statutes, and my laws.*

In the above verse, God very clearly states that He gave Abraham "commandments, statutes and laws". These I believe to be the "first edition" of the Ten Commandments that were passed down through generations "orally". I say this in part also because of the following:

Genesis 39:7 to 10 *And it came to pass after these things, that his master's wife cast her eyes upon Joseph; and she said, Lie with me.*

8 But he refused, and said unto his master's wife, Behold, my master wotteth not what is with me in the house, and he hath committed all that he hath to my hand;

9 There is none greater in this house than I; neither hath he kept back any thing from me but thee, because thou art his wife: how then can I do this great wickedness, and sin against God?

10 And it came to pass, as she spake to Joseph day by day, that he hearkened not unto her, to lie by her, or to be with her.

How did Joseph know that "adultery" with his masters wife was a "great wickedness, and a sin against God". The only way he could possibly have understood this act to be sinful, is if he had heard it from others. If it had been orally passed down through generations.

Successions of Abrahams "seed" sinned against God, but these were a people "chosen" by God. These were the Hebrew nation; these people became the nation of Israel.

Deuteronomy 7:6 to 9 *For thou art an holy people unto the LORD thy God: the LORD thy God hath chosen thee to be*

a special people unto himself, above all people that are
upon the face of the earth.
7 The LORD did not set his love upon you, nor choose you,
because ye were more in number than any people; for ye
were the fewest of all people:
8 But because the LORD loved you, and because he would
keep the oath which he had sworn unto your fathers, hath
the LORD brought you out with a mighty hand, and
redeemed you out of the house of bondmen, from the hand
of Pharaoh king of Egypt.
9 Know therefore that the LORD thy God, he is God, the
faithful God, which keepeth covenant and mercy with them
that love him and keep his commandments to a thousand
generations;
God had made a covenant with these people and God never
breaks His word. Omniscient God also had said that the
Savior of the world would come out of this nation. The
Messiah, the long hoped for deliverer, would come from
Abrahams seed.
Galatians 3:16 *Now to Abraham and his seed were the*
promises made. He saith not, And to seeds, as of many; but
as of one, And to thy seed, which is Christ.
Matthew 1:1 to 17 *The book of the generation of Jesus*
Christ, the son of David, the son of Abraham.
2 Abraham begat Isaac; and Isaac begat Jacob; and Jacob
begat Judas and his brethren;
3 And Judas begat Phares and Zara of Thamar; and Phares
begat Esrom; and Esrom begat Aram;
4 And Aram begat Aminadab; and Aminadab begat
Naasson; and Naasson begat Salmon;
5 And Salmon begat Booz of Rachab; and Booz begat Obed
of Ruth; and Obed begat Jesse;
6 And Jesse begat David the king; and David the king
begat Solomon of her that had been the wife of Urias;
7 And Solomon begat Roboam; and Roboam begat Abia;
and Abia begat Asa;

8 And Asa begat Josaphat; and Josaphat begat Joram; and Joram begat Ozias;
9 And Ozias begat Joatham; and Joatham begat Achaz; and Achaz begat Ezekias;
10 And Ezekias begat Manasses; and Manasses begat Amon; and Amon begat Josias;
11 And Josias begat Jechonias and his brethren, about the time they were carried away to Babylon:
12 And after they were brought to Babylon, Jechonias begat Salathiel; and Salathiel begat Zorobabel;
13 And Zorobabel begat Abiud; and Abiud begat Eliakim; and Eliakim begat Azor;
14 And Azor begat Sadoc; and Sadoc begat Achim; and Achim begat Eliud;
15 And Eliud begat Eleazar; and Eleazar begat Matthan; and Matthan begat Jacob;
16 And Jacob begat Joseph the husband of Mary, of whom was born Jesus, who is called Christ.
17 So all the generations from Abraham to David are fourteen generations; and from David until the carrying away into Babylon are fourteen generations; and from the carrying away into Babylon unto Christ are fourteen generations.

Abrahams seed, the Hebrews, the nation of Israel, all sinned in numerous ways through Satanic temptation leading to disobedience to God. Although there were numerous punishments, God never breaks His word and repentance by the peoples was always followed by forgiveness and love. God shows mercy repeatedly. Abraham had a son name Isaac, who in turn had a son name Jacob. It was through Jacob that the nation of Israel became named.

Genesis 32:27/28 *And he said unto him, What is thy name? And he said, Jacob.*

28 And he said, Thy name shall be called no more Jacob, but Israel: for as a prince hast thou power with God and with men, and hast prevailed.

We now move on to Act Five for the angels in heaven. The punishment by God for the Hebrew nation. The nation of Israel was to be exiled in Egypt.

During this exile, Israel had become even more corrupted by Satan. In addition, they had forgotten all the verbal laws (commandments) which had been handed down through the generations. Again, the love and grace of God would be seen. God heard the cries of His oppressed beloved Israel and He remembered His covenant with Abraham, Isaac and Jacob.

Exodus 2:23/24 *And it came to pass in process of time, that the king of Egypt died: and the children of Israel sighed by reason of the bondage, and they cried, and their cry came up unto God by reason of the bondage.*

24 And God heard their groaning, and God remembered his covenant with Abraham, with Isaac, and with Jacob.

God would raise up a savior to lead them out of bondage, and it would be Moses.

Exodus 2:2 to 5 *And there went a man of the house of Levi, and took to wife a daughter of Levi.*

2 And the woman conceived, and bare a son: and when she saw him that he was a goodly child, she hid him three months.

3 And when she could not longer hide him, she took for him an ark of bulrushes, and daubed it with slime and with pitch, and put the child therein; and she laid it in the flags by the river's brink.

4 And his sister stood afar off, to wit what would be done to him.

5 And the daughter of Pharaoh came down to wash herself at the river; and her maidens walked along by the river's side; and when she saw the ark among the flags, she sent her maid to fetch it.

Moses was born to a Hebrew woman at a time when Pharaoh was killing all Hebrew male babies at birth. It was noted that Moses was a "goodly" child. Some scholars understand this to signify that he was born circumcised. In those days this was a sign of future greatness, especially in relationship to God. God never shared with me whether this was true or not.

Pharaoh's daughter adopted the baby Moses and raised him as her own. God's hand was upon Moses and He appointed him to lead the nation of Israel out of their Egyptian bondage.

Exodus 3:9 to 12 *Now therefore, behold, the cry of the children of Israel is come unto me: and I have also seen the oppression wherewith the Egyptians oppress them.*

10 Come now therefore, and I will send thee unto Pharaoh, that thou mayest bring forth my people the children of Israel out of Egypt.

11 And Moses said unto God, Who am I, that I should go unto Pharaoh, and that I should bring forth the children of Israel out of Egypt?

12 And he said, Certainly I will be with thee; and this shall be a token unto thee, that I have sent thee: When thou hast brought forth the people out of Egypt, ye shall serve God upon this mountain.

With God's protection and guidance, Moses would deliver the nation of Israel out of Egypt. In return for forgiveness, deliverance and salvation, God would again ask only for obedience. Again, God would keep things very simple, but to remove any confusion, this time God's commandments would be written down. These are what we know as the Ten Commandments. In addition, God would also give Moses laws by which the people should live. These laws would relate to all aspects of life and would ensure that the righteousness and love of God prevailed.

Exodus 24:12 *And the LORD said unto Moses, Come up to me into the mount, and be there:* and *I will give thee tables of stone, and a law, and commandments which I have written; that thou mayest teach them.*

Regrettably, before Moses could even share with the delivered nation of Israel the commandments and laws of God, they had already sinned again against God. Moses was so angry that he broke the tablets of stone written by and given to him by God.

Exodus 32:15 to 21 *And Moses turned, and went down from the mount, and the two tables of the testimony were in his hand: the tables were written on both their sides; on the one side and on the other were they written.*

16 And the tables were the work of God, and the writing was the writing of God, graven upon the tables.

17 And when Joshua heard the noise of the people as they shouted, he said unto Moses, There is a noise of war in the camp.

18 And he said, It is not the voice of them that shout for mastery, neither is it the voice of them that cry for being overcome: but the noise of them that sing do I hear.

19 And it came to pass, as soon as he came nigh unto the camp, that he saw the calf, and the dancing: and Moses' anger waxed hot, and he cast the tables out of his hands, and brake them beneath the mount.

20 And he took the calf which they had made, and burnt it in the fire, and ground it to powder, and strawed it upon the water, and made the children of Israel drink of it.

21 And Moses said unto Aaron, What did this people unto thee, that thou hast brought so great a sin upon them?

Once more, the all loving ever forgiving and ever merciful God told Moses not to worry, and to just make two more tablets of stone. Moses did as God had told him to do and he took the new tablets and presented them to God on Mount Sinai.

Exodus 34:1 to 7 *And the LORD said unto Moses, Hew thee two tables of stone like unto the first: and I will write upon these tables the words that were in the first tables, which thou brakest.*
2 And be ready in the morning, and come up in the morning unto mount Sinai, and present thyself there to me in the top of the mount.
3 And no man shall come up with thee, neither let any man be seen throughout all the mount; neither let the flocks nor herds feed before that mount.
4 And he hewed two tables of stone like unto the first; and Moses rose up early in the morning, and went up unto mount Sinai, as the LORD had commanded him, and took in his hand the two tables of stone.
5 And the LORD descended in the cloud, and stood with him there, and proclaimed the name of the LORD.
6 And the LORD passed by before him, and proclaimed, The LORD, The LORD God, merciful and gracious, longsuffering, and abundant in goodness and truth,
7 Keeping mercy for thousands, forgiving iniquity and transgression and sin, and that will by no means clear the guilty; visiting the iniquity of the fathers upon the children, and upon the children's children, unto the third and to the fourth generation.

Again, we and the remaining angels in heaven, witness first hand the pure love and mercy continually extended by God to His chosen people. Regrettably, repeatedly throughout hundreds of years, God's people would continue to be tempted by Satan. They would commit every evil known to humankind, adultery, incest, rape, murder, bestiality and worse. The angels in heaven could clearly contrast the ways of Satan, to the all loving, ever merciful and gracious ways of God.

God had given His instruction twice; once verbal then written. Next, the God of pure love would give Himself.

In the next act of this play, what the angels would witness would involve the greatest sacrifice ever seen by humankind. The God of creation would sacrifice His only begotten Son, Jesus Christ. Jesus would come to earth, not as the all powerful creator of every living thing, but as a lowly human being.

Remember the most famous verse in the bible?

John 3:16 *For God so loved the world, that he gave his only begotten Son, that whosoever believeth in him should not perish, but have everlasting life.*

Hopefully, by the end of this chapter this verse will mean much more to you than it does now.

Remember also that God gave a free will to Lucifer, all the angels and all humankind. God is love and He uses love, never force! After hearing the simple gospel message of Jesus, we can choose to "believeth" or not. My favorite bible verse is this:

Hebrews 10:38 *Now the just shall live by faith: but if any man draw back, my soul shall have no pleasure in him.*

"The just, shall live, by faith". When we choose of our own free will to have faith in Jesus Christ, our spirit will be justified, and we will live eternally. Remember, it is the righteousness of Christ that "justifies" our spirit.

Remember what God told Ezekiel to tell the nation of Israel?

Ezekiel 33:12/13 *Therefore, thou son of man, say unto the children of thy people, The righteousness of the righteous shall not deliver him in the day of his transgression: as for the wickedness of the wicked, he shall not fall thereby in the day that he turneth from his wickedness; neither shall the righteous be able to live for his righteousness in the day that he sinneth.*

13 When I shall say to the righteous, that he shall surely live; if he trust to his own righteousness, and commit iniquity, all his righteousnesses shall not be remembered;

but for his iniquity that he hath committed, he shall die for it.

As a non-Christian, if we trust in our own righteousness and sin only once, then ALL of our other righteousnesses shall not be remembered and we shall die! As a Christian, we have the opportunity to repent and be forgiven.

I pray to you again, choose Jesus and live!

So, what else do we know about Jesus?

Jesus was God's Son, but He became fully human. Jesus stripped Himself of all power and He laid aside His majesty. Jesus became just like you and me with all of our vulnerabilities and temptations. He gave Himself up to demonstrate His love to His Father in heaven and humanity on planet earth. Jesus would be love personified, yet He would suffer more than any human. Jesus would manifest to humankind the love of God, the pure love of God even throughout the most horrendous suffering.

Jesus is the Lamb of God. He is the Lamb that was slain. Revelation 12:10/11 *And I heard a loud voice saying in heaven, Now is come salvation, and strength, and the kingdom of our God, and the power of his Christ: for the accuser of our brethren is cast down, which accused them before our God day and night.*

11And they overcame him by the blood of the Lamb, and by the word of their testimony; and they loved not their lives unto the death.

Have you ever seen a Lamb? Picture that purity, honesty, softness, trusting, vulnerability, joyfulness, totally blemish free. Lacking completely any violence, hatred, malice, selfishness.

Isaiah 53:7 *He was oppressed, and he was afflicted, yet he opened not his mouth: he is brought as a lamb to the slaughter, and as a sheep before her shearers is dumb, so he openeth not his mouth.*

Years ago, humankind sacrificed the blood of lambs and goats as an offering to God for their sins. Jesus became the once and for all sin offering for the whole world. The only way to "overcome" Satan and live is by the Blood of the Lamb, your testimony, and not to love this life other than to be a witness of the truth. Love the life that is to come next and ensure your guarantee of it by loving Jesus Christ. Christians can do nothing of themselves, but in and through Jesus they can become more than conquerors.

Jesus came so that God could be manifested on earth. The only way to know God is to know Jesus. Anyone who claims to know God and yet denies Jesus needs to seriously question which god they know.

John 14:7 to 11 *If ye had known me, ye should have known my Father also: and from henceforth ye know him, and have seen him.*

8 Philip saith unto him, Lord, shew us the Father, and it sufficeth us.

9 Jesus saith unto him, Have I been so long time with you, and yet hast thou not known me, Philip? he that hath seen me hath seen the Father; and how sayest thou then, Shew us the Father?

10 Believest thou not that I am in the Father, and the Father in me? the words that I speak unto you I speak not of myself: but the Father that dwelleth in me, he doeth the works.

11 Believe me that I am in the Father, and the Father in me: or else believe me for the very works' sake.

God is love, if we don't have love we don't have God!

Jesus is God, if we don't have Jesus we don't have love!

1st John 4:8 to 16 *He that loveth not knoweth not God; for God is love.*

9 In this was manifested the love of God toward us, because that God sent his only begotten Son into the world, that we might live through him.

10 Herein is love, not that we loved God, but that he loved us, and sent his Son to be the propitiation for our sins.
11 Beloved, if God so loved us, we ought also to love one another.
12 No man hath seen God at any time. If we love one another, God dwelleth in us, and his love is perfected in us.
13 Hereby know we that we dwell in him, and he in us, because he hath given us of his Spirit.
14 And we have seen and do testify that the Father sent the Son to be the Saviour of the world.
15 Whosoever shall confess that Jesus is the Son of God, God dwelleth in him, and he in God.
16 And we have known and believed the love that God hath to us. God is love; and he that dwelleth in love dwelleth in God, and God in him.

Do not confuse the agape love of God, with the worldly love of humankind. What is the agape love of God? To see God we need to see Jesus. How did Jesus manifest this "agape" love?
Jesus was patient and longsuffering. Jesus was never envious or jealous. Jesus was gentle, kind and gracious. Jesus was never conceited or puffed up. Jesus did not brag or boast. Jesus never behaved in an incorrect manner, He was never unseemly and never acted disgracefully. Jesus was never irritated, He never flew off into a temper even when provoked. Jesus was never selfish, He was also never pleased when others made mistakes. Jesus always stood for truth and never had evil thoughts. Jesus was trustworthy and had total faith. Jesus was full of hope and endured all things with great fortitude. These traits perfectly demonstrate the "agape" love of God.
John confirmed that perfect love can only come from and through Lord Jesus.

1st John 4:17 to 21 *Herein is our love made perfect, that we may have boldness in the day of judgment: because as he is, so are we in this world.*
18 There is no fear in love; but perfect love casteth out fear: because fear hath torment. He that feareth is not made perfect in love.
19 We love him, because he first loved us.
20 If a man say, I love God, and hateth his brother, he is a liar: for he that loveth not his brother whom he hath seen, how can he love God whom he hath not seen?
21 And this commandment have we from him, That he who loveth God love his brother also.
1st John 5:1 to 3 Whosoever believeth that Jesus is the Christ is born of God: and every one that loveth him that begat loveth him also that is begotten of him.
2 By this we know that we love the children of God, when we love God, and keep his commandments.
3 For this is the love of God, that we keep his commandments: and his commandments are not grievous.
Pause for a moment to consider the agape love of our Lord Jesus. Compare it to the actions of Satan and evil doers in the world because this is exactly what the angels in heaven are doing. Let's go back for a moment to see Jesus as a small boy. The very first recorded words of our Lord Jesus were:
Luke 2:49 *And he said unto them, How is it that ye sought me? wist ye not that I must be about my Father's business?*
Even at the tender age of 12 years, Jesus was interested in one thing and it was not Himself. It was all about sacrificing Himself to fulfill His duty to His Father's will and purpose for Him on this earth. The first and overriding duty of Satan is to himself. This is the basic Satanic philosophy. Remember, the first to "fall" in God's creation was Satan. Self is the greatest enemy of humankind, it caused the fall of the first and it will cause the fall of the last. Self is the last enemy that we will all face in this

world. Jesus is all about denial of self to ensure that God's will and love always come first. Let's read God's words again to see this incredible self-sacrificial love of God in action.

Matthew 16:21 to 23 *From that time forth began Jesus to shew unto his disciples, how that he must go unto Jerusalem, and suffer many things of the elders and chief priests and scribes, and be killed, and be raised again the third day.*

22 Then Peter took him, and began to rebuke him, saying, Be it far from thee, Lord: this shall not be unto thee.

23 But he turned, and said unto Peter, Get thee behind me, Satan: thou art an offence unto me: for thou savourest not the things that be of God, but those that be of men.

Jesus had just told His disciples that He **MUST GO** into Jerusalem to face terrible torture and suffering carried out by the religious leaders. These chief priests would ultimately crucify Him through death on the cross, but He would rise again on the third day. Peter tried desperately to dissuade Jesus from going because he did not want Jesus to suffer and die. Peter's heart was loving towards Jesus, but he suffered from a human condition. Jesus had already explained that He **MUST GO** to Jerusalem and the reasons for this. If He did not obey God and sacrifice Himself, then I would not be writing this, and you would not be reading it! Satan knew these things and that is why he spiritually influenced Peter to say what he did. Peter was a man, and he had the love of a man towards Jesus. Peter loved Jesus and he did not want Jesus to suffer and die for nothing. Peter could see nothing to be gained from dying other than failure. Despite everything that Jesus had previously said to Peter including the resurrection life, the building of a great church and heaven, Peter was blinded to see only death and failure. I think it fair to say that all of us would have behaved in exactly the same way as Peter. Praise be to God that Jesus saw self-sacrifice as victory not failure. Now let's get back to the love of God.

Jesus gave His life for you and I. What is more important and to always be remembered, Jesus willingly gave His life so that those chief priests also could be saved! Jesus suffered more than any human so that the chief priests, who tortured and ultimately crucified Him, could be saved! That, is the ultimate demonstration of the love of God!

Do you want to see how paradise on earth can be achieved? Do you want to live in a utopian world? If your answer is yes, then you have just read the way to achieve it. Believe in Jesus Christ and follow Him!

I've spoken numerous times that our audience are the angels in heaven. Before continuing, let me qualify this statement from the word of God. In this chapter, the Apostle Paul is giving a revelation of the "church" (the meaning of church being a body or group of believers in Jesus Christ, not a building) to Christian believers in Ephesus.

Ephesians 3:1 to 13 *For this cause I Paul, the prisoner of Jesus Christ for you Gentiles,*

2 If ye have heard of the dispensation of the grace of God which is given me to you-ward:

3 How that by revelation he made known unto me the mystery; (as I wrote afore in few words,

4 Whereby, when ye read, ye may understand my knowledge in the mystery of Christ)

5 Which in other ages was not made known unto the sons of men, as it is now revealed unto his holy apostles and prophets by the Spirit;

6 That the Gentiles should be fellowheirs, (No longer is it only for the nation of Israel, now through Jesus eternal life is available to all) *and of the same body, and partakers of his promise in Christ by the gospel:*

7 Whereof I was made a minister, according to the gift of the grace of God given unto me by the effectual working of his power.

8 Unto me, who am less than the least of all saints, is this grace given, that I should preach among the Gentiles the unsearchable riches of Christ;

9 And to make all men see what is the fellowship of the mystery, which from the beginning of the world hath been hid in God, who created all things by Jesus Christ:

10 To the intent that now unto the principalities and powers in heavenly places (The angels in heaven) *might be known by the church the manifold wisdom of God,*(Believers in Jesus Christ by their actions in faith, will teach the angels in heaven! Angels will learn of God's wisdom by watching humankind).

*11 According to the eternal purpose which he purposed in Christ Jesus our Lord(*This is God's perfect will and purpose*):*

12 In whom we have boldness and access with confidence by the faith of him.

13 Wherefore I desire that ye faint not at my tribulations for you, which is your glory.

Also, we can read more confirmation from the words that God gave to Peter:

1st Peter 1:12/13 *Unto whom it was revealed, that not unto themselves, but unto us they did minister the things, which are now reported unto you by them that have preached the gospel unto you with the Holy Ghost sent down from heaven; which things the angels desire to look into.*(The angels in heaven "desire to look into" the glory of the wisdom and love of God through His plan for humankind through belief in His Son, Jesus Christ)

13 Wherefore gird up the loins of your mind, be sober, and hope to the end for the grace that is to be brought unto you at the revelation of Jesus Christ;(In other words, if you are a Christian, understand fully the Almighty responsibility which you have).

I said that you would be challenged to believe like never before. I asked you also to suspend your disbelief. This next passage is the main reason why. You see, not only are the angels in heaven learning of God's wisdom through the actions of humankind, they are also learning from all the rest of God's creation.
Not only are Christians eagerly and anxiously awaiting and praying for Christ the Redeemer to come and save them, all the rest of God's creation are doing exactly the same thing! Already, I can hear non-believers and even some Christians saying, "Surely he can't mean animals, birds and fishes?" Not only do I mean those, but plant life as well!
Remember, God gave humankind "dominion" over all of His creation.
Remember also that God's meaning of "dominion" or "kingship" (read in chapter First Man the Truth) is totally different to what it has come to symbolize today. In simple language, humans were charged by God with lovingly taking care of all of His creation. Regrettably, after sin entered through Adam and Eve, Satan then gave humankind understanding of the knowledge that was now within us. This understanding was of the most horrendous kind which led humankind to subject all other creatures to the horrors of Satan. Horrendous pain and suffering have been and still are being inflicted upon animals, birds, and fishes. The Satanic influence on humankind is also inflicting this suffering upon trees and plants.
Every time suffering occurrs they cry out to God. We might not hear their cries, but every angel in heaven does. The whole of God's creation groans with pain and suffering because they have been forced by humankind to do things for which they were never created. They cry out to God to deliver them from the horrors of this earth and make no

mistake, God hears their cries. The good news is that they will all be delivered at the coming of the Redeemer.

Can we possibly believe this?

Again, don't take my word for it, take the word of God!

Romans 8:18 to 25 *For I reckon that the sufferings of this present time are not worthy to be compared with the glory which shall be revealed in us.*

19. *For the earnest expectation of the creature waiteth for the manifestation of the sons of God.*

20. *For the creature was made subject to vanity, not willingly, but by reason of him who hath subjected the same in hope.*

21. *Because the creature itself also shall be delivered from the bondage of corruption into the glorious liberty of the children of God.*

22. *For we know that the whole creation groaneth and travaileth in pain together until now.*

23. *And not only they, but ourselves also, which have the firstfruits of the Spirit, even we ourselves groan within ourselves, waiting for the adoption, to wit, the redemption of our body.*

24. *For we are saved by hope: but hope that is seen is not hope: for what man seeth, why doth he hope for?*

25. *But if we hope for that we see not, then do we with patience wait for it.*

Now answer these very simple questions honestly, the Holy Spirit will do the rest!

Was a fish created to be kept in a glass bowl?

Was a bird created to be kept in a cage?

Was a desert plant created to be grown in Northern America or Europe?

Was an equatorial tree created to be grown in a North American or European garden? If you have ever tried to do either of these two you will know the answer!

After witnessing every event on earth from the moment of Satan's arrival, all the heavenly host will be in complete agreement. They will have witnessed first hand the wisdom and pure love of God. Now, after witnessing the pure evil of Satan, they will be fully accepting of God's judgement and punishment. So that only pure love and righteousness prevail in the new eternal kingdom, Satan and his angel followers will be destroyed forever. Satan, and all who loved evil, will spend eternity apart from God. Consider the analogy of the prison where the warden opens every cell door, switches off the air conditioning and lights, then secures the entrance so that no one can ever get out. Scream and cry as they may, the warden will be long gone and what is more important, they cannot escape through death! This is described more graphically in the chapter, Third Man.

Let's now look more closely at our Dear Lord and Savior, Jesus Christ.
First, I want you to see that He is God and that He is pure love. Also, I want you to remember the carnival procession that I spoke of before. When the head of the procession has passed us, are we then looking at the future beginning of that procession. Or are we looking at its and our past? Hopefully these few verses from the Apostle Paul might help.
Colossians 1:9 to 18 *For this cause we also, since the day we heard it, do not cease to pray for you, and to desire that ye might be filled with the knowledge of his will in all wisdom and spiritual understanding;*
10 That ye might walk worthy of the Lord unto all pleasing, being fruitful in every good work, and increasing in the knowledge of God;
11 Strengthened with all might, according to his glorious power, unto all patience and longsuffering with joyfulness;

12 Giving thanks unto the Father, which hath made us meet
to be partakers of the inheritance of the saints in light:
13 Who hath delivered us from the power of darkness, and
hath translated us into the kingdom of his dear Son:
14 In whom we have redemption through his blood, even
the forgiveness of sins:
15 Who is the image of the invisible God, the firstborn of
every creature:
16 For by him were all things created, that are in heaven,
and that are in earth, visible and invisible, whether they be
thrones, or dominions, or principalities, or powers: all
things were created by him, and for him:
17 And he is before all things, and by him all things consist.
18 And he is the head of the body, the church: who is the
beginning, the firstborn from the dead; that in all things he
might have the preeminence.

Interesting to read "He is before all things, and by Him all
things consist". Also, "He is the head of the body, the
church: who is the beginning, the firstborn from the dead".
Jesus Christ is the beginning, but He also came to earth and
died and then rose again to be the firstborn from the dead.
Every believer in Jesus will be "born again". Their old
sinful self will die, but from that "death" they will be
reborn. This is the church, this is the beginning, this is the
body of Christ on earth today. I say today, because this sin
filled earth will pass away. There will be a new heaven and
earth that will be inhabited by "born again" Christians.
God told humanity this in the Old Testament, but we know
that humanity didn't believe it!
Isaiah 65:17 *For, behold, I create new heavens and a new*
earth: and the former shall not be remembered, nor come
into mind.
God reminded humanity again in the book of Revelation.
Revelation 21:1 to 7 *And I saw a new heaven and a new*
earth: for the first heaven and the first earth were passed
away; and there was no more sea.

2 And I John saw the holy city, new Jerusalem, coming down from God out of heaven, prepared as a bride adorned for her husband.

3 And I heard a great voice out of heaven saying, Behold, the tabernacle of God is with men, and he will dwell with them, and they shall be his people, and God himself shall be with them, and be their God.

4 And God shall wipe away all tears from their eyes; and there shall be no more death, neither sorrow, nor crying, neither shall there be any more pain: for the former things are passed away.

5 And he that sat upon the throne said, Behold, I make all things new. And he said unto me, Write: for these words are true and faithful.

6 And he said unto me, It is done. I am Alpha and Omega, the beginning and the end. I will give unto him that is athirst of the fountain of the water of life freely.

7 He that overcometh shall inherit all things; and I will be his God, and he shall be my son.

God never complicates anything. To overcome, to inherit and to become His son; we need only to believe!

John 3:16 *For God so loved the world, that he gave his only begotten Son, that whosoever believeth in him should not perish, but have everlasting life.*

Remember, God is omniscient (all knowing) and He knew that Satan would lead a rebellion in heaven. God, because of His nature, could only solve this problem through pure love, otherwise all the heavenly host would simply see Him as a tyrant dictator.

God had to create the perfect stage where all things would become new. Satan would be the ruler and every person would have a free will. Through the Old Testament, God would tell the world about everything that had already happened and that was to happen. The Old Testament would reveal Jesus Christ and His coming to the world.

God knew that the world would not believe the "word" of the Old testament. So God sent His Son Jesus into the world and Jesus would become the "living word"; the "word made flesh Who came and dwelt amongst us".

John 1:1 to 14 *In the beginning was the Word, and the Word was with God, and the Word was God.*

2 The same was in the beginning with God.

3 All things were made by him; and without him was not any thing made that was made.

4 In him was life; and the life was the light of men.

5 And the light shineth in darkness; and the darkness comprehended it not.

6 There was a man sent from God, whose name was John.

7 The same came for a witness, to bear witness of the Light, that all men through him might believe.

8 He was not that Light, but was sent to bear witness of that Light.

9 That was the true Light, which lighteth every man that cometh into the world.

10 He was in the world, and the world was made by him, and the world knew him not.

11 He came unto his own, and his own received him not.

12 But as many as received him, to them gave he power to become the sons of God, even to them that believe on his name:

13 Which were born, not of blood, nor of the will of the flesh, nor of the will of man, but of God.

14 And the Word was made flesh, and dwelt among us, (and we beheld his glory, the glory as of the only begotten of the Father,) full of grace and truth.

After thousands of years of sin and unbelief how would God, now as a normal human being named Jesus, convince the whole of humanity of the perfection of pure love?

Even today with instant global communication it would be difficult for one person to get this message through to all humankind. So how would Jesus do it?

Remember, Jesus was fully human, He had exactly the same capabilities as you or I. This is a very important statement because it remains true today.

Jesus used the most powerful weapon that ever was or will be created. Jesus used the Sword of the Spirit, the word of God. We know it better as the Holy Bible.

Romans 1:16 *For I am not ashamed of the gospel of Christ: for it is the power of God unto salvation to every one that believeth; to the Jew first, and also to the Greek.*

It doesn't get much more powerful than the power of God! What else did Jesus have? He had exactly the same thing that any believer has access to; the Holy Spirit!

Immediately after Jesus was baptized by John in the water, He was baptized by the Holy Spirit. He was then led into the wilderness to be tempted by Satan. How did Jesus overcome Satan?

By the Sword of the Spirit, the word of God!

Matthew 4:3 to 11 *And when the tempter came to him, he said, If thou be the Son of God, command that these stones be made bread.*

4 But he answered and said, It is written, Man shall not live by bread alone, but by every word that proceedeth out of the mouth of God.

5 Then the devil taketh him up into the holy city, and setteth him on a pinnacle of the temple,

6 And saith unto him, If thou be the Son of God, cast thyself down: for it is written, He shall give his angels charge concerning thee: and in their hands they shall bear thee up, lest at any time thou dash thy foot against a stone.

7 Jesus said unto him, It is written again, Thou shalt not tempt the Lord thy God.

8 Again, the devil taketh him up into an exceeding high mountain, and sheweth him all the kingdoms of the world, and the glory of them;
9 And saith unto him, All these things will I give thee, if thou wilt fall down and worship me.
10 Then saith Jesus unto him, Get thee hence, Satan: for it is written, Thou shalt worship the Lord thy God, and him only shalt thou serve.
11 Then the devil leaveth him, and, behold, angels came and ministered unto him.

Every time Jesus quoted from the old Testament, "It is written", "It is written"; Satan was beaten! Nothing has changed! When Satan attacks, simply arm yourself with the greatest weapon ever created, the Holy Bible!
This still doesn't answer the communication problems. Jesus has no cellphone, computer or even motorized means of transport so how will He manifest God and His love to the world?
There was considerable unbelief and so one way to create publicity was through miraculous acts. There were far too many to list here, but I'm sure we all know about water into wine and the loaves and fishes. These miracles drew large crowds, but in the overall scheme of things they would never get the message through to the whole world.
The answer we are looking for is the Holy Spirit, the Spirit of Truth, also known as the Comforter. Remember, we are all spirit beings and our "understanding" of knowledge that is within can only come from three sources. We can get "wisdom" or "understanding" from the world and Satan. We can also get it from God above through the Holy Spirit, the Spirit of Truth.
Jesus knew that His physical manifestation of the love of God on earth was about to end. Through Christian believers and with the Almighty power of the Holy Spirit, Jesus would continue to be manifested throughout the

whole world! In addition, His miraculous story would never be forgotten.

Matthew 16:18 *And I say also unto thee, That thou art Peter, and upon this rock I will build my church; and the gates of hell shall not prevail against it.*

After two thousand years of Satan doing everything he can to destroy the church, it is stronger than ever!

Again, can we believe that Satan will never prevail against believers in Jesus? Once more, let's see what God says:

1st Peter 1:3 to 5 *Blessed be the God and Father of our Lord Jesus Christ, which according to his abundant mercy hath begotten us again unto a lively hope by the resurrection of Jesus Christ from the dead,*

4 To an inheritance incorruptible, and undefiled, and that fadeth not away, reserved in heaven for you,

5 Who are kept by the power of God through faith unto salvation ready to be revealed in the last time.

Seems very clear to me. Reserved in heaven for every believer in Jesus is an "incorruptible inheritance, undefiled that will **never** fadeth away". Doesn't get any better than that! Just to add even more reinforcement, "Reserved" in Greek is Tereo (TAY-REH-O). Tereo in the military sense means to guard from loss. The eternal inheritance promised to all Christians is being "guarded" in heaven by God. Nothing and no one ever takes anything away from God!

Remember, the church is the body of Christ here on earth. Jesus and the love of God will be manifested through the whole world by churches and Christians. Of course, there will be absolute hatred and violence towards Christians and the church in the same way as it was with Jesus. Nevertheless, it will be the total contrast in lifestyles of believers against non-believers that will be witnessed by the angels in heaven. This is the reason we are all here!

Before Jesus left this earth, He made a promise to His disciples. Jesus never breaks His promise and it is His words that I want to end this chapter with. I do not believe it necessary to say anything else.

John 15:1 to 27 *I am the true vine, and my Father is the husbandman.*

2 Every branch in me that beareth not fruit he taketh away: and every branch that beareth fruit, he purgeth it, that it may bring forth more fruit.

3 Now ye are clean through the word which I have spoken unto you.

4 Abide in me, and I in you. As the branch cannot bear fruit of itself, except it abide in the vine; no more can ye, except ye abide in me.

5 I am the vine, ye are the branches: He that abideth in me, and I in him, the same bringeth forth much fruit: for without me ye can do nothing.

6 If a man abide not in me, he is cast forth as a branch, and is withered; and men gather them, and cast them into the fire, and they are burned.

7 If ye abide in me, and my words abide in you, ye shall ask what ye will, and it shall be done unto you.

8 Herein is my Father glorified, that ye bear much fruit; so shall ye be my disciples.

9 As the Father hath loved me, so have I loved you: continue ye in my love.

10 If ye keep my commandments, ye shall abide in my love; even as I have kept my Father's commandments, and abide in his love.

11 These things have I spoken unto you, that my joy might remain in you, and that your joy might be full.

12 This is my commandment, That ye love one another, as I have loved you.

13 Greater love hath no man than this, that a man lay down his life for his friends.

14 Ye are my friends, if ye do whatsoever I command you.

15 Henceforth I call you not servants; for the servant knoweth not what his lord doeth: but I have called you friends; for all things that I have heard of my Father I have made known unto you.

16 Ye have not chosen me, but I have chosen you, and ordained you, that ye should go and bring forth fruit, and that your fruit should remain: that whatsoever ye shall ask of the Father in my name, he may give it you.

17 These things I command you, that ye love one another.

18 If the world hate you, ye know that it hated me before it hated you.

19 If ye were of the world, the world would love his own: but because ye are not of the world, but I have chosen you out of the world, therefore the world hateth you.

20 Remember the word that I said unto you, The servant is not greater than his lord. If they have persecuted me, they will also persecute you; if they have kept my saying, they will keep yours also.

21 But all these things will they do unto you for my name's sake, because they know not him that sent me.

22 If I had not come and spoken unto them, they had not had sin: but now they have no cloke for their sin.

23 He that hateth me hateth my Father also.

24 If I had not done among them the works which none other man did, they had not had sin: but now have they both seen and hated both me and my Father.

25 But this cometh to pass, that the word might be fulfilled that is written in their law, They hated me without a cause.

26 But when the Comforter is come, whom I will send unto you from the Father, even the Spirit of truth, which proceedeth from the Father, he shall testify of me:

27 And ye also shall bear witness, because ye have been with me from the beginning.

John 16:1 to 14 *These things have I spoken unto you, that ye should not be offended.*

2 They shall put you out of the synagogues: yea, the time cometh, that whosoever killeth you will think that he doeth God service.

3 And these things will they do unto you, because they have not known the Father, nor me.

4 But these things have I told you, that when the time shall come, ye may remember that I told you of them. And these things I said not unto you at the beginning, because I was with you.

5 But now I go my way to him that sent me; and none of you asketh me, Whither goest thou?

6 But because I have said these things unto you, sorrow hath filled your heart.

7 Nevertheless I tell you the truth; It is expedient for you that I go away: for if I go not away, the Comforter will not come unto you; but if I depart, I will send him unto you.

8 And when he is come, he will reprove the world of sin, and of righteousness, and of judgment:

9 Of sin, because they believe not on me;

10 Of righteousness, because I go to my Father, and ye see me no more;

11 Of judgment, because the prince of this world is judged.

12 I have yet many things to say unto you, but ye cannot bear them now.

13 Howbeit when he, the Spirit of truth, is come, he will guide you into all truth: for he shall not speak of himself; but whatsoever he shall hear, that shall he speak: and he will shew you things to come.

14 He shall glorify me: for he shall receive of mine, and shall shew it unto you.

Amen. Come, Dear Lord Jesus.

First Man-The TRUTH

The next three chapters contain the main reasons for writing this book. I will try to write them as God gave them to me. I pray that the **PURE TRUTH** herein contained will not only bring all people to a knowledge and acceptance of God as the Creator of all things, but that it will also bring together both creationists and evolutionists. We are all seekers after the truth and for centuries both these groups of people have battled each other for supremacy. Both presented their case and both were right, but both were also wrong.

Matthew 10:34 to 36 *Think not that I am come to send peace on earth: I came not to send peace, but a sword.*
35 For I am come to set a man at variance against his father, and the daughter against her mother, and the daughter in law against her mother in law.
36 And a man's foes shall be they of his own household.
Jesus speaks here about the Sword of the Spirit, the Word of God, our Holy Bible. The words in the book that you are now reading are not mine; the Holy Spirit gave them to me. The Spirit of Truth gave me the words and they are **PURE TRUTH.** Jesus is very clear, "a man's foes shall be they of his own household". After centuries of reputations being dependent upon it, I know that both evolutionists and Christian creationists will oppose the words that are about to be read. This is despite the fact that all of these words come from the Sword of the Spirit, the Holy Bible.

Jesus always speaks the truth. The main opposition to this book will not come from evolutionists; it will come from Christian creationists.

Are evolutionists truly so vain as to think that the earth and everything in it are all the results of an explosion in space? Are Christian creationists truly so blinded by their belief that they refuse to accept the obvious advances made by science and it's technology in being able to correctly date our planet and everything that's lived upon it?

King David put it perfectly when he wrote this some three thousand years ago: -

Psalm 2:1 *Why do the heathen rage, and the people imagine a vain thing?*

David could not understand why the world was in such a mess. More importantly, David could not understand why people preferred to believe people rather than believe God. David questioned the insanity of vanity. Quite interesting, David's son Solomon, who was acknowledged to be the wisest king whoever lived, also commented upon the "vanity" of humankind.

Ecclesiastes 1:2 *Vanity of vanities, saith the Preacher, vanity of vanities; all [is] vanity.*

Despite possessing wisdom beyond that of any human, Solomon acknowledged that apart from God there is nothing. Solomon also was a "seeker after the truth", but he realized that apart from God, all was "vanity."

Ecclesiastes 1:13/14 *And I gave my heart to seek and search out by wisdom concerning all [things] that are done under heaven: this sore travail hath God given to the sons of man to be exercised therewith.*

14 I have seen all the works that are done under the sun; and, behold, all [is] vanity and vexation of spirit.

Solomon uses this same expression in another verse: -

Ecclesiastes 2:11 *Then I looked on all the works that my hands had wrought, and on the labour that I had laboured to do: and, behold, all [was] vanity and vexation of spirit, and [there was] no profit under the sun.*

Basically, what Solomon was saying was that at the end of it all, apart from God everything was meaningless. Despite being the wisest, richest man on earth and being able to do everything he wanted, it was all futile and impermanent. Solomon realized that the only permanent and meaningful thing was his spirit life and relationship to God. You see, we are all eternal spirit beings housed in a mortal body that will die. This physical life is very short, but our spirit life lasts forever!

If you are a non-Christian reading this you might find the last statement odd. Let me again make a suggestion to better help position your mind. Imagine that you only have thirty minutes left to live, who will you turn to then? Think about this very carefully, in only 30 minutes time you will be dead, at that very moment who will you cry out to? Will it be the idols you have worshiped all your life? Your bank balances, your large house, your large car, alcohol, or drugs? None of these will be able to help you at this moment. No matter how hard you cry out to them, I guarantee they will not answer. You will be totally alone and might I suggest; severely afraid.

On the other hand, a Christian will be totally at peace because they know where they are going and to Whom. They won't be in fear of leaving anything behind because they were not enslaved by "worldly" goods. True Christians never get "trapped" by the "trappings of success." Over the course of their life, however long or short, they will have come to know Jesus Christ as their Savior and at that very moment when He is needed most, He will be there.

What qualifies me to say these things? Very simply and once more let's look at the word of God.

Matthew 28:20 *Teaching them to observe all things whatsoever I have commanded you: and, lo, I am with you always, even unto the end of the world. Amen.*

Was Jesus alive and well when He made this promise? No, He wasn't. Jesus had already been crucified, buried and risen. Jesus appeared to the disciples after His death and He can do exactly the same again at any time.

Jesus doesn't lie, when He makes a promise He keeps it. When a Christian needs the Lord Jesus, He will be there for them.

Also, consider very carefully this other scenario. You have a terminal illness, but a great physician offers you a deal. He can guarantee to treat you 100% successfully and give you life, but you have to promise him one thing. He asks you to "believe" that he can cure you. That's all he asks, nothing more, nothing less. What do you think your answer would be? Might I suggest that every person on this planet in that situation would answer, "yes I promise to believe that you can cure me".

Every human on this planet will physically die, but there is a Great Physician named Jesus Christ Who can guarantee eternal life. Not just a few short years, or fifty, or eighty; but eternal life. What do we have to sacrifice or give to Jesus in exchange for the greatest gift ever? All we have to do is to believe on Him. Don't just take my word for it, take the word of Almighty God.

John 3:16 *For God so loved the world, that he gave his only begotten Son, that whosoever believeth in him should not perish, but have everlasting life.*

If you are a non-believer in any of the last two situations then take heart. If you have a terminal illness then know this, Jesus never placed time limits on conversions. Whether you have thirty days left to live or only thirty-seconds, it's never too late. It matters not how badly you may have lived your life, Jesus is ready and waiting to forgive you. Jesus gave His life for you, please don't miss your opportunity to give what remains of your earthly life to Him so that He might give you eternal life. If you are reading this now and you have a terminal illness, then please go and read the last two chapters from the gospel of John. When I wrote that Jesus appeared to the disciples after His death, this wasn't just a one-off fluke. After his death and resurrection, Jesus appeared on countless occasions to many people over many days. On one occasion He appeared to more than 500 people! Again, can we believe this? This is what the Apostle Paul wrote.

1st Corinthian 15:4 to 8 *And that he was buried, and that he rose again the third day according to the scriptures:*
5 And that he was seen of Cephas, then of the twelve:
6 After that, he was seen of above five hundred brethren at once; of whom the greater part remain unto this present, but some are fallen asleep.
7 After that, he was seen of James; then of all the apostles.
8 And last of all he was seen of me also, as of one born out of due time.

Please, please believe, because this is the Truth, the **PURE TRUTH** from God!

Now to get back to the script!
We are taught by "great men", that we and our planet evolved out of an explosion in space... what vanity! Even more incredible is the fact that most people imagine this vain thing! To think that by chance the oceans have always had just enough water in them. To imagine that evaporation of sea water by the sun to give us rain is because of an explosion in space. To imagine that rivers flow into the sea by chance, and that just enough water from those rivers goes into the sea (which never overflows) by chance. To imagine it's by chance that the sun, the moon, winds, etc., all coordinate perfectly so that life on earth can exist. To imagine that these things and many, many more happened by coincidence because of an explosion in space? Truly, what an incredibly vain insect man is!
Ask yourself, "Has the greatest of the great of these men throughout the history of humankind, ever created

anything"? The simple answer is no! Great men have invented things and made things, but they have only ever used what already existed. Think about it, no human however intelligent, has ever created (brought into existence, a causing to be out of nothing) anything and they never will. Almighty God is **THE** only One who creates. Man cannot even create one humble blade of grass! We live today in the most technologically advanced age humankind has ever experienced, yet even the greatest of the great cannot even create a simple blade of grass! Have any of the greatest of the great of these men ever given life to anything? Again, the answer is a resounding no! No man on earth has ever given breath or blood to anything. Yet these great men expect us to believe that everything came from an explosion in space? Truly, this is vanity at it's extreme and the sad thing is that people imagine this vain thing.

I say all of these things to prepare your heart, and more importantly to know that what you are about to read has come from God and not me. I can align myself perfectly with Solomon and say that apart from God, I am absolutely nothing at all. I wish that I were able to boast that I was capable of writing what is about to come next, but I can't. What you are about to read is exactly what God, through the direct power of the Holy Spirit, told to me. Every person can read the bible, but **"UNDERSTANDING"** of it can come only through the manifestation of the Holy Spirit in that persons life. Job 32:8 *But [there is] a spirit in man: and the INSPIRATION of the Almighty giveth them UNDERSTANDING.*
Moses was inspired by the Holy Spirit to write the truth of creation. We read this truth in Genesis, the first book of the bible which was written by Moses. In the book of Genesis, God Himself through the Holy Spirit through Moses tells

us the **PURE TRUTH** of creation. We then have a "free will" choice to believe it or not.

This is what Jesus said:

Luke 16:31 *And he said unto him, If they **hear not** Moses and the prophets, neither will they be persuaded, though one rose from the dead.*

John 5:46/47 *For had ye believed Moses, ye would have believed me: for he wrote of me.*

*47 But if **ye believe not** his writings, how shall ye believe my words?*

God told Moses that there was water in space, Moses believed God. How do we know this? Again, let's look at the word of God:

Genesis 1:6 to 8 *And God said, Let there be a **firmament** in the **midst of the waters**, and let it divide the waters from the waters.*

7 And God made the firmament, and divided the waters which [were] under the firmament from the waters which [were] above the firmament: and it was so.

*8 And God **called the firmament Heaven***

Most people mistakenly think the "firmament" to be our planet earth. If we look at the original Hebrew word RAQIYA we can see that "firmament" is our sky, our atmosphere, our universe.

RAQIYA (RAW-KEE-AH) translated is "an expanse, visible arch of the sky." If we look from one horizon on our left, upward and over to the horizon on our right, we form an "arch in the sky."

God told Moses that He divided the waters in space to create our "universe." This is what God refers to as "heaven." For millenniums, Moses was ridiculed because everyone said that there was no water in space. We now know that there are billions of tons of water in space, there may even be water on Mars!

Moses believed God, what a tragedy that the religious leaders of the day did not believe Moses, hopefully history will not repeat itself again.

If we cannot believe the **TRUTH** that was written by Moses, then we will struggle to believe in Jesus. I pray with every breath in my body that you believe what you are about to read.

Let me first pre-empt a few possible questions.

A. The original scriptures by Moses were a continuous writing, they did not contain the paragraphs and chapters that we see today.

B. The prophet Isaiah lived approximately 700 years after Moses, but you will see that God spoke to Isaiah using exactly the same words concerning the sequence of creation. As we read the book of Isaiah, we will see exactly the same sequence of words used by God to describe the development and history of humankind as the ones found in the book of Genesis.

Isaiah 43:7 *[Even] every one that is called by my name: for I have **created** him for my glory, I have **formed** him; yea, I have **made** him.*

First, God uses the word **"created."**

Secondly, God uses the word **"formed."**

Thirdly, God uses the word **"made."**

The importance and sequence of these words and the understanding of them, will become clear as you read further.

We can play around with our English translations of all of these words, but not with the original Hebrew. The Hebrew definitions of these words translated are very clear and precise. They do not leave any room for misinterpretation or change.

CREATE or BARA (baw-raw) in Hebrew is an all-inclusive word meaning a causing to be by God, the omnipotent power or force. It includes that this "causing to be" is out of nothing. This word CREATE or CREATED appears only three times in the 1st Chapter of Genesis and it is used specifically when there is an entirely new beginning, it is not used anywhere else. The word "made" is used many times, but for all evolutionists reading this, the word CREATE or CREATED is used specifically in relation to:

HEAVEN and EARTH. Genesis 1, Verse 1.
EVERY LIVING CREATURE. Genesis 1, Verse 21.
MAN IN HIS OWN IMAGE. Genesis 1, Verse 27.
There was NO evolution from Ape to man because ALL living things were CREATED! This was creation complete, HEAVEN and EARTH, EVERY LIVING CREATURE, and MAN (humankind both male and female). God's "creation" was complete.

FORMED or YATSAR (yaw-tsar) in Hebrew means to fashion out of something that is already made. To shape or to mould into a form a material or object that you already have. In other words to make a new thing out of something that you already have.

Hopefully, you will start to get God's message.
Humankind had already been "created", but Second Man (as I call him) was "Formed." There was NO evolution from Ape to Second Man. Second Man was "formed" by God out of His existing material!

MADE or ASAH (aw-saw) in Hebrew and in the context of Genesis means the completed, finished work. This is the finality of God's accomplishments, the result is complete humankind on earth, exactly and perfectly made to enable the fulfillment of God's plan for humankind.

Basically, this is what I call Third Man. This is you and I.

C. How can God do all this in just six days? We hear and read that a day to God is like a thousand years, and a thousand years to God is like a day. Let me ask you to simply appreciate that God is God and He can do **ALL** things. Again, let me try to help you to adjust your mind. Was Genesis and creation at the beginning, or was it at the end? Many people naturally would say that it was history and therefore in the past, but isn't the start in the future? Was this not the start, and therefore not in the past, but at the beginning? Imagine a carnival procession that is half way past where you are standing. Is the head of the procession in the past or are you looking at it's beginning or it's start? Are you in that processions past, or is it in yours? This is difficult for me to put into words, but if nothing else it will make you think.

On the 27 June 1960, I died and was taken into what I believe was heaven and the presence of God. I was eight years old, God allowed me to come back to earth and live, but he kept my best friend, Philip Lawton. It's a complete story for another time. For now let me just say this, at the exact second that the car hit me, every millisecond of my eight-year life went before me. Not just certain moments of my eight years, every millisecond right back into my mother's womb! I was then taken out of my mothers womb and transported to heaven. Communication took place and I was then brought back to earth and into my physical body. My story on this has never changed and there are countless numbers of people who can verify what I say. I always described it like a reel of old cinema film. Every frame of my eight-year life captured on film and going before my eyes in less than a millisecond! Since that day in 1960, I viewed time differently than most other people and it held no boundaries to me. The point of this

156

sharing is to confirm from personal experience that God has no problem "creating" the heaven, earth and EVERYTHING in it in six days!

2nd Corinthian 12:1 to 7 *It is not expedient for me doubtless to glory. I will come to visions and revelations of the Lord.*
2 I knew a man in Christ above fourteen years ago, (whether in the body, I cannot tell; or whether out of the body, I cannot tell: God knoweth;) such an one caught up to the third heaven.
3 And I knew such a man, (whether in the body, or out of the body, I cannot tell: God knoweth;)
4 How that he was caught up into paradise, and heard unspeakable words, which it is not lawful for a man to utter.
5 Of such an one will I glory: yet of myself I will not glory, but in mine infirmities.
6 For though I would desire to glory, I shall not be a fool; for I will say the truth: but now I forbear, lest any man should think of me above that which he seeth me to be, or that he heareth of me.
7 And lest I should be exalted above measure through the abundance of the revelations, there was given to me a thorn in the flesh, the messenger of Satan to buffet me, lest I should be exalted above measure.
I do not for one-second compare myself to such a great man as the Apostle Paul, but I can say truthfully that I had exactly the same experience. That experience qualifies me to speak with authority about time because I had a unique experience of it.

D. In the early hours of a dark and damp October morning in 2005, the Holy Spirit appeared to me. From that moment God began to speak to me on a regular basis and revealed to me the **PURE TRUTH** that I share with you now. None of this was by my design. Truly, the last thing I ever wanted to be was a Christian, but praises be to God that He had other ideas.

E. If First Man didn't have a Soul (mind, will, emotions) or Knowledge, how come archeologists have discovered artifacts, cave drawings , etc., from millions of years ago? First Man had basic instincts in exactly the same way as animals do. We know that a bird does not have a mind like ourselves, does this prevent it from constructing a very elaborate nest?
We know that Squirrels don't posses a brain like ourselves, does this prevent them for planning for the winter by burying nuts?
We know that Salmon can navigate thousands of miles of ocean to get to their spawning river without any compass or GPS. Do they posses a human mind or spirit?
We have already read that our bodies can and do behave totally independently of our mind, will and brain. First Man simply used this function more than humankind does today.

F. If death did not come into the world until the Fall of Man in Eden, what happened to the millions of humans and animals before this event?
Death was in the world before humankind was taken by God into the garden of Eden.
Quite a bold statement to make! How can this be qualified? Again, let's look at the word of God. First, there is nothing in the bible up to Genesis chapter 2 verse 8 that says death was NOT in the world. I can already hear you screaming, "That doesn't mean that it was"! You would be quite justified in saying this, but let's go to the word of God again.

Genesis 2:8 *And the LORD God planted a garden eastward in Eden; and there he put the man whom he had formed.*

Garden in Hebrew is GAN which is taken from GANAN (GAW-NAN) meaning a defended, protected, hedged area. In other words, a very special area. What would it need to be protected and defended from if not death?

Eden in Hebrew is EDEN (AY-DEN) and translated it is the region of Adam's home (in other words a specially protected area formed by God for humankind at that moment in the creation process), or humankind's home. Another fair description would be that Eden was "paradise" on earth. In this very special area of planet earth there was no death only eternal life. There was eternal life in Eden because God tells us that it contains the Tree of Life. God specifically commanded humankind to eat of the Tree of Life. This wasn't a suggestion, it was a commandment from Almighty God. Anyone who eats from the Tree of Life will live forever and they will never see death. It is IMPOSSIBLE to eat from the Tree of Life and die!

Genesis 2:16 *And the LORD God commanded the man, saying, Of every tree of the garden thou mayest freely eat:*

My simple question now is, if death was not already in the rest of planet earth at this moment in creation, then why would God bother to provide this very special protected and defended area which contained the Tree of Life? What is more important, why would God Command humankind to eat from it?

Let's look at more words from God.

Genesis 2:17 *But of the tree of the knowledge of good and evil, thou shalt not eat of it: for in the day that thou eatest thereof thou shalt surely die.*

I think it fair to say that God would not make this statement unless He had already protected humankind from death by way of the Tree of Life. I think it also fair to assume that death was in the rest of the world at this moment. Why do I say this?

Let's look at more of God's words.

Genesis 3:21 *Unto Adam also and to his wife did the LORD God make coats of skins, and clothed them.*

The Hebrew word for SKINS is OWR (ORE), translated this is Skin, Hide, Leather. In other words, God clothed them with animal skins. To skin an animal, you have to first kill the animal. The animal has to die. Death had to be in the rest of planet earth so that these animals could be killed for their hide or skins.

Now that the preparation is complete, let's look at what God tells us.

Genesis 1:1 to 31 *In the beginning God **created** the heaven and the earth.*

2 And the earth was without form, and void; and darkness [was] upon the face of the deep. And the Spirit of God moved upon the face of the waters.

3 And God said, Let there be light: and there was light.

4 And God saw the light, that [it was] good: and God divided the light from the darkness.

5 And God called the light Day, and the darkness he called Night. And the evening and the morning were the first day.

*6 And God said, Let there be a firmament in the **midst of the waters**, and let it divide the waters from the waters.*

7 And God made the firmament, and divided the waters which [were] under the firmament from the waters which [were] above the firmament: and it was so.

8 And God called the firmament Heaven. And the evening and the morning were the second day.

9 And God said, Let the waters under the heaven be gathered together unto one place, and let the dry [land] appear: and it was so.

10 And God called the dry [land] **Earth***; and the gathering together of the waters called he Seas: and God saw that [it was] good.*

11 And God said, Let the **earth** *bring forth grass, the herb yielding seed, [and] the fruit tree yielding fruit after his kind,* **whose seed [is] in itself, upon the earth***: and it was so.*

12 And the **earth** *brought forth grass, [and] herb yielding seed after his kind, and the* **tree yielding fruit, whose seed [was] in itself***, after his kind: and God saw that [it was] good.*

13 And the evening and the morning were the third day.

14 And God said, Let there be lights in the firmament of the heaven to divide the day from the night; and let them be for signs, and for seasons, and for days, and years:

15 And let them be for lights in the firmament of the heaven to give light upon the **earth***: and it was so.*

16 And God made two great lights; the greater light to rule the day, and the lesser light to rule the night: [he made] the stars also.

17 And God set them in the firmament of the heaven to give light upon the **earth***,*

18 And to rule over the day and over the night, and to divide the light from the darkness: and God saw that [it was] good.

19 And the evening and the morning were the fourth day.

20 And God said, Let the waters bring forth abundantly the moving creature that hath life, and fowl [that] may fly above the **earth** *in the open firmament of heaven.*

21 **And God created** *great whales, and every living creature that moveth, which the waters brought forth abundantly, after their kind, and every winged fowl after his kind: and God saw that [it was] good.*

22 And God blessed them, saying, Be fruitful, and multiply, and fill the waters in the seas, and let fowl multiply in the **earth***.*

23 And the evening and the morning were the fifth day.
24 And God said, Let the **earth** *bring forth the living creature after his kind, cattle, and creeping thing, and beast of the* **earth** *after his kind: and it was so.*
25 And God made the beast of the **earth** *after his kind, and cattle after their kind, and every thing that creepeth upon the* **earth** *after his kind: and God saw that [it was] good.*
26 And God said, Let us make man in our image, after our likeness: and let **them** *have dominion over the fish of the sea, and over the fowl of the air, and over the cattle, and over all the* **earth***, and over every creeping thing that creepeth upon the* **earth***.*
27 So God created man in his [own] image, in the image of God created he him; **male and female created he them.**
28 And God blessed **them***, and God said unto* **them***, Be fruitful, and multiply, and replenish the* **earth***, and subdue it: and have dominion over the fish of the sea, and over the fowl of the air, and over every living thing that moveth upon the* **earth***.*
29 And God said, Behold, I have given you every herb bearing seed, which [is] **upon the face of all the earth***, and every tree, in the which [is] the fruit of a tree yielding seed; to you it shall be for meat.*
30 And to every beast of the **earth***, and to every fowl of the air, and to every thing that creepeth upon the* **earth***, wherein [there is] life, [I have given] every green herb for meat: and it was so.*
31 And God saw every thing that he had made, and, behold, [it was] very good. And the evening and the morning were the sixth day.
Genesis 2:1 to 4 *Thus the* **heavens and the earth were finished***, and* **all the host of them.** *And on the seventh day God ended his work which he had made; and he rested on the seventh day from all his work which he had made.*

3 And God blessed the seventh day, and sanctified it:
because that in it he had rested from all his work which
God created and made.
4 These [are] **the generations of the heavens and of the**
earth when they were created*, in the day that the LORD*
God made the **earth** *and the heavens,*

Let's now assume that this was the end of the bible, what
would it tell us?
First, it would give us the sequence as already discussed,
"created," "formed" and "made", but it would give us
another sequence which is of vital importance.
Let's re-visit Genesis and look more closely at what God
tells us about the "sequence" of events.
1, God created light and divided it from darkness.
2, God divided the waters and a firmament was created, this
being our sky, universe and heaven.
3, God gathered the waters together and created dry land.
This was our earth and seas.
4, God said let the earth bring forth grass and fruit trees.
5, God created our sun, moon and stars.
6, God gave us our day and our night.
7, God created every living creature that lives in the waters
and every fowl (bird) that may fly above the earth. Up to
verse 23, earth was now complete. This is what we know
from scientists to be pre-historic earth. Please read the
chapters "A Summary of Creation" and "Genesis Chapters
1 to 5 a slightly different version" to confirm this truth.
"And the evening and the morning were the fifth day", the
age of pre-historic earth was complete. Next, would come
the age of all the wild animals and humankind; the "Hunter
Gatherer". Nothing else would be "**created**" other than
humankind. From this moment all new animals, birds,
fishes, etc., would be "**formed**" or "**made**" from the
existing creature and out of the earth!

8, We now move from the "pre-historic" age to the "hunter gatherer" age, but before humankind arrived. In verses 24 and 25, the "earth brought forth" and "God made" the beasts of the "earth". Very important here to note the use of the word "earth" and not "field". This was the age of every wild animal that "Hunter Gatherer" humankind would live with.

God created every other living creature except for humankind.

At this very moment in our history, we were not yet "created."

It is of critical importance that this sequence is accepted. These are the words of Almighty God, not of me. God never gave me time lines, today we have experts who can determine those things. God simply gave me the **PURE TRUTH**.

If we continue this sequence by way of the word of God, we see that humankind follows afterwards.

God does not complicate things, He keeps it very simple.

9, In verse 26, God said "Let us make man in our image, after our likeness." Humankind now entered upon an earth which had been created complete. Complete like it is today? No, complete as it was millions or billions of years ago.

What would it tell us about humankind?

It would tell us that First Man was a "spirit being" in a human body.

Genesis 1:26 *And God said, **Let us make man in our image**, after our likeness: and let **them** have dominion over the fish of the sea, and over the fowl of the air, and over the cattle, and over all the earth, and over every creeping thing that creepeth upon the earth.*

We know that "God is spirit", because Jesus told us and therefore if God made us in His image, then we are spirit beings.

John 4:24 *God [is] a Spirit: AND they that worship him must worship [him] in spirit and in truth.* We know that First Man was "created" as a "spirit being" that was to be housed in a "flesh" body because later in Genesis, God Himself tells us this:

Genesis 6:3 *And the LORD said, My spirit shall not always strive with man, for that he also [is] flesh: yet his days shall be an hundred and twenty years.*

So, we know from the word of God that First Man was a "spirit being" housed in a "flesh" body, which enabled him to exist on earth as it had been **created** at that time.

Also of critical importance, is to note that the Hebrew word for humankind, or man, is ADAM (AW- DAWM). We can get sidetracked because of translations into thinking that Adam was just one man, he wasn't.

Could this be the biggest deceit ever by Satan? Has Satan tricked the majority of humankind for thousands of years into believing that Adam was just one man?

God did not just create ONE MAN and ONE FEMALE. God said very clearly in verse 26, "let THEM have dominion." In numerous other verses' God refers to "them" in the plural. It was not coincidence, but God-incidence when we read:

Genesis 2:1 *Thus the heavens and the earth were finished, and **all the host** of them.*

Genesis 2:4 *These [are] **the generations** of the heavens and of the earth when they were **created**, in the day that the LORD God made the earth and the heavens,*

God tells us that "the heavens and the earth were finished, and ALL THE HOST of them." God never said that only ONE MAN and ONE FEMALE had been created!

The Hebrew for HOST is TSABA (TSAW-BAW) and translated it means "mass of persons!" Not just ONE MAN and ONE FEMALE!

Also, very clearly we read "these ARE THE GENERATIONS of the heavens and of the earth." The Hebrew for GENERATIONS is TOLEDAH (TO-LED-AW). It comes from a root word "to bear young" and translated it means, "Family descent, history, birth, generations." This fact will become more important later when we learn from God about Second Man. Second Man was "**formed**" by God and you will read about him in the next chapter.

In addition, God was very clear in telling us that NOTHING had yet been PLANTED.

Genesis 1:11 *"And God said, Let the earth bring forth grass, the herb yielding seed, [and] the fruit tree yielding fruit after his kind, **whose seed [is] in itself, upon the earth**: and it was so."*

All the fruit and vegetables that humankind needed were upon the earth, not planted in it. All humankind had to do was to "gather" it up and eat it. This was the First Man that archaeologists call the "hunter gatherer."

This simple, yet massively important statement by God, was confirmed to Moses again in the following verse:

Genesis 1:12 *"And the earth brought forth grass, [and] herb yielding seed after his kind, and the tree yielding fruit, **whose seed [was] in itself**, after his kind: and God saw that [it was] good."*

Nothing had been planted because the seed was still in "itself" NOT in the ground! Have you ever known a seed to grow unless it has first been planted IN THE GROUND? God didn't want to leave it there, this point is so important that He gave it to us again just in case we missed it on the first two occasions!

Genesis 2:4/5 *These [are] the generations of the heavens and of the earth when they were **created**, in the day that the LORD God made the earth and the heavens,*

*5 And every plant of the field **before it was in the earth**, and every herb of the field **before it grew**: for the LORD God had not caused it to rain upon the earth, and [there was] not a man to till the ground.*

Sorry to labour the point, but what does Jesus say?

John 12:24 *Verily, verily, I say unto you, Except a corn of wheat fall into the ground and die, it abideth alone: but if it die, it bringeth forth much fruit.*

When Jesus says "verily" it's important. When Jesus says "verily", "verily" it's ultra important and imperative that it be believed without question. "Except a corn of wheat fall INTO the ground and die, it abideth alone". In other words unless it is planted INTO the earth, it will never grow and reproduce.

It doesn't come more plain and simple than this, " *And every plant of the field **before it was in the earth**, and every herb of the field **before it grew**"*:

Before it was in the earth, not after! Before it grew and not after it had been planted in the earth and started to grow!

In addition, God tells us that "God had not caused it to rain upon the earth, and there was not a man to till the ground." In other words, the earth had not yet received any rain, and First Man had not yet been taught how to "farm" or cultivate the ground!

Every fruit and vegetable that First Man (hunter gatherer) needed was there on the earth's surface. At this moment in humankinds development man didn't need a Soul or Knowledge, these would come later. Right now he instinctively felt hunger and instinctively ate that which God had placed for him to gather.

Again, let me try to pre-empt two questions that you might have:

First, if there was no rain, from where did First Man get his water? It's really quite simple. He would have gotten his water from the "fruit tree yielding fruits" which might be a coconut or any number of fruit trees that provide fruit which is full of juice. We know that ALL of God's "creative" work had ended and so First Man had access to water melon and countless other plants that contained water.

Furthermore, why didn't these plants and fruit trees rot? I would ask a question in answer to this question. What would make them rot? Assume that there would be something that would cause them to rot. If this is so then I believe that God very simply replaced these plants and trees every night. Why do I say this? I say it simply because we know from the word of God that God has already proven Himself capable of doing such things. Let,s see from God's words this TRUTH.

Exodus 16:1 to 15 *And they took their journey from Elim, and all the congregation of the children of Israel came unto the wilderness of Sin, which [is] between Elim and Sinai, on the fifteenth day of the second month after their departing out of the land of Egypt.*

2 And the whole congregation of the children of Israel murmured against Moses and Aaron in the wilderness:

3 And the children of Israel said unto them, Would to God we had died by the hand of the LORD in the land of Egypt, when we sat by the flesh pots, [and] when we did eat bread to the full; for ye have brought us forth into this wilderness, to kill this whole assembly with hunger.

*4 Then said the LORD unto Moses, Behold, **I will rain bread from heaven for you**; and **the people shall go out and gather a certain rate every day**, that I may prove them, whether they will walk in my law, or no.*

5 And it shall come to pass, that on the sixth day they shall prepare [that] which they bring in; and it shall be twice as much as they gather daily.

6 And Moses and Aaron said unto all the children of Israel, At even, then ye shall know that the LORD hath brought you out from the land of Egypt:

7 And in the morning, then ye shall see the glory of the LORD; for that he heareth your murmurings against the LORD: and what [are] we, that ye murmur against us?
8 And Moses said, [This shall be], when the LORD shall give you in the evening flesh to eat, and in the morning bread to the full; for that the LORD heareth your murmurings which ye murmur against him: and what [are] we? your murmurings [are] not against us, but against the LORD.
9 And Moses spake unto Aaron, Say unto all the congregation of the children of Israel, Come near before the LORD: for he hath heard your murmurings.
10 And it came to pass, as Aaron spake unto the whole congregation of the children of Israel, that they looked toward the wilderness, and, behold, the glory of the LORD appeared in the cloud.
11 And the LORD spake unto Moses, saying,
12 I have heard the murmurings of the children of Israel: speak unto them, saying, At even ye shall eat flesh, and in the morning ye shall be filled with bread; and ye shall know that I [am] the LORD your God.
13 And it came to pass, that at even the quails came up, and covered the camp: and in the morning the dew lay round about the host.
14 And when the dew that lay was gone up, behold, upon the face of the wilderness [there lay] a small round thing, [as] small as the hoar frost on the ground.
15 And when the children of Israel saw [it], they said one to another, It [is] manna: for they wist not what it [was]. And Moses said unto them, This [is] the bread which the LORD hath given you to eat.

We can see clearly from the verses above that God "rained bread from heaven," and that He did it so that "the people shall go out and gather a certain rate every day."

First, can we believe this to be true? The "Exodus" of the nation of Israel out of Egypt is referred to more than one hundred and fifty times in the bible, so I think it fair to say it's true.

Did God feed just a few people? From numerous records it is calculated that at this moment in its history, the nation of Israel numbered in between two and three million people. Did God feed these people for just a day or two? Not exactly, God fed these people on a daily basis for forty years!

I think it's fairly safe to assume that God could feed His original "creation" regardless of its size or duration.

God tells us very, very clearly that *"These [are] the generations of the heavens and of the earth when they were created."* Notice what God says, "these are," not maybe or could be, these **ARE**.

At this very moment, be it millions or billions of years ago, our earth and everything that God at that moment wanted to be in it, had been **created**.

God had created an earth that was "perfect" for First Man, the hunter gatherer. No "knowledge" or "conscious" thought was necessary for this man. When he felt pangs of hunger, he just ate like an animal would.

This is First Man complete, he did not have a name, knowledge or soul, simply because at this moment, he did not need them to fulfill God's plan.

You might well now question, "What about our spirit?" Remember what God told us:

Job 32:8 *But [there is] a spirit in man: and the inspiration of the Almighty giveth them understanding.*

Well, our spirit is there to give us "understanding", but without "knowledge" (which would come to us later), there is nothing to "understand." I can "know" every word in the bible, but if I do not understand it; it's useless! Similarly, if I have no "knowledge" of the bible, then my "understanding" or "spirit" is useless. God's timing is always perfect and our spirit would become engaged later in God's development plan for us.

I'd like to mention here humankind's evolutionary graph because it will become important later. Does no one ever question why for millions or billions of years, humankind's evolutionary graph flatlined? If we were "evolving," surely there should have been upward movements in its trajectory? God-incidentally, I prefer to use this word than coincidentally, you will learn that humankind's line on the graph started to move upwards at the exact time of the appearance of Second Man. Second Man is referred to by evolutionists as the "farmer," and you will read about him in the next chapter.

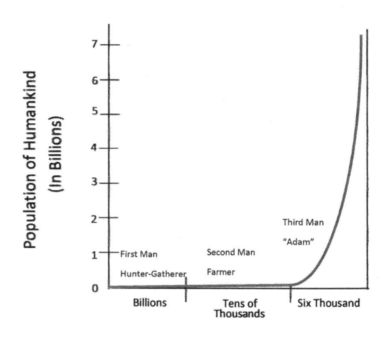

Before moving on, let me end with a couple of other interesting facts.

We all know that Darwinian evolutionists believe we evolved from Apes. One of the factors in this is that early human remains showed clearly that First Man was covered in body hair. Remember that God told us that "these are the generations of the heaven and earth WHEN they were created." Well, we now know that clothing was not provided by God until He confronted Third Man Adam after he ate of the tree.

Genesis 3:21 *Unto Adam also and to his wife did the LORD God make coats of skins, and clothed them.*

It's clear that both Adam and Eve had no clothing until God made it for them, but we know that God is a perfectionist. Does anyone think that God would leave humankind in a very hot climate like Israel or Africa (both countries where archeologists say the remains of First Man have been discovered) without protection? Let me suggest to you that God created First Man covered in hair as a means of protection against the sun. It is now known by scientists that excess body hair is a means of keeping the body cool, not as was first thought to keep them warm! It also protected our skin from burning. We did not evolve from Apes. We were just "created" perfectly!

In addition, I'd like to comment upon "nutcracker" man. This was a man that lived in Africa more than one million years ago. After research, the scientists discovered that this "hominid" had powerful jaws, huge teeth and may have preferred to eat grass. Recent further studies indicated to these scientists that not only did "nutcracker" man like to eat grass, but he also liked soft fruit! Was this First Man? Also, we now know that two million years ago, again in Africa, humans lived on a diet of trees, bushes and fruit. Researchers made this discovery by zapping fossilized teeth with a laser. Carbon that was released from the enamel provided clear evidence of this food. Also, very interesting, was that the diet contained both protein and soluble sugars, vital to life on earth. Was this also First Man?

Is it coincidence or God-incidence that the most complete and oldest human skeleton ever discovered was found in "The Cradle of Humankind?" The Cradle of Humankind is a World Heritage site in, you guessed it, Africa! It's no coincidence at all!

All of these earliest archaeological discoveries fall within an area known as the "Fertile Crescent." The term "Fertile Crescent", was coined by James Henry Breasted of the University of Chicago. It is a crescent-shaped area of land encompassing large parts of the Middle East and Africa. Is it coincidence, or God-incidence, that the whole of the Old and New Testament Bibles relate to this area? Is it coincidence, or God-incidence, that the famous Garden of Eden was in this area? Is it coincidence, or God-incidence, that there has never been a more fertile area of land on this earth than the Fertile Crescent? Is it coincidence, or God-incidence, that there is no other area on earth that contains more numerous or greater archaeological sites relating to the complete and oldest known history of humankind? Hopefully you are getting the picture, but I will write more on the Fertile Crescent in the next chapter. Let's now get back to First Man, the Hunter Gatherer.

Let me just remind you of what God said to Moses:

Genesis 1:11 *And God said, Let the earth bring forth **grass**, the herb yielding seed, [and] the **fruit tree yielding fruit** after his kind, whose seed [is] in itself, upon the earth: and it was so.*

Is this coincidental, or is it God-incidental, that ALL evidence concerning earliest humanity confirms them to be grass, herb and fruit eaters? I'll let you decide.

Also, it's worth pointing out that at this moment in "creation", God intended First Man to be a vegetarian! How do we know this? Let's look again at what God said:

Genesis 1:28 to 30 *And God blessed them, and God said unto them, Be fruitful, and multiply, and replenish the earth, and subdue it: and have dominion over the fish of the sea, and over the fowl of the air, and over every living thing that moveth upon the earth.*

29 And God said, Behold, **I have given you every herb bearing seed, which [is] upon the face of all the earth, and every tree, in the which [is] the fruit of a tree yielding seed; to you it shall be for meat.**

30 And to every beast of the earth, and to every fowl of the air, and to every thing that creepeth upon the earth, wherein [there is] life, [I have given] every green herb for meat: and it was so.

"To you it shall be for meat," or in other word's; food. At this moment in creation we were to be vegetarians.

If we look very carefully, although God gave humankind "dominion" over all creatures, our "meat" or food was to come from "every herb bearing seed and every tree in which is the fruit of a tree yielding seed!" At this moment in creation, God never intended that humankind should eat animals!

Equally as important is to fully understand the word "dominion" as God at this time intended for it to be understood. In the same way as a king has "dominion" over his domain and all of his subjects, we were given "dominion" over all creatures. However, God's idea of kingship is somewhat different to it's understanding today. Kingship in God's eyes, is a privileged position of authority whereby the king **"serves"** his subjects; ensures their total **"security"** by giving them a **"peaceful"** life and most importantly, leads them in **"Godly"** ways. Regrettably, successive kings over centuries have all fallen short of this God given model and God's original "dominion" is totally different today than was ever intended.

Let me also be so bold as to suggest that at this moment in creation all animals were also vegetarian. Why do I say this? Again what did God say?

Genesis 1:30 *And to every beast of the earth, and to every fowl of the air, and to every thing that creepeth upon the earth, wherein [there is] life, [I have given] every green herb for meat: and it was so.*

God tells us very clearly, "I have given every green herb for meat (food), and it was so." The green herbs were all the food every animal or bird needed for survival. At this moment in "creation" animals didn't kill one another and neither did humankind kill animals. Let me suggest to you that at this moment in "creation", animals and humankind lived together peacefully. The exact moment in humankinds history on earth at which they started to kill animals for food has not been shared with me by God. Purely personally, I would like to think that it came immediately after sin entered the world through the "fall" of Adam, who I call Third Man, but from the word of God I cannot prove it. More realistically, it might well be at the arrival of Second Man, the "farmer." Second Man, as we will learn in the next chapter, had a "soul". Not only did he need protein to sustain it, but he was taught by God to farm animals.

Also, another very important point to remember is what I said earlier, that if the bible ended at Genesis 2:4 what would we have?

Genesis 2:4 *These [are] the generations of the heavens and of the earth when they were **created**, in the day that the LORD God made the earth and the heavens,*

We would have humankind with body and spirit only. In addition, every other living thing on land, sea and in the air had been created. Food and drink for every living thing was upon the earth simply to be "gathered" and eaten. There had been no rain and there were no seasons. Most importantly, until this moment God had on every occasion

176

referred to the "**earth**." In the next chapter, we will learn that in connection to Second Man (the farmer), God refers to "**fields**" and not the "**earth**." In the original Hebrew, there are very clear differences between the translations of these two words and the significance of this cannot be understated.

I do also believe that there were periods of crossover between First and Second Man. Regrettably, from the word of God I cannot prove it. I believe that First Man was still on the earth during the early period of Second Man, and that Second Man was still on the earth during the early period of Third Man. This I believe goes part way to answering questions concerning "giants in the earth" referred to in Genesis 6:

Genesis 6:4 *There were giants in the earth in those days; and also after that, when the sons of God came in unto the daughters of men, and they bare [children] to them, the same [became] mighty men which [were] of old, men of renown.*

Recent scientific evidence goes some way to providing confirmation of First, Second and Third Man. David Reich of Harvard Medical School in Boston, Massachusetts presented his findings at a Royal Society meeting in London.

His DNA research revealed that humans have a mystery ancestor yet to be identified. Research compared DNA from Neanderthals and the other group of ancient humans, known as the Denisovans. Genome research identified that "Denisovans harbour ancestry from an unknown archaic population, unrelated to Neanderthals".

Is this mystery ancestor First Man?

Were the Denisovans Second Man?

As stated earlier, God never spoke to me about this, but if nothing else, hopefully it will lead to more discussion.

I know little or nothing about these scientific developments, but I pray that Christians who do will research this further to establish that once more God's word aligns itself perfectly with that of current scientific research.

Before moving onto the next chapter "Second Man," let me refer you to more of what God said to Moses.

Genesis 2:4 to 8 *And every plant of the field before it was in the earth, and every herb of the field before it grew: for the LORD God had not caused it to rain upon the earth,* **and [there was] not a man to till the ground.**
6 But there went up a mist from the earth, and watered the whole face of the ground.
7 And the LORD God formed man [of] the dust of the ground, and breathed into his nostrils the breath of life; and man became a living soul.
8 And the LORD God planted a garden eastward in Eden; and there he put the man whom he had formed.

The key words here are " **[there was] not a man to till the ground.** Or, to use the scientists' and evolutionist's words, there was not a "farmer." There was no man who planted and grew his own food, because God had not yet **caused it to rain upon the earth**. No wonder First Man was covered in body hair. It must have been very hot without cooling rain!

Let me now share with you the words of Paul, the great Apostle. The man who had a miraculous encounter with Jesus Himself on the road to Damascus and was thereby given almighty revelation by God. What Paul wrote was about one thousand, seven hundred years after Moses, but again I hope you will see the God-incidence.

Acts 14:15 to 17 *And saying, Sirs, why do ye these things? We also are men of like passions with you, and preach unto you that ye should turn from these vanities unto the living God, which made heaven, and earth, and the sea, and all things that are therein:*

16 Who in times past suffered all nations to walk in their own ways.

17 Nevertheless he left not himself without witness, in that he did good, and gave us rain from heaven, and fruitful seasons, filling our hearts with food and gladness.

Paul tells us in exactly the same sequence about the creation of "heaven," "earth," "the sea" and everything else. He then speaks of humankind walking in their own ways (First Man was a walker without "knowledge" who simply walked and gathered), until God gave "rain from heaven." The rain brought about Second Man, the "farmer" who enjoyed "fruitful seasons", that "filled his heart with food and gladness." First Man never had "knowledge" or "fruitful seasons" because everything that he needed was "upon" the ground. Also, it had not yet rained and there were no "seasons." On the other hand, Second Man the "farmer," had to have rain and "seasons" to enable him to grow the various crops that were provided to him, but that had not yet been planted. Was it coincidental that Paul wrote this, or God-incidental?

These are not coincidence. They are God-incidence!

I do sincerely hope that by now you will believe in God as the creator of all things. More important, that you will believe evolutionists and creationists to be both half right, but also half wrong. If you still need more convincing, then I pray the next two chapters will help you to believe that God is the Creator and that Jesus Christ is the Savior of all humankind.

Second Man-The TRUTH

In the previous chapter we learnt that First Man (hunter gatherer) was "created" by God with a body and a spirit. The spirit was to give us access to understanding of knowledge (conscience), which would come to us at a later stage in our development. We also learnt that our body totally independently of spirit or soul, could already do certain things.

Our bodies breathe without thought. This obviously keeps us supplied with oxygen and alive. Our bodies walk without thought. They tell us when they are hungry and again, without thought we eat. Along with these things, our bodies also have sexual urges (for reproduction) and bowel movement urges (to expel waste products) again, both without thought. All of these actions are what we might refer to as "instincts," and this was how First Man lived on planet earth however many millions or billions of years ago. The word of God does not give us exact dates, but as we have already read, it is very simplistic and clear concerning our "creation."

Now, I want to share with you what God shared with me concerning Second Man or as evolutionists call him, the "farmer." You will see very clearly and simply from the word of God that again there was no evolution from Apes or anything else. Second Man was "formed" by God in a very defined way and for a very specific purpose.

Again, let's read the word of God to know the TRUTH.

Genesis 2:2 to 5. *And on the seventh day God **ended his*** ***work*** *which he had made; and he rested on the seventh day from all his work which he had made.*
3 And God blessed the seventh day, and sanctified it: because that in it he had rested from all his work which God created and made.
*4 These [**are**] the generations of the heavens and of the earth when they were **created**, in the day that the LORD God made the earth and the heavens,*
*5 And every plant of the field **before it was in the earth**, and every herb of the field **before it grew**: for the LORD God **had not caused it to rain upon the earth**, and [there was] **not a man to till the ground.***

God had now "ended his work," First Man, the heavens, earth and everything in them had now been "created." God again told us that every plant and herb was upon the earth, but not growing in it for two reasons. First God "had not caused it to rain upon the earth, and second, there was "Not a man to till the ground."

Now, let's get back to Second Man and look again at what God said:
Genesis 2:6 to 9 *But there went up a mist from the **earth**, and **watered the whole face of the ground.***
*7 And the LORD **God formed man** [of] the dust of the ground, and **breathed into his nostrils the breath of life; and man became a living soul**.*
*8 And **the LORD God planted a garden** eastward in Eden; and there **he put the man** whom he had formed.*
*9 And **out of the ground made the LORD God to grow** every tree that is pleasant to the sight, and good for food; the tree of life also in the midst of the garden, and the tree of knowledge of good and evil.*

God tells us that "there went up a mist from the earth." Critical here to note the word "earth" not "field." This was the first rain, and it wasn't at this moment in creation limited to certain areas. It "watered the whole face of the ground."

This of course is vital before the planting of seed. Seed will not grow without water.

In addition, we can see that God "formed" man and "breathed into his nostrils the breath of life. Man became a living soul." We know from the previous chapter that the original Hebrew word for formed is "YATSAR," which means to "fashion out of something that is ALREADY made." "To shape or to mould into a form a material or object that **you have already made**."

We know from this that God took His original "creation" First Man, and "shaped, fashioned and moulded" him into Second Man. We can see also that at this moment, man was also given a "soul." There was no evolution from Apes.

If we need more support for this TRUTH, let's again look at the word of God:

1st Timothy 2:13 *For Adam was first **formed**, then Eve.*

Confirmation truth from the Apostle Paul that Second Man was moulded, shaped or fabricated out of something which was already in existence! The Greek word that Paul used for "formed" is PLASSO (PLAS-SO) and this is exactly the same translation as the Hebrew word used by Moses in the book of Genesis! I'm certain your question now is, "how was First Man Formed out of the dust of the ground"? Regrettably, God did not share this process with me. After millions of years, humankind still does not possess a brain capable of creating a simple grass seed. So I think consideration of this answers the question. My brain is infinitely too small to comprehend and process such complexity as the process of "forming" a human.

This is Second Man, "Formed" out of First Man and given a "soul." This human now had a body, spirit and a soul, but still no "knowledge" or "conscience."

Remember from a previous chapter that our soul is what makes us who we are as individuals. Our soul is our mind, our emotions and our will, the free will that God gave to us. Our soul is what makes us recognizable, not physically but intellectually. It gives us an awareness of our surroundings and of our environment. Our soul enables us to sin, to believe, to prosper and to love God. At this moment in our history, we still don't have "knowledge" and so you might well ask, how did we "know" how to "farm." How did we "know" how to plant and grow things?

Again, what does God tell us:

Genesis 2:8/9 *And **the LORD God planted a garden eastward in Eden**; and there he put the man whom he had formed.*

*9 And out of the ground made the **LORD God to grow every tree** that is pleasant to the sight, and good for food; the tree of life also in the midst of the garden, and the tree of knowledge of good and evil.*

Genesis 2:15 *And the **LORD God took the man, and put him into the garden of Eden** to **dress it** and to keep it.*

Again, it's very simple, "The Lord God planted a garden eastward in Eden; and there He put the man whom He had "formed." Man didn't plant a garden; God did. Man didn't make things grow; God did.

If we show a dog, horse, parrot, etc., how to do something, even without a common language they will be able to copy what we do. Second Man did exactly this. Let me give you a better example. We hear a song numerous times on the radio and we are then able to hear that song so perfectly in our heads that we can sing along to it. What's more amazing is that we could do exactly the same, even if the song was in a language that we didn't even understand! You can replay and hear perfectly in your head, the songs that you heard on the radio sung in a foreign language that you don't understand. Remember, our soul is our mind, our will and our emotions. It is what gives us an awareness of our surroundings, because it connects us to ourselves and our body is what connects us to the world and the things in it. We might not "know" (knowledge that Second Man does not yet possess) what a radio is or understand the language of the song we are listening to, but within a few hearings of that song we can play it back perfectly in our minds and even sing along to it!

At that moment in our history we now had a soul. Again, look closely at God's words. The "LORD God took the man, and put him into the garden of Eden." First Man (Hunter/Gatherer) was obviously NOT in the garden of Eden at this moment in our history. First Man was not just "one man." Remember from the previous chapter that the "heavens and the earth were finished, and ALL the HOST of them." At this moment in our history First Man was all over the earth, the earth was "populated" by First Man the Hunter Gatherer. God now moved onto the next part of His plan and He "Planted a garden eastward in Eden." God planted this garden not man, but what else does it tell us? In addition, "Out of the ground made the LORD God to grow every tree." Man didn't plant or make trees grow; God did!

Why did the Lord God say "Eastward"? Might I suggest to you that all the other previous activity took place in Africa as most of the archaeological evidence suggests. We know from historical manuscripts that Eden was in the Middle East, is this not "Eastward" from Africa?

This garden is situated within an area more commonly known today by archaeologists as the "fertile crescent." It was an area that archaeologists discovered as being in the Middle East. It was the most fertile land on earth tens of thousands of years ago, and many farming implements have been discovered there including seeds. Discoveries made in this area suggest that man first "farmed" there some forty-thousand years ago or more. As with First Man, God never gave me any indications of time lines and so Second Man might have "farmed" there, forty, fifty or even one hundred thousand years ago! We know from skeletal and cultural remains that this whole area contains more sites of historical human activity than anywhere else on earth. Apart from great rivers such as the Jordan, Euphrates, Tigris, etc, that provided perfect irrigation of the land, the whole area also had a perfect climate to encourage growth of all manner of plants. Was it coincidence, or God-incidence, that this area also produced (according to expert archaeologists) wild progenitors of the founding eight Neolithic crops, which were all vital to early agriculture? Crops that we know as wheat, barley, chick pea, lentil, etc. Let me remind you again of what God said: Genesis 1:11 *And God said, Let the earth bring forth* **grass***, the herb yielding seed, and the fruit tree yielding fruit after his kind, whose seed is in itself, upon the earth: and it was so.*

Are wheat, barley, etc, not all members of the Poaceae family, or **GRASS** family?

Was it coincidence, or God-incidence, that this whole area (according to expert archaeologists) led to historical discoveries of more species of edible plants than any other area on earth?

Was it coincidence, or God-incidence, that this area gives archaeological evidence of being the first on earth to be inhabited by four of the most important domesticated animals vital to farming? Evidence of cows, goats, pigs and sheep are there in abundance. Only evidence of the horse is missing, but even that has been found very close by. I'll discuss farm animals in more detail later, right now I think you may have a question. "How could cattle live in what we know as a largely desert ridden area"? We know from our archaeological friends that years ago this whole area was humid and green!

Was it coincidence, or God-incidence, that geneticists from Stanford University found evidence of gluten sensitive and lactose intolerant genes that began to emerge in populations expanding into Europe and beyond some 10,000 years ago? Well, you may find it more God-incidence when you learn that these originated out of wheat and milk allergies that came from humans who migrated out of Africa some 60,000 years ago, and who took farming methods into Europe, the America's and the rest of the World!

Truly, I don't know why any Christian should be surprised that scientific evidence fits perfectly with the Word of God, and vice versa.

Let me leave you with another thought and word from God. Genesis 3:23 *Therefore the LORD God sent him forth from the garden of Eden, to **till the ground from whence he was taken.***

After Adam & Eve ate of the forbidden fruit, they were "sent forth from the garden of Eden to TILL THE GROUND FROM WHENCE HE WAS TAKEN"! In other words, humankind had been taught by God how to farm both animals and crops, and now they were being sent back to Africa to farm exactly the same area from where he was at first taken from! It's no coincidence that archaeologists have found more evidence of farming in North Africa; it's God-incidence!

Understandably, some of you may now ask, "What happened to Eden?" If this area has been proven by archaeologists to have been the birthplace of farming and containing the most fertile soil on earth, why is it now a desert? The obvious answer is climate change and of course we know that's possible. I want to give you a different answer. It is something that will be explained later, not by me, but from the word of God.

Let's now get back to where we were. God simply took His original "creation," and "formed" him into Second Man. He then took Second Man into the most fertile area on earth, and taught him to farm!
We can see that now "out of the ground made the LORD God to grow every tree." It's very clear to see that it was God, not man who first farmed. God had taught Second Man how to "farm." If we look at verse 15, this is confirmed to us because the translation of "dress" is to "cultivate."
.

Let's now go back to the word of God to see what else it tells us.
Genesis 2:9 to 20. *And out of the ground **made the LORD God to grow** every tree that is pleasant to the sight, and good for food; the tree of life also in the midst of the garden, and the tree of knowledge of good and evil.*
10 And a river went out of Eden to water the garden; and from thence it was parted, and became into four heads.
11 The name of the first [is] Pison: that [is] it which compasseth the whole land of Havilah, where [there is] gold;
12 And the gold of that land [is] good: there [is] bdellium and the onyx stone.
13 And the name of the second river [is] Gihon: the same [is] it that compasseth the whole land of Ethiopia.
14 And the name of the third river [is] Hiddekel: that [is] it which goeth toward the east of Assyria. And the fourth river [is] Euphrates.

*15 And the **LORD God took the man, and put him into the garden of Eden** to **dress** it and to keep it.*

16 And the LORD God commanded the man, saying, Of every tree of the garden thou mayest freely eat:

17 But of the tree of the knowledge of good and evil, thou shalt not eat of it: for in the day that thou eatest thereof thou shalt surely die.

18 And the LORD God said, [It is] not good that the man should be alone; I will make him an help meet for him.

*19 And out of the ground the LORD God **formed every beast of the field, and every fowl of the air;** and brought [them] unto Adam to see what he would call them: and whatsoever Adam called every living creature, that [was] the name thereof.*

*20 And Adam gave names to all **cattle, and to the fowl of the air, and to every beast of the field;** but for Adam there was not found an help meet for him.*

Let's once more examine the word of God. Remember in the last chapter, I spoke of the importance in remembering the Hebrew definitions for the words, "earth" and "fields." If we look, we will see the huge significance of the next revelation that God gave to me.

The Hebrew word for "earth" is ERETS (EH-RETS). Translated, this is "the earth at large, a land, country, nations, wilderness, world".

The Hebrew word for "field" is SADEH or SADAY (SAW-DAH-EE). Translated this is "to spread out, a field (as flat), country, field, ground, land, soil."

I think any fair minded person would concede a simple difference in these words. The word "earth" as seen in Genesis refers to our planet earth. The word "field" as seen in Genesis refers to an agricultural field, a "farmers" field; a Second Man farmers field!

Genesis 2:4 *"These [are] the generations of the heavens and of the earth when they were created, in the day that the LORD God made the earth and the heavens,"*

Remember what was said in the previous chapter, "These ARE the generations," not maybe, or could be, these are! Up to this moment in the "creation" of our planet and everything in it concerning First Man, God had used the word "earth." Never once referring to anything that may connect to "farming." After Genesis 2:4, except for reference to worldwide rain, in every other reference to humankind and animals God uses the word "field." This is because Second Man was the original farmer.

Of course, I'm sure that still there will be people who read this as mere coincidence. As for me, when God spoke to me to share this TRUTH, that's all it was, **PURE TRUTH**. If you are still not convinced, there's more, much more! Before Genesis 2:4, God had spoken about all of "creation", including fish (*"Whales and every living creature that moveth which the waters brought forth"*), and "fruit trees." Does no one question why God does not mention these when He talks about "fields?" Sorry to keep it so simple, but fish and fruit trees don't immediately spring to mind when referring to original farming. More important, does no one ever question why when God talks about fields, He always talks about the type of animal that can be "farmed," and the "plants and herbs" (various grasses like wheat, barley, maize, rice, etc.) that can be "farmed". It is to be hoped that you are now getting the message, but if you still need convincing, here it is. After God talked about Second Man whom He had "formed," God also talked about "beasts of the field." Were these the same "beasts" that were spoken of in connection with First Man the Hunter Gatherer? No, they were not!

God is now telling us about Second Man, the farmer, and we all know that farmers need "farm" animals. They need domesticated "beasts" that God "formed" specifically for them!

Remember again the Hebrew translations, "formed" and "created." God very simply took His existing "creatures" and "formed" them into domestic farm animals and He tells us this very clearly in Genesis 2:19/20

Genesis 2:19/20 *And out of the ground the LORD God* ***formed every beast of the field, and every fowl of the air;*** *and brought [them] unto Adam to see what he would call them: and whatsoever Adam called every living creature, that [was] the name thereof.*

*20 And Adam gave names to all **cattle, and to the fowl of the air, and to every beast of the field;** but for Adam there was not found an help meet for him.*

Sorry to repeat myself, but it doesn't get any clearer than this! "Every beast of the field" being every farm animal that we know so well today. At this moment in God's plan for humankind, a new and unique breed of animal and bird were needed. These would be of a type that could easily be "farmed." Let's get back for a moment to the Fertile Crescent into which God planted Eastward the Garden of Eden. We know that the Sahara desert stretches from West to East North Africa. We also know that today it would be impossible to farm cattle in this desert due to extreme heat, lack of water or soil. We also know that 10,000 years ago it was lush, green and perfect for farming. We also know that the North Eastern tip of the Libyan Sahara desert comes within the Fertile Crescent. Is it coincidence, or God-incidence, that farmers were keeping cows for their milk in this area 7,000 years ago? British scientists found microscopic stains of dairy products on cooking pots from this area and discovered that milk was a very important part of humankind's diet at this time. In addition, rock art found in this region depicts cattle herding among early pastoral humankind. Also, faunal evidence demonstrates that sheep and goats were also together and being farmed in the same area.

Also, I find it interesting when I consider that so many things were fashioned by our ancestors out of animals; their skins, organs and bones. Again, was this a slow evolutionary process? Not at all, it was simply as God wanted it to be so that His plan for humankind could be fulfilled.

Again, let me remind you of the "independent" nature of our bodies. When we are cold, we shiver. When we are hot, we sweat. No thought is required to do these things. In exactly the same way, if we cover ourselves with something when we are cold, we don't need to think that we are getting warmer. Additionally, if we get too close to fire we don't need to think to get burnt! We will know exactly when this happens and like the foreign song heard on the radio, we will remember it!

So now, the question must be how did Second Man the farmer reproduce? What about Second Woman? Notice here that I use the word "Woman." This is of great importance and significance because if you will remember in relation to First Man, God used the word "female." Again, let's read what God has to tell us:

Genesis 2:18 to 25 *And the LORD God said, [It is] not good that the man should be alone; I will make him an **help meet for him.***

19 And out of the ground the LORD God formed every beast of the field, and every fowl of the air; and brought [them] unto Adam to see what he would call them: and whatsoever Adam called every living creature, that [was] the name thereof.

*20 And Adam gave names to all cattle, and to the fowl of the air, and to every beast of the field; but for Adam there was not found an **help meet for him**.*

21 And the LORD God caused a deep sleep to fall upon Adam, and he slept: and he took one of his ribs, and closed up the flesh instead thereof;
*22 And the rib, which the LORD God had taken from man, **made he a woman**, and brought her unto the man.*
23 And Adam said, This [is] now bone of my bones, and flesh of my flesh: she shall be called Woman, because she was taken out of Man.
24 Therefore shall a man leave his father and his mother, and shall cleave unto his wife: and they shall be one flesh.
*25 And they were **both naked**, the man and his wife, and were **not ashamed**.*

Three things immediately are made apparent.

First, God tells us that He "made" a Woman and second, He uses the word "woman." Thirdly, God refers to his "father and his mother".

I'm certain your question now is, how was Woman "made" from the rib of Second Man? Regrettably, God did not share this process with me. Again, I refer you to humankind's inability to create even a grass seed. My brain is simply infinitely too small to comprehend and process such complexity.

Also, it's very important to note that God does **NOT** use the word "Eve". This is simply because "Eve" has not yet arrived. "Eve", the originator of you and I, does not appear until the next chapter. At this moment in time, women were in every way complete, but without one thing, that thing being "knowledge". Knowledge would come after one of these women ate from the Tree of Knowledge. The woman who committed this act of disobedience would from that moment become the individual who we all know as "Eve".

Sorry to be so obvious concerning the third point, but why would God use the words "father and mother", if Adam and Eve were the first and only two humans on the planet? The simple answer is because they were not!

Genesis 3:20 *And Adam called his wife's name Eve; because she was the mother of all living.*

The Hebrew for mother is EM (AME), translated it is "mother", "bond of the family". All of humankind from this moment on would be "bonded" to "Eve". Every one of us are descended from this woman.

Ask yourself a very simple question. Throughout the whole creative process, "IF" there was just one woman, why would God wait until Genesis Chapter 3 Verse 20 to call her by name?

Very simply, one of the "women" ate of the fruit, offered her husband some and both at that moment received "knowledge" of all things. From this pivotal moment on, both can be seen as Adam and Eve, two individuals. Before this moment, we have Second Man as a species of both men and women occupying an area of our planet known as the Garden of Eden.

If you are a female reading this let me ask you to pay particular attention to what comes next. So many groups of people today tend to denigrate females in scripture to be second class citizens. God never intended it to be this way. When we study closely the word of God, woman was made by God to be able to help man in ways that God did Himself. Such was the importance of womankind to creation.

At this point, let's look at the original Hebrew words: The Hebrew for "Female" is NEQEBAH (NEK-AY-BAW) "the sexual form." It is taken from NAQAB (NAW-KAB) meaning to puncture, or to perforate with more or less violence, pierce, bone with holes. In other words we can see that God's original "created" female was described by God in a very mechanical way, not in a womanly, motherly, intelligent way. The very first "female" creation was just like the very first "male" creation, a functioning body with a spirit and that's all.

Now let's contrast this with the Hebrew word that God gave to Moses for "woman," we see huge differences. The Hebrew for "Woman" is ISHSHAH (ISH-SHAW) and translated from its root words, it speaks of a complete woman, a wife, adulterer. It means to be an individual, with character, a champion, great, dignified, mortal, a servant. In other words, a perfectly "finished" human with a soul, because it's our soul which gives us all these things.

Genesis 2:22 *And the rib, which the LORD God had taken from man, **made he a woman**, and brought her unto the man.*

This is Second Woman. This is not just a "female," or a body with a spirit. This is now a body, with a spirit, with a character or "soul," "made" by God out of "existing material", but now "finished" and complete.

How important was this "woman" or these "women"? To understand the answer to this question, let's again take a look at the word of God, and it's original Hebrew translation.

Genesis 2:18 *And the LORD God said, [It is] not good that the man should be alone; I will make him an **help meet for him.***

The Hebrew for "Help meet" is EZER (A-ZER) and translated it means "help or assistance especially in times of difficulty." This in itself makes women very important, but what else do we know from God about this? Apart from the two mentions of "help meet" in Genesis 2, Verses 18 and 20, the same Hebrew word occurs a further twenty times in the bible. What I found interesting was that on EVERY other occasion in the bible where these words are mentioned, they refer to help directly from, and by God Himself. What is less commonly known is that further research has proven this translation to be somewhat simplistic. The Hebrew word EZER comes from two root words, one meaning to "rescue, to save," and the other meaning "to be strong." As I read the other scriptures where this Hebrew word is used, something became quite obvious to me. In relation to God, it denotes God as the deliverer, the savior, the protective shield, the power and strength.

I then pondered upon Genesis 3:20:
Genesis 3:20 *And Adam called his wife's name Eve; because she was the mother of all living.*
"She was the mother of all living". At this moment in the creation of humankind on this earth, every human yet to be born would have "Eve" as their mother. There would be no more "creation", "forming" or "making" by God. All living humankind would now come from "Eve". I think it fair to say that in God's eyes women are very important. God knew that this was the "finished" human. His creative work on humankind was complete.
Deduce from this what you will, but one thing is certain, God never made women to be second class citizens!
Let me add one final thought, not from God, but from myself. If the originally "created" "female" had been perfect for Second Man, then why did God "make" Second Woman out of the "formed" Second Man who now had a soul? Truly, I pray that you can see the simplicity of God's work through God's own sequential words.

Also, I refer again to humankinds evolutionary graph which for millions and billions of years had flatlined. What does this graph do now at the arrival of Second Man? Scientists show very clearly that humankinds "evolution" suddenly started to increase at the appearance of the "farmer." Was this because God had given us a soul? Or was it as the Darwinians suggest that we progressed out of Apes!

As we consider these things let me present something of interest. It is known that our brains use 20 to 25% of our total energy requirements. After being given a "soul", it is fairly safe to assume that our brains would become more active and therefore require more protein to provide our energy. Did God teach us to "farm" to solve this problem? Hopefully this question will at least lead to more investigation and discussion.

Is not man's neo-cortex much larger and greatly different to that of other mammals? Could the word of God not be a more simple explanation as to the truth of how humankind suddenly jumped from being a "hunter gatherer" to a "farmer?" If nothing else, I pray that this paragraph stirs the experts into researching the possibility of a link between humankinds change from a smaller to a larger neo-cortex. Did this change occur around the same time as "farming" was first discovered? In addition, as we read in the next chapter about Third Man, consider why humankind's brain developed to an even larger extent. Was this purely coincidental to provide us with a brain of sufficient size to accommodate our new "knowledge," or was it God-incidental?

One thing is certain, after flatlining for billions of years, and then moving up during the period of Second Man, humankind's line on the graph rose exponentially after the fall of Adam, whom I refer to as Third Man. Was this because we now had "knowledge", as the word of God tells us? Or was it purely coincidental that our line starts to move up exponentially six or seven thousand years ago to coincide exactly with Adam's fall? Remember, that Adam ate from the Tree of Knowledge. Adam didn't eat an Apple or a Banana! He ate from the Tree of Knowledge! Truly, I believe man's vanity is total if we believe anything other than this to be God-incidental!

Remember from a previous chapter, we learnt that it is our soul that enables us to sin. Well, now let's see this in action for the first time. In the next chapter, let's see how Third Man Adam or you and I came into being.

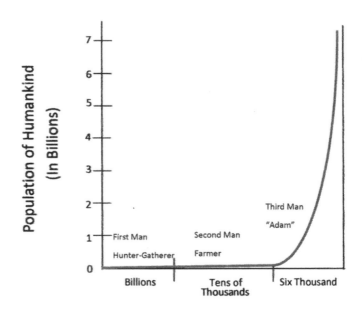

Third Man - The TRUTH

We now know from the word of God that First Man, the "Hunter Gatherer," did not "evolve" from Apes. We also now know from the word of God that Second Man, the "Farmer," did not "evolve" from Apes. Now, we refer again to the word of God to read the TRUTH about Third Man. Third Man, or you and I, also did not "evolve" from Apes.

Remember where we left Second Man, the "Farmer?" Second Man, or countless numbers of humankind, both men and women with spirit and soul, were now "farming" in a part of the Middle East which God called Eden. In addition, the "females" of this humankind had now been made out of a rib from the "formed" males. These "females" were now no longer just "females," they were now "woman." You will remember from the previous chapter the significant difference between "female" and "woman." These "women" were complete. They became wives, were individuals with character because they now had a soul (mind, will and emotions).

God said "I will make him an help meet." God also said, "made He a woman."

Let me just remind you of the Hebrew word for "Made." It is ASAH which translated is "the completed or finished work." This is the finality of God's accomplishments regarding humankind. Out of one of these women would come offspring who were exactly and perfectly "made" by God, and who could then go on to fulfill God's perfect plan for humankind.

So, here we have humankind farming exactly as taught by God, in an area of the Middle East that possessed the most fertile soil ever known to humankind. An area that we know as the Garden of Eden. We read again confirmation of this from the word of God:

Genesis 2:15 to 25 *And the LORD God took the man, and put him **into the garden of Eden** to **dress it and to keep it.***
16 And the LORD God commanded the man, saying, Of every tree of the garden thou mayest freely eat:
*17 But **of the tree of the knowledge of good and evil, thou shalt not eat of it**: for in the day that thou eatest thereof **thou shalt surely die**.*
*18 And the LORD God said, [It is] not good that the man should be alone; **I will make** him an help meet for him.*
19 And out of the ground the LORD God formed every beast of the field, and every fowl of the air; and brought [them] unto Adam to see what he would call them: and whatsoever Adam called every living creature, that [was] the name thereof.
20 And Adam gave names to all cattle, and to the fowl of the air, and to every beast of the field; but for Adam there was not found an help meet for him.
21 And the LORD God caused a deep sleep to fall upon Adam, and he slept: and he took one of his ribs, and closed up the flesh instead thereof;
*22 And the rib, which the LORD God had taken from man, **made he a woman**, and brought her unto the man.*
23 And Adam said, This [is] now bone of my bones, and flesh of my flesh: she shall be called Woman, because she was taken out of Man.
24 Therefore shall a man leave his father and his mother, and shall cleave unto his wife: and they shall be one flesh.
*25 And they were **both naked**, the man and his wife, and **were not ashamed**.*

We see again the important words, "God took the man and put him into the garden," "To dress it and to keep it." "Both naked and were not ashamed." They didn't "know" they were naked, because at that moment they had no "knowledge."

We can also see that God threatened humankind for the first time with death. God told humankind that if they ate from the tree of knowledge, they would surely die. God knew what was coming next and that death would eventually prove to be a blessing to us!

God never shared with me the time line of Second Man's farming period in the Middle East, but the next event ended it and brought about Third Man, or you and me.

Revelation 12:7 to 12 *And there was war in heaven: Michael and his angels fought against the dragon; and the dragon fought and his angels,*

8 And prevailed not; neither was their place found any more in heaven.

9 And the great dragon was cast out, that old serpent, called the Devil, and Satan, which deceiveth the whole world: he was cast out into the earth, and his angels were cast out with him.

10 And I heard a loud voice saying in heaven, Now is come salvation, and strength, and the kingdom of our God, and the power of his Christ: for the accuser of our brethren is cast down, which accused them before our God day and night.

11 And they overcame him by the blood of the Lamb, and by the word of their testimony; and they loved not their lives unto the death.

12 Therefore rejoice, [ye] heavens, and ye that dwell in them. Woe to the inhabiters of the earth and of the sea! for the devil is come down unto you, having great wrath, because he knoweth that he hath but a short time.

A war had taken place in heaven. Satan and a rebellious number of angels had fought with Michael. Satan was cast down to earth and as we read from the word of God, he had "great wrath."

Satan set about the destruction of earth and of all humankind who dwelt therein. Unfortunately, Satan couldn't achieve this objective until humankind had knowledge and God knew this. God has a plan for every age and His plan for this age would now come into being. Until this moment, Satan and his rebellious angels had been powerless, but that would now change.

Remember, humankind at this moment in our history had a spirit and a soul, but they had no "knowledge." Satan knew that the only way he could destroy humankind would be to get them to eat of the Tree of Knowledge. Once humankind had ALL knowledge, then Satan could ensure that humankind was given by him the spiritual "Understanding" of that knowledge. Of course, the spiritual understanding given by Satan would only relate to the "knowledge" of evil!

Let's again read the word of God:

Genesis 3:1 to 7 *Now the serpent was more subtil than any beast of the field which the LORD God had made. And he said unto the woman, Yea, hath God said, Ye shall not eat of every tree of the garden?*
2 And the woman said unto the serpent, We may eat of the fruit of the trees of the garden:
3 But of the fruit of the tree which [is] in the midst of the garden, God hath said, Ye shall not eat of it, neither shall ye touch it, lest ye die.
4 And the serpent said unto the woman, Ye shall not surely die:

5 For God doth know that in the day ye eat thereof, then your eyes shall be opened, and **ye shall be as gods, knowing good and evil**.
6 And when the woman saw that the tree [was] good for food, and that it [was] pleasant to the eyes, and a tree to be desired to make [one] wise, she took of the fruit thereof, and did eat, and gave also unto her husband with her; and he did eat.
7 And the eyes of them both were opened, and they **knew that they [were] naked***; and they sewed fig leaves together, and made themselves aprons.*

Satan did that which was necessary; he tempted one of the women into eating of the tree of knowledge.
We read from the word of God, "The eyes of them both were opened, and they 'knew that they were naked".
At this very moment, Third Man (or you and I), came into being. One "farmer" and his wife now had "knowledge". These would become our ancestors whom we know as "Adam" and "Eve." These two humans were now complete. They are as complete as you or me! They now had access spiritually through either God or Satan to the **UNDERSTANDING** of **ALL** knowledge.

Genesis 3:8 to 24 *And they heard the voice of the LORD God walking in the garden in the cool of the day: and Adam and his wife hid themselves from the presence of the LORD God amongst the trees of the garden.*
9 And the LORD God called unto Adam, and said unto him, Where [art] thou?
10 And he said, I heard thy voice in the garden, and I was afraid, **because I [was] naked***; and I hid myself.*
11 And he said, **Who told thee that thou [wast] naked?**
Hast thou eaten of the tree, whereof I commanded thee that thou shouldest not eat?

203

12 And the man said, The woman whom thou gavest [to be] with me, she gave me of the tree, and I did eat.

13 And the LORD God said unto the woman, What [is] this [that] thou hast done? And the woman said, The serpent beguiled me, and I did eat.

14 And the LORD God said unto the serpent, Because thou hast done this, thou [art] cursed above all cattle, and above every beast of the field; upon thy belly shalt thou go, and dust shalt thou eat all the days of thy life:

15 And I will put **enmity between thee and the woman**, and between **thy seed and her seed**; it shall bruise thy head, and thou shalt bruise his heel.

16 Unto the woman he said, I will greatly multiply thy sorrow and thy conception; in sorrow thou shalt bring forth children; and thy desire [shall be] to thy husband, and he shall rule over thee.

17 And unto Adam he said, Because thou hast hearkened unto the voice of thy wife, and hast eaten of the tree, of which I commanded thee, saying, Thou shalt not eat of it: **cursed [is] the ground** for thy sake; in sorrow shalt thou eat [of] it all the days of thy life;

18 **Thorns also and thistles shall it bring forth to thee**; and thou shalt eat the herb of the field;

19 In the sweat of thy face shalt thou eat bread, till thou return unto the ground; for out of it wast thou taken: for dust thou [art], and unto dust shalt thou return.

20 And Adam called his wife's name Eve; because she was the **mother of all living**.

21 Unto Adam also and to his wife **did the LORD God make coats of skins, and clothed them.**

22 And the LORD God said, Behold, the **man is become as one of us**, to **know good and evil**: and now, lest he put forth his hand, and take also of the tree of life, and eat, and **live for ever**:

*23 Therefore the LORD God **sent him forth from the garden of Eden**, to till the ground from whence he was taken.*
*24 **So he drove out the man**; and he placed at the east of the garden of Eden Cherubims, and a flaming sword which turned every way, to keep the way of the tree of life.*

From this moment, the God inspired writing of Moses in the book of Genesis would follow the genealogy of one man and his wife; Adam and Eve! Both you and I are descended from these two humans. We are of Adam's seed and passed down to us through this seed is **ALL** knowledge. There was no evolution from Apes, we were "created," we were "formed" and finally "made."
Before leaving the word of God and discussing "knowledge" in more detail, let me just add a couple of final points.
Why would God make them coats of skins and clothe them? It was nothing to do with embarrassment, because originally they were naked before God anyway. Did our ancestors now farm planet earth dressed in animal skins simply because they copied God in how to make them? Third Man now had all the "formed" domesticated farm animals to take with him out of Eden and from which to get his hides for clothing.

According to scientists and archeologists, at this moment in humankinds history there was about one million people on earth. So after millions and billions of years, humankind added up to about one million people. Today, just six or seven thousand years after Adam, our population is about eight billion! May I suggest to you that without this "knowledge," it would be impossible for humankind to grow as exponentially as we have done.

Also, Satan said that "ye shall be as gods." Are not the genetic scientists of today "creating" life in test tubes? Does this not make them "god like?"

In June of 2010, it was reported in the Daily Mail newspaper that SYNTHIA had been "created". Craig Venter, a biologist, had "created" artificial life by using synthetic cells to make a "designer microbe". Other scientists accused him of "playing God".

God shared with me a massive truth concerning this and when God so chooses, it will be revealed. It relates however, to the end of this earth and is therefore not for this book, but for another time.

A large part of the "fertile crescent" as it was known, is now a desert. What happened to all the fertile soil? Of course, we all know about climate change, but what does God say?

God tells us very clearly.

Genesis 3:17 *And unto Adam he said, Because thou hast hearkened unto the voice of thy wife, and hast eaten of the tree, of which I commanded thee, saying, Thou shalt not eat of it: cursed is the ground for thy sake; in sorrow shalt thou eat of it all the days of thy life;*

God cursed the ground and it became desolate.

Humankind was now taken out of this wonderful paradise. God "drove" out the man! One translation of the word "drove", is to "drive away," another is to "expatriate."

God also wanted to ensure that Third Man would eventually die; that he would not live forever. God ensured this by removing the Tree of Life and by giving us death. I said earlier that "death" would prove to be a blessing to us. Why ever would I say this? How could death possibly be a blessing to us?

We know that "knowledge" would not only be of "good", but also "evil." This "evil" would not just be the odd bad thing. It would be the most vile, degrading, violent, perverse, bodily sickening evil that most people cannot even imagine. Try to picture yourself locked up in a high security prison in a very hot and lawless country. The cells either side of you contain the most violent, perverted, sadistic criminals on the face of this planet. These are men who delight in inflicting the worse possible pain on both men, women and animals. These are men who get pleasure out of violating the human body in the most extreme ways. It's hot and it's ultra scary, but it's going to get worse! The warden of this prison decides he's had enough. He instructs the guards to switch off the air conditioning, the lights, open every cell door, open every other door and then proceed to the main entrance locking it behind them. You are now in a hot, dark prison with no protection whatsoever and you cannot escape! You are locked in! You cry out, but the warden doesn't hear because he is long gone. The rest I'll leave to your imagination, but this best describes a Godless earth without death! People would have to live forever in fear and suffering of the most heinous kind. Praise God that He loves us too much to allow this scenario, that's why He gave us death.

Also, and most important; God gave us death so that humankind would turn to Jesus as their only hope of salvation. Without death, there is no need for Jesus!

The Lord God never shared with me exactly what happened to all the other "farmers" or human beings. My own personal view is that after Adam and Eve sinned against God and were driven out of Eden, all remaining human beings were driven out also.

You may well now ask, "what then happened to all the other farmers or human beings with spirit and soul, but no knowledge?" I believe in what God told me happened to them. They all died in the great flood at the time of Noah, or before through simple degeneration and natural death.

Now, let's get back to the word of God and what Satan said. "Ye shall be as gods, knowing good and evil." In other words, you will "know" everything! This "everything" is within us. It is within each one of us, but we are only given "understanding" of it, through spiritual means. Even everything about God's kingdom is within us, but how do I know this? Jesus tells us that it is.

Luke 17:21 *Neither shall they say, Lo here! or, lo there! for, behold, the kingdom of God is within you.*

What else does Jesus say about that which is within us?

Matthew 15:16 to 19 *And Jesus said, Are ye also yet without understanding?*

17 Do not ye yet understand, that whatsoever entereth in at the mouth goeth into the belly, and is cast out into the draught?

18 But those things which proceed out of the mouth come forth from the heart; and they defile the man.

*19 For **out of the heart proceed evil thoughts, murders, adulteries, fornications, thefts, false witness, blasphemies:***
Confirmation again that knowledge of evil is within us. Understanding of this evil "knowledge" will be given to us by Satan and his demons.

Praises be to God that understanding of "knowledge" of good is also given to us by the Holy Spirit.

God gave us all a "free will" and with this we can choose who our spirit listens to, God or Satan.

All of these words have now brought us to the most important topic, that of "knowledge" and our completion as human beings.

Remember in a previous chapter, I wrote that we could "know" every word in the bible and yet not understand it. I once had a parrot who "knew" lots and lots of words, regrettably he understood none of them. My parrot was very clever, but as with Second Man it was simple word association. My dog "knows" the word cookie, but he doesn't understand what a cookie is, he just loves the taste! Now, let me bring you into a deeper "understanding." We know what morality is and let's keep it very simple, it is a knowledge of good or bad. We "know" what is good or bad. Though no one ever taught us this, even from the earliest we "knew" what was right and what was wrong. You had a bad thought, how do you know it's bad? We have a "conscience," from where did we get this "conscience," and what is it?

We all know that from birth, babies "know" how to behave badly. Ever hear the saying, "He's got the devil in him today?" It might be more true than we think! Even in the womb, a baby can be influenced and given "understanding." The baby already has "knowledge" of everything, but through spiritual forces directly it can be given "understanding." Much more important, indirect spiritual forces acting through the mother or father will give "understanding" to the baby. Still more important, words spoken by the mother or father, under spiritual influence whether known or not, can have an impact on the baby throughout the whole of its life. These influences can be for good, or they can be for evil. How do we know that babies in the womb can be influenced by words spoken by either parent or others? Again, let's look at the word of God.

Luke 1:41 *And it came to pass, that, when Elisabeth heard the salutation of Mary, the babe leaped in her womb; and Elisabeth was filled with the Holy Ghost:*

The leaping baby was John the Baptist! John had just heard the good news about the coming of our Lord and Savior, Jesus Christ!

Moving on from the baby, what about the early child, the young child? Let us think back. Without any teaching or words from adults, we all "knew" exactly when we had done something wrong. Our "conscience" told us so! So what is our "conscience" and how can it "tell" us when we do wrong? It is our "conscience" that teaches us "morals." Without any instruction from adults at all, young children and early adults "know" immediately that their words or actions were "morally" right or "morally" wrong.

Before continuing with God's own words, let me just give simple definitions of the word CONSCIENCE.

The Greek word for conscience is SUNEIDESIS. This word is made up of two words, SUN meaning "with", and OIDA meaning "to know."

The Latin is CONSCIENTIA meaning "with knowledge." So, it's fair to deduce that our conscience is all knowledge, but "with" something else. That something else is "understanding", or to use a scriptural word, "wisdom."

My own personal belief is that "understanding" comes to us through our spirit. Understanding can be given to our spirit in three ways; through the world and worldly things; through our spirit from Satan; or through our spirit from Almighty God. One thing is certain, the greatest of all these is "understanding" or "wisdom" given from God. Every human on this planet has access to the "understanding" of ALL knowledge, but that can only ever come to us after our spirit has become "justified" through our total belief in Jesus Christ. Increasingly, this Godly "wisdom" and "understanding" will be given to us as we become more and more "sanctified."

God will only share the mysteries and wonders with a Holy, new and undefiled spirit. You will possess this "justified" spirit immediately you become "Born Again" through your belief in Jesus Christ as the Messiah, Son of God and Savior of Humankind.

This Godly "wisdom" will not be given immediately. Our earthly bodies, minds and brains simply couldn't take it, but when we are given a "glorified" body, then ALL will be "known" and "understood."

210

How do I know this? God told me.

1st Corinth 13:9 to 12 *For we know in part, and we prophesy in part.*

10 But when that which is perfect is come, then that which is in part shall be done away.

11 When I was a child, I spake as a child, I understood as a child, I thought as a child: but when I became a man, I put away childish things.

12 For now we see through a glass, darkly; but then face to face: now I know in part; but then shall I know even as also I am known.

Paul tells the church in Corinth the truth. Using very simple words, he confirms to them that our knowledge now is only "part" complete. He explains that our prophesies are only "partly" complete, but he gives them a guarantee. That guarantee is certain. When our Lord Jesus Christ comes, that which is in part shall be done away with. When our Lord Jesus Christ comes, every believing Christian that ever was or ever will be, will "know even as I am known." No longer will we "see through a glass darkly," EVERYTHING will be revealed.

When our Lord comes, or we go to be with Him, nothing at all will be hidden. We will all be like a completely open book. Whatever we may exhibit on the outside through our attitudes or personalities, we will no longer be able to conceal the truth of what's in our hearts. The inner most secrets of our hearts will be laid bare for all to see.

Hebrews 4:12 *For the word of God [is] quick, and powerful, and sharper than any twoedged sword, piercing even to the dividing asunder of soul and spirit, and of the joints and marrow, and [is] a discerner of the thoughts and intents of the heart.*

Notice it's the "WORD OF GOD" that is the discerner. Your bible reads you, and Jesus is "The Word made flesh."

We will be able to see the hearts of others and nothing whatsoever will be hidden again. We will "know" others exactly as the Lord knows us. Some will be very happy, but others will be very ashamed. On this day, we will truly see "the pure in heart" and those who never were as pure as their earthly persona made them appear to be. This is why the Apostle Paul stresses repeatedly that the most important thing is love. God prepares every Christian for His Kingdom and the day in which we will see Him. Hopefully, this will help some to understand better the beatification process, and it's Almighty importance.

Ephesians 3:11 to 17 *According to the eternal purpose which he purposed in Christ Jesus our Lord: 12 In whom we have boldness and access with confidence by the faith of him. 13 Wherefore I desire that ye faint not at my tribulations for you, which is your glory. 14 For this cause I bow my knees unto the Father of our Lord Jesus Christ, 15 Of whom the whole family in heaven and earth is named, 16 That he would grant you, according to the riches of his glory, to be strengthened with might by his Spirit in the inner man; 17 That Christ may dwell in your hearts by faith; that ye, being rooted and grounded in love,*

"Dwell" translated means a "settling in," being completely at home as though it was your own home. When any Christian reaches this point, the "thoughts and intents" of our hearts could not be bettered! When Christ dwells within your hearts, you have access to ALL understanding. Is this possible? Let's read what God says:

John 14:23 *Jesus answered and said unto him, If a man love me, he will keep my words: and my Father will love him, and we will come unto him, and make our abode with him.*

Also consider this, we hear that the Kingdom of God is "within us," what do we understand by this?

Luke 17:21 *Neither shall they say, Lo here! or, lo there! for, behold, the kingdom of God is within you.*

"Kingdom" translated is the "foundation of power." We know that ALL knowledge is already within us, but how do we get access to the "power" that Luke writes about? We get access to the "understanding" of that power when the One Who created us dwells within our hearts! Again, it's important to understand the translation correctly.

"Within" translated is the Greek word ENTOS (EN-TOS) which means "inside or within." Not as some bibles translate as "among or in your midst", but INSIDE YOU! This Almighty POWER or knowledge of it, we already have. However, it will only be made active and we will only ever understand it, if Jesus settles down and makes His home within our hearts.

Remember what Matthew said:

Matthew 5:8 *Blessed [are] the pure in heart: for they shall see God.*

When Jesus "dwells within" our hearts, they WILL be pure! This purification process is available to all who truly believe; believe being the operative word.

Our hearts naturally contain every evil and understanding of this evil is given freely by Satan. How do we know this? Again, let's look at the word of God:

James 3:13 to 17 *Who [is] a wise man and endued with knowledge among you? let him shew out of a good conversation his works with meekness of wisdom.*

14 But if ye have bitter envying and strife in your hearts, glory not, and lie not against the truth.

15 This wisdom descendeth not from above, but [is] earthly, sensual, devilish.

16 For where envying and strife [is], there [is] confusion and every evil work.

17 But the wisdom that is from above is first pure, then peaceable, gentle, [and] easy to be intreated, full of mercy and good fruits, without partiality, and without hypocrisy.

Remember also what God said:

Matthew 15:17 to 20 *Do not ye yet understand, that whatsoever entereth in at the mouth goeth into the belly, and is cast out into the draught?*
18 But those things which proceed out of the mouth come forth from the heart; and they defile the man.
19 For out of the heart proceed evil thoughts, murders, adulteries, fornications, thefts, false witness, blasphemies:
20 These are [the things] which defile a man: but to eat with unwashen hands defileth not a man.

The entire worst of the worst is already within us. When Satan said eat and you will have ALL knowledge he wasn't kidding! If we need more confirmation of this, here it is again from the word of God:

Matthew 15:11 *Not that which goeth into the mouth defileth a man; but that which cometh out of the mouth, this defileth a man.*

Mark 7:14 to 23 *And when he had called all the people [unto him], he said unto them, Hearken unto me every one [of you], and understand:*
15 There is nothing from without a man, that entering into him can defile him: but the things which come out of him, those are they that defile the man.
16 If any man have ears to hear, let him hear.
17 And when he was entered into the house from the people, his disciples asked him concerning the parable.
18 And he saith unto them, Are ye so without understanding also? Do ye not perceive, that whatsoever thing from without entereth into the man, [it] cannot defile him;
19 Because it entereth not into his heart, but into the belly, and goeth out into the draught, purging all meats?
20 And he said, That which cometh out of the man, that defileth the man.

21 For from within, out of the heart of men, proceed evil thoughts, adulteries, fornications, murders,
22 Thefts, covetousness, wickedness, deceit, lasciviousness, an evil eye, blasphemy, pride, foolishness:
23 All these evil things come from within, and defile the man.

How can we confirm and be certain that our "wisdom" or "understanding" comes from three sources?
We can all agree that we are taught by our parents, teachers and through other worldly means.
It is to be hoped that we can all agree, that Satan and his demonic spirits provide all of our understanding of evil and all things Satanic. Both of these sources were confirmed by James in Chapter 3 Verses 13 to 17, but what about our "wisdom" or "understanding" from God?
It is widely accepted that the "wisest" human ever to inhabit planet earth was Solomon. Why was Solomon so wise and from where did this "wisdom" come? Once more let's look at the word of God:
1st Chronicles 22:11/12 *Now, my son, the LORD be with thee; and prosper thou, and build the house of the LORD thy God, as he hath said of thee. 12 Only the LORD give thee wisdom and understanding, and give thee charge concerning Israel, that thou mayest keep the law of the LORD thy God.*
It's quite obvious from the words of his father David, that only from God could this type of "wisdom" and "understanding" come.
When we look at the original Hebrew word for wisdom, it is SEKEL (SEH-KEL) which comes from SAKAL (SAW-KAL), both meaning "intelligent, expert instruction, prosper, good success, understanding, behave self, consider, make wise." Also, let's look at the translation for "understanding." The Hebrew word used here is BIYNAH (BEE-NAW) which comes from the word BIYN (BENE).

Both words translated mean "perfect understanding, separate mentally, to distinguish, discern, inform, instruct, have intelligence, be prudent, skillful, wisely man", etc. I think it fair to say that all of these things together could only come from God, but again let's look for more confirmation.

Proverbs 2:6 *For the LORD giveth wisdom: out of his mouth [cometh] knowledge and understanding.*

Daniel 9:20 to 22 *And whiles I [was] speaking, and praying, and confessing my sin and the sin of my people Israel, and presenting my supplication before the LORD my God for the holy mountain of my God; 21 Yea, whiles I [was] speaking in prayer, even the man Gabriel, whom I had seen in the vision at the beginning, being caused to fly swiftly, touched me about the time of the evening oblation. 22 And he informed [me], and talked with me, and said, O Daniel, I am now come forth to give thee skill and understanding.*

Daniel 10:18 to 21 *Then there came again and touched me [one] like the appearance of a man, and he strengthened me, 19 And said, O man greatly beloved, fear not: peace [be] unto thee, be strong, yea, be strong. And when he had spoken unto me, I was strengthened, and said, Let my lord speak; for thou hast strengthened me. 20 Then said he, Knowest thou wherefore I come unto thee? and now will I return to fight with the prince of Persia: and when I am gone forth, lo, the prince of Grecia shall come. 21 But I will shew thee that which is noted in the scripture of truth: and [there is] none that holdeth with me in these things, but Michael your prince.*

It doesn't get much better than that. God sent both Gabriel and Michael to give Daniel heavenly "wisdom" or "understanding."

I give all the praise, honor and glory to God in giving my personal example. I had been reading my bible since 1987 and yet I didn't UNDERSTAND a word! I KNEW all the words, but I did not UNDERSTAND them. Immediately after I was baptized in the Spirit, I began to UNDERSTAND more. After the Holy Spirit appeared to me in 2005, the whole bible became like A, B, C. I UNDERSTOOD as never before. My eyes had been opened, I could now see the TRUTH, the **PURE TRUTH**.

The "moral" guiding light of our soul, is our "conscience" (knowledge with). One definition of conscience is: The awareness of a moral or ethical aspect to ones conduct together with the urge to prefer right over wrong.
When we have a thought, we may not have any idea where the thought came from, yet we immediately "know" whether that thought is good, bad or indifferent. All "good" comes from God. All evil comes from Satan. Our "understanding" of that thought is presented to us immediately, we then have our own free will given by God to choose one or the other. We choose to dismiss one as being evil or to keep one as being good.
If we have the most horrendous thought possible, let me suggest that it is not your thought at all. I suggest that the thought was planted there by Satan as a temptation. The problem comes if we accede to that thought and turn it into an action. If this takes place then you need spiritual help. It is impossible to combat Satan without the help of God through the Holy Spirit. Remember even Jesus was tempted. Remember also, Jesus has already won that battle for us.

Someone once said, "Conscience is not made to manufacture truth, but to seek it". Knowledge that is within all of us, is permanently seeking truth or understanding so that it may come into "being".

We are all "seekers after the truth." My advice is to seek the higher God given truth and live. Not to seek the lower Satanic truth and die, not just physically, but spiritually also and for eternity.

What does the word of God tell us about those who seek the Satanic truth?
1st Timothy 4:1/2 *Now the Spirit speaketh expressly, that in the latter times some shall depart from the faith, giving heed to seducing spirits, and doctrines of devils; 2 Speaking lies in hypocrisy; having their conscience seared with a hot iron;*

As the Apostle Paul says, "Some shall depart from the faith, giving heed to seducing spirits, and doctrines of devils: Speaking lies in hypocrisy." These people will listen to Satan and be seduced by him. They will then be so far from the **PURE TRUTH** of God that they will even tell lies about their lies! Their conscience has become so hardened through sin that it even lies to itself. What else do we learn? "Having their conscience seared with a hot iron." What does this mean? It means that these people have allowed their knowledge to become like a wound which has been cauterized. The cauterized wound became hardened, crusted over and is therefore totally insensitive. It means that these people are now totally insensitive to the truth. Even when the truth is presented to them, they cannot understand it because they have become desensitized.
Paul speaks that this is what we will see in "the latter times." Do you see more and more of these people today than you did years ago?

I have written much more about "knowledge" than I originally intended, but hopefully you will find it useful. Before leaving this section let me just add one final thought.

The final action of our "conscience" (knowledge with) in this life here on earth, is the fear of death. The very last thing we will understand is death. It's hard for me to imagine being at this pinpoint, pivotal moment and never to have known my Lord and Savior Jesus Christ. Why do I say this? I say it because as a Christian, as a believer, death to me has lost its power.

1st Corinthian 15:52 to 57 *In a moment, in the twinkling of an eye, at the last trump: for the trumpet shall sound, and the dead shall be raised incorruptible, and we shall be changed.*

53 For this corruptible must put on incorruption, and this mortal [must] put on immortality.

54 So when this corruptible shall have put on incorruption, and this mortal shall have put on immortality, then shall be brought to pass the saying that is written, **Death is swallowed up in victory. 55 O death, where [is] thy sting? O grave, where [is] thy victory?** *56 The sting of death [is] sin; and the strength of sin [is] the law. 57 But thanks [be] to God, which giveth us the victory through our Lord Jesus Christ.*

Confirmation positive from the Apostle Paul that death holds no fear for Christians. This fear and action have been removed by Christ's death and resurrection. If we need more confirmation, then here it is:

2nd Timothy 1:9/10 *Who hath saved us, and called [us] with an holy calling, not according to our works, but according to his own purpose and grace, which was given us in Christ Jesus before the world began, 10 But is now made manifest by the appearing of our Saviour Jesus*

*Christ, **who hath abolished death**, and hath brought life and immortality to light through the gospel:*

Here the Apostle Paul tells us very clearly that our Lord Jesus Christ "abolished" death. If we check the definition of abolish it is to "formally put an end to/Annulment." If we define still further, it is to "obliterate the effect or existence of." Further still, "To make of no effect!"

So this is the end of the story of the creation of humankind, every creature and of planet earth on which we all live. I do sincerely hope that you will all be able to understand my words. I hope that you will now be able to see the **PURE TRUTH** of the creation process. There were three very definite stages in our creation, all of which bring us to the present day human, you and I.
God created every one of us for one reason, to glorify Himself through our love, belief in and commitment to Jesus Christ.
We all have a body, spirit, soul and "knowledge", but most important; a free will.
I pray that each one of you will use your free will to seek the **PURE TRUTH** in the only One in Whom it can be found; Jesus Christ.

God never gave me time-lines for the periods before or after these key moments in creation, but again as with First Man, if this was the end of the bible, what would we have? We would have Second Man and Woman who had been placed by God in the most fertile land on earth. God had given them rain and taught them how to plant and cultivate plants and herbs in "fields." These are the plants and herbs that were previously "upon the face of the earth." In addition, God had now "formed" from His original "creation," "beasts of the field, fowl of the air and cattle" and given them to Second Man. These newly "formed" animals would be what we know today as "livestock", or "domesticated" farm animals. They would include, sheep, goats, horses, pigs, ducks, geese, turkey's, chicken's , etc. We know that "jungle fowl" was the ancestor of our domestic chickens. Was this a slow evolutionary process? No, not at all, it was simply as God tells us in His word, He "formed" them specifically for Second Man.

I find it quite interesting to learn that many thousands of years ago, both Egyptians and Romans used chicken eggs to make both bread and cakes. In addition, we also know that early clothing was made from animal skins, in fact items too numerous to mention were fashioned out of skin, bones and organs of "farmed" animals.

Regrettably, Second Man could not keep the commandment of God. Despite having been taught by God how to farm in the most fertile agricultural area on earth, Second Man was tempted by Satan and succumbed to him. This human being and his wife, now had knowledge of everything within themselves. This is who I refer to as Third Man. These two humans can now be referred to as "Adam and Eve". These are our ancestors and through Noah we can trace our lineage directly back to them.

After this transgression, God drove Adam, Eve and all the other Second Man "Farmers" out of Eden. They were sent back to "till" (farm) the area of land (North Eastern Africa) from where they were originally taken from. Knowledge of sin was now in the world and as we read in our Holy Bibles, Satan immediately set about giving "understanding" of evil to those with knowledge. Eden, and eternal life on this earth were to be no more.

There was nothing evolutionary about all of this process. God simply created, formed and made humankind so that His plan could be fulfilled.

We are reliably informed by archeologists that the "birthplace of civilization," or the "cradle of civilization" is in an area of Iraq. Has no one ever questioned that it was in this area that humankind first gained "knowledge?" Is it coincidence or God-incidence that Eden or the Fertile Crescent is in exactly the same place as archeologists tell us is the "birthplace of civilization?"

I'm not an educated man, but even I can answer that one! There was no big bang! We did not evolve from apes! There is an Almighty God and He created everything and it is as simple, and as awesome, as that.

I am reminded of the warning from Peter, who in a few short verses gave us the beginning and the end. Peter never doubted Moses or the holy prophets. Peter was a simple, uneducated fisherman, but he came to know the **PURE TRUTH** and stood upon this **PURE TRUTH** until his death. I pray with every breath in my body, that you will do the same. The day of fire and judgement is coming, don't delay. Accept Jesus Christ as your Lord and Savior today because you may not have the opportunity tomorrow! Does a burglar let you know what time of night he will break into your house? In the same way our Lord Jesus doesn't tell us on which day He will return, but one thing is 100% certain, He will return.

On that day, what manner of person will you be? I pray to God that you will be a "Christian," a believer in Jesus Christ and the Almighty God of creation.

2nd Peter 3:1 to 11 *This second epistle, beloved, I now write unto you; in [both] which I stir up your pure minds by way of remembrance:*
2 That ye may be mindful of the words which were spoken before by the holy prophets, and of the commandment of us the apostles of the Lord and Saviour:

3 Knowing this first, that there shall come in the last days scoffers, walking after their own lusts,

4 And saying, Where is the promise of his coming? for since the fathers fell asleep, all things continue as [they were] from the beginning of the creation.

5 For this they willingly are ignorant of, that by the word of God the heavens were of old, and the earth standing out of the water and in the water:

6 Whereby the world that then was, being overflowed with water, perished:

7 But the heavens and the earth, which are now, by the same word are kept in store, reserved unto fire against the day of judgment and perdition of ungodly men.

8 But, beloved, be not ignorant of this one thing, that one day [is] with the Lord as a thousand years, and a thousand years as one day.

9 The Lord is not slack concerning his promise, as some men count slackness; but is longsuffering to us-ward, not willing that any should perish, but that all should come to repentance.

10 But the day of the Lord will come as a thief in the night; in the which the heavens shall pass away with a great noise, and the elements shall melt with fervent heat, the earth also and the works that are therein shall be burned up.

*11 [Seeing] then [that] all these things shall be dissolved, **what manner [of persons] ought ye to be** in [all] holy conversation and godliness,*

The end of this age, and this earth as we know it, is closer than we think. Everything shall be burned up in fervent heat and all things shall be dissolved. Peter then asks this question:

What manner of persons ought ye to be?

I pray that having read the **PURE TRUTH** herein contained, you will be a Christian.

A Summary of Creation

As previously explained, I am not a professional writer and the **PURE TRUTH** contained in this book comes not from my words, but those of Almighty God. The sole purpose of God sharing with me the **PURE TRUTH** of Creation, is contained mainly in the three chapters First, Second and Third Man. As I proofread these chapters it became apparent to me that non-Christians, and even some Christians, may struggle to fully understand the simplicity and enormity of God's revelation. These chapters rightly contain the words of God, but there are many of them and the terminology therein contained may not be fully understood by all.

I therefore feel challenged to put into my own words, a brief summary of the revelation of the **PURE TRUTH** of creation so that everyone might understand. This is that summary and I pray that its simplicity will help every reader to come to an understanding of the **TRUTH.**

First, as I researched the Hebrew and Greek translations for the words; man, Adam, male and mankind, I was alerted to the GREAT DECEPTION! From the very beginning, Satan tricked translators into using the word "Adam" instead of human beings or humankind. As a consequence, Christians for thousands of years have been deceived into thinking that every "Adam" in the bible relates to one man and it doesn't! In certain instances, "Adam" does refer to one man, but in others it translates into humankind as a species! Throughout my own Christian life until this point, I had always had the mind set that Adam was just one man. I too had been deceived by Satan. Praises be to God; not anymore!

Why I should have been so surprised at this centuries old deception I do not know. God told us all very clearly what to expect. The Apostle Paul tells us in his letter to the Corinthians.

2nd Corinthian 4:4 *In whom the god of this world hath blinded the minds of them which believe not, lest the light of the glorious gospel of Christ, who is the image of God, should shine unto them.*

The "god of this world" being none other than the "accuser of the brethren" himself, Satan!

Now that the GREAT DECEPTION has been exposed, let me continue to give you an easy to understand summary of the three key chapters.

First, we read from the word of God that there was a sequence of events or a time line. God created the earth and everything in it EXCEPT humankind! What? I hear you say! Yes, that's right! Up to verse 23 of the first chapter of Genesis humankind did not exist. The earth was complete, but only inhabited by waterborne, airborne and land-based creatures. Humankind had not yet been created! I don't like to use scientific terminology, but to better help you understand, I will. This was simply prehistoric earth, human beings had yet to arrive.

How long ago was this? God never gave me the answer, but I have no reason to disbelieve our expert scientists and so it's millions or even billions of years ago.

Then in verse 26 of Genesis chapter one, humankind first arrived on this earth.

God "created" (a causing to be out of nothing) humankind in His image. God is Spirit and First Man (first human beings) was a spirit living inside a human body. This First Man had no soul or knowledge. This man lived on planet earth millions or billions of years ago and he is what we commonly know today as the Hunter Gatherer. Every food that First Man needed was provided for him by God, all he had to do was to "gather" it and eat it.

At this moment in the history of Humankind, First Man didn't need a soul (mind, will and emotions) because

Lucifer (Satan) was still in heaven with God. Our omniscient God knew what was coming next. There would be a rebellion in heaven led by Lucifer and supported by many angels. To accommodate and fulfill His plan for humankind through pure love, God would have to take action on earth and in heaven.

First, God prepared the earth to accept a new humankind that would possess a soul (mind, will and emotions). This newly prepared earth would contain the means by which the new humankind could obtain the on-hand protein necessary to sustain and increase a brain that could encompass all knowledge
Second, God had to cast down to this newly prepared earth, Lucifer (Satan) and his angels (demons)
These two sentences provide the most important key to unlock and understand God's master plan.

Very simply, God is love. God could simply have destroyed Lucifer and his supporters, but love does not destroy. This was the pivotal moment in humankinds history. Love had to prevail and conquer evil. Lucifer told all the host of heaven that pure evil was the best way. God had to prove to all the host of heaven that love was the best way, but God had to do this by using humankind. From this pivotal moment in humankinds history, we became participants in the greatest play on earth. We would be given a free will by God with access to Himself to enable us to overcome evil through our belief in the word of God. From this pivotal moment, all the heavenly host (the Angels who remained in Heaven) are watching and learning from humankind. They see our behavior in following Satan and evil, or our behavior in following Jesus Christ and love. Before the end of this age, earth will witness evil like never before. Evil will multiply and manifest itself in ways currently unimaginable. Make no mistake, however much Christians will suffer (and they will suffer immensely), the love of God through His Son Jesus Christ, will prevail and be victorious.

Now, let's get back to our Summary of Creation!
God then had to give these new humans access to all "knowledge" of both good and evil.
This was the arrival of humankind which I call "Second Man."
There was no evolutionary process. Second Man was "Formed" by God out of First Man and by using the "dust of the ground".
God now had to create a garden that would contain the Tree of Knowledge, and it would be into this garden that God would place Second Man. This "garden" is more commonly known as the "Garden of Eden." It was the most fertile land on earth, and it is known today to have been within the "Fertile Crescent."
God now gave rain to the earth, moreover He planted everything that was required in the Garden of Eden. God now gave the increase and everything He planted grew.
God then took some of the First Man humans and "Formed" (to shape or model out of existing) them using the dust from the ground. In addition, God breathed into these humans and they then became living souls. So Second Man now has a spirit and a soul (mind, will, emotions). In addition, Second Man has been taught by God to "farm" not just agriculture, but also animals. This is the human who evolutionists call the "farmer." There was no evolutionary process. God did it in an instant so that His plan for humankind could be fulfilled.
Second Man "farmed" both crops and animals within the "Garden of Eden" within the Fertile Crescent area, hundreds of thousands or even millions of years ago. There was no evolutionary process. Second Man was "formed."

Now came the critical moment in the history of this age of humankind. Lucifer and his rebellious angels were cast out of heaven by God and thrown to earth.

Satan, as Lucifer is now known, was determined to show the remaining angels in heaven that he was right. That his evil ways were better than the good ways of God.

Remember that God had now given humankind a soul (free will, mind and emotions). They could now "choose" who to follow, God, by whom they were "formed", or Satan who had now appeared in their midst.

This, yet again, is now a critical moment in the understanding of creation.

At this moment in our history, part of our earth (the Garden of Eden) was populated with human beings with spirits and souls who "farmed" the earth as taught by God, but who had no "knowledge."

Satan, who by the way had been given power on earth by God, now sought to exercise that power in a way that would have an impact on humankind throughout this whole present age.

Satan realized that the only way he could exercise this power, would be to trick one of the "formed" human beings into obtaining "knowledge," which of course would be of good AND evil!

This is that key moment of deception I wrote about earlier. Satan tricked Eve into eating of the Tree of Knowledge. Eve then encouraged Adam to eat also.

At this very moment in the bible, we can now view Adam and Eve as separate human beings. Before this moment, view the word Adam as meaning humankind and you will see the deception!

From this moment on in the bible, we can follow the genealogy of two individuals. Adam and Eve from this moment on became our ancestors and we can trace ourselves right back to them.

We can also follow the spiritual battle that continues to rage. The spirit of Satan influencing us to do evil, and the Holy Spirit instructing us in all righteousness.

I'm certain at this point that you will all have a question. What happened to all the other human beings whom God had "formed" and placed in Eden?

I ask myself exactly the same question! God never gave me the answer, but being a Christian I believe totally in the Holy Bible. God removed the Tree of Life and cursed the ground. I believe that Eden became no more. We know that God drove out humankind from Eden and they were expatriated to the area from where they were originally taken from. An area I believe to be in North East Africa. Also, I believe that death, which had not been originally allowed to get into the protected Eden, came again. God's words concerning death can be found in more detail in the chapter, First Man.

In addition, in my bible it tells of a great flood and only one man and his family survived, together with the animals. My own personal belief is in the story of Noah and his Ark. I believe that God caused huge rains together with massive earthquakes. The result of this was a "global tsunami." A tsunami like the one in Japan in 2011, but one that rolled over the whole landmass of earth.

SEQUENCE OF CREATION.

1. Genesis 1:2 to 5 *And the earth was without form, and void; and darkness [was] upon the face of the* **deep**. *And the Spirit of God moved upon the face of the waters. 3 And God said, Let there be light: and there was light. 4 And God saw the light, that [it was] good: and God divided the light from the darkness. 5 And God called the light Day,*

and the darkness he called Night. And the evening and the morning were the first day.

The Hebrew word for DEEP is TEHOM (TEH-HOME) meaning MASS of WATER. The Spirit of God came upon a mass of water in space. God illuminated the area surrounding the mass of water. God divided the illumination from the darkness of space and called (proclaimed) this division, Day and Night.

2. Genesis 1:6 to 8 *And God said, Let there be a firmament in the midst of the waters, and let it divide the waters from the waters. 7 And God made the firmament, and divided the waters which [were] under the firmament from the waters which [were] above the firmament: and it was so. 8 And God called the firmament Heaven. And the evening and the morning were the second day.*

God divided the mass of water and surrounded it with what we know as our sky and atmosphere, our outer space.

3. Genesis 1:9/10 *And God said, Let the waters under the heaven be gathered together unto one place, and let the dry [land] appear: and it was so. 10 And God called the dry [land] Earth; and the gathering together of the waters called he Seas: and God saw that [it was] good.*

God created the land mass of our planet earth and the "gathered together" water, God now called seas. God never revealed the next sentence to me. These are my own words. As I look at ancient world maps, our land mass appears to originally have been one land mass which became separated over the years by tectonic plate movements. I don't believe it to be coincidence that this fits perfectly with God's original creation.

4. Genesis 1:11 to 13 *And God said, Let the earth bring forth grass, the herb yielding seed, [and] the fruit tree yielding fruit after his kind, whose seed [is] in itself, upon the earth: and it was so. 12 And the earth brought forth grass, [and] herb yielding seed after his kind, and the tree yielding fruit, whose seed [was] in itself, after his kind: and God saw that [it was] good. 13 And the evening and the morning were the third day.*

God provided all the plants and trees, but the seed remained within them. They were upon the earth, but not yet planted in it.

5. Genesis 1:14 to 19 *And God said, Let there be lights in the firmament of the heaven to divide the day from the night; and let them be for signs, and for seasons, and for days, and years: 15 And let them be for lights in the firmament of the heaven to give light upon the earth: and it was so. 16 And God made two great lights; the greater light to rule the day, and the lesser light to rule the night: [he made] the stars also. 17 And God set them in the firmament of the heaven to give light upon the earth, 18 And to rule over the day and over the night, and to divide the light from the darkness: and God saw that [it was] good. 19 And the evening and the morning were the fourth day.*

God created the Sun, Moon and all the Stars and Planets in our Solar System. These gave us our time of seconds, minutes, hours, days, weeks, months and years. They also gave us navigational aids and most important, they provided our seasons. In other words they would provide our weather systems.

6. Genesis 1:20 to 23 *And God said, Let the waters bring forth abundantly the moving creature that hath life, and*

fowl [that] may fly above the earth in the open firmament of heaven. 21 And God created great whales, and every living creature that moveth, which the waters brought forth abundantly, after their kind, and every winged fowl after his kind: and God saw that [it was] good. 22 And God blessed them, saying, Be fruitful, and multiply, and fill the waters in the seas, and let fowl multiply in the earth. 23 And the evening and the morning were the fifth day.

God created the first life forms on earth. These were the Mass of Minute Animals that Wriggle, Creep and Swarm Abundantly! These are the Flying Creatures with wings not necessarily covered with Feathers! These are the Land and Sea Monsters, Sea Serpents, Dragons! In other words, planet earth at this moment in creation was what we know as Prehistoric. The Pikaia gracilens recently discovered by scientists is not our ancestor. These are very simply the Mass of Minute Animals that Wriggle, Creep and Swarm! This Flatworm that lived 500 million years ago is not what we "evolved" from! It was "created" by God. We are not descended from two inches long worms and we are not descended from Apes. We were created by God!
The Flying Creatures without Feathers and the Sea Monsters and Dragons are very simply what we have come to know as Prehistoric animals!
How do I know about "Mass of Minute Animals that Wriggle, Sea Monsters and Dragons etc"? Very simply from the Hebrew translation that you will read all about in the chapter "Genesis Chapters 1 to 5 - A Slightly Different Version". Regrettably, centuries of translation have changed the words of Moses. The arch deceiver Satan may have enjoyed it while it lasted, but not anymore! His deception is over.
Ask yourselves two very simple questions.

Is it coincidence or God-incidence, that all the archaeological scientific discoveries of creatures millions of years old, do **NOT** relate to dogs, cats, birds, sheep, goats, cows, horses or chickens?

Is it coincidence or God-incidence that **ALL** Prehistoric archaeological discoveries relate to Mass of Minute Animals that Wriggle, Creep and Swarm Abundantly?

Land and Sea Monsters, Sea Serpents, Dragons and Flying Creatures without Feathers?

Again, you don't have to be a nuclear physicist to answer both questions correctly!

The earliest fossils of domestic dogs date from 33,000 years ago. The earliest domestic cat fossils date from 10,000 years ago.

The earliest fossils of Flatworms, Dinosaurs etc are at least 250 million years old!

I'll leave you to decide whether you believe in coincidence, or God-incidence.

And the evening and the morning were the fifth day. At this moment in creation prehistoric earth was complete. This ended God's creation of the Prehistoric age. God never shared with me the timescale. I have no reason to disbelieve the scientific experts. This could have been hundreds of millions, or even billions of years ago.

Next, would come all the wild animals and birds that we know so well today. It is very important at this point that you "close the door" on prehistoric earth.

Now, we can open a new door that will herald in earth as we know it today. We can also open a "new door" that will herald in all the "wild" animals that humankind has lived with throughout our history.

I am compelled at this point to ask again a simple question. Do highly intelligent brains genuinely believe that humankind occupied this planet for millions of years and progressed in absolutely no way at all? By some miraculous means humankind in only the last seven thousand years or less developed exponentially beyond all expectation purely by coincidence?

Again believe me, this was not coincidence, it was God-Incidence!

7. Genesis 1:24/25 *And God said, Let the earth bring forth the living creature after his kind, cattle, and creeping thing, and beast of the earth after his kind: and it was so. 25 And God made the beast of the earth after his kind, and cattle after their kind, and every thing that creepeth upon the earth after his kind: and God saw that [it was] good.*

God then created all the other creatures on earth that we know today. These were all created after the Prehistoric period. These are the wild animals and birds. It is important to note that these creatures do not include the more "domesticated" ones that we know so well today. These are the "beasts of the EARTH not FIELD. They do not include what we know to be our "farm" animals, the ones that would provide our on-hand protein.

8. Genesis 1:26 to 31 *And God said, Let us make man in our image, after our likeness: and let them have dominion over the fish of the sea, and over the fowl of the air, and over the cattle, and over all the earth, and over every creeping thing that creepeth upon the earth. 27 So God created man in his [own] image, in the image of God created he him; male and female created he them. 28 And God blessed them, and God said unto them, Be fruitful, and multiply, and replenish the earth, and subdue it: and have dominion over the fish of the sea, and over the fowl of the air, and over every living thing that moveth upon the earth.*

235

29 And God said, Behold, I have given you every herb bearing seed, which [is] upon the face of all the earth, and every tree, in the which [is] the fruit of a tree yielding seed; to you it shall be for meat. 30 And to every beast of the earth, and to every fowl of the air, and to every thing that creepeth upon the earth, wherein [there is] life, [I have given] every green herb for meat: and it was so. 31 And God saw every thing that he had made, and, behold, [it was] very good. And the evening and the morning were the sixth day.

Genesis 2:1 to 5 *Thus the heavens and the earth were finished, and all the host of them. 2 And on the seventh day God ended his work which he had made; and he rested on the seventh day from all his work which he had made. 3 And God blessed the seventh day, and sanctified it: because that in it he had rested from all his work which God created and made. 4 These [are] the generations of the heavens and of the earth when they were created, in the day that the LORD God made the earth and the heavens, 5 And every plant of the field before it was in the earth, and every herb of the field before it grew: for the LORD God had not caused it to rain upon the earth, and [there was] not a man to till the ground.*

God created First Man. God created humankind. These first humans were what we know today to be "hunter gatherers." Nothing had been planted, they simply had to "gather" the food up and eat it. God tells us very clearly, "These are the generations of the heavens and of the earth." Earth was complete for that moment in time. There was no evolutionary process. Nothing had been planted in the ground because, "the LORD God had not caused it to rain upon the earth, and there was not a man to till the ground." In other words, farming had yet to arrive! How long was planet earth like this? I don't know. God never told me.

Also, another very important point to note, who did "man" have dominion over? Did God say "man" had dominion over all the prehistoric creatures? Not in my Holy Bible He didn't! Very clearly, God says that He gave "man" dominion over all the wild animals that were created after the end of the prehistoric age! Why ever would God do this? Very simply, "man" had not even been "created" until AFTER the prehistoric age! Again, I sincerely pray that even the least among us can see the simplicity of God's words.

9. Genesis 2:6 to 17 *But there went up a mist from the earth, and watered the whole face of the ground. 7 And the LORD God formed man [of] the dust of the ground, and breathed into his nostrils the breath of life; and man became a living soul. 8 And the LORD God planted a garden eastward in Eden; and there he put the man whom he had formed. 9 And out of the ground made the LORD God to grow every tree that is pleasant to the sight, and good for food; the tree of life also in the midst of the garden, and the tree of knowledge of good and evil. 10 And a river went out of Eden to water the garden; and from thence it was parted, and became into four heads. 11 The name of the first [is] Pison: that [is] it which compasseth the whole land of Havilah, where [there is] gold; 12 And the gold of that land [is] good: there [is] bdellium and the onyx stone.*
13 And the name of the second river [is] Gihon: the same [is] it that compasseth the whole land of Ethiopia. 14 And the name of the third river [is] Hiddekel: that [is] it which goeth toward the east of Assyria. And the fourth river [is] Euphrates. 15 And the LORD God took the man, and put him into the garden of Eden to dress it and to keep it. 16 And the LORD God commanded the man, saying, Of every tree of the garden thou mayest freely eat: 17 But of the tree

*of the knowledge of good and evil, thou shalt not eat of it:
for in the day that thou eatest thereof thou shalt surely die.*

God provided rain to planet earth. Out of First Man, the
Hunter Gatherer, God "formed" Second Man, who we will
eventually come to know as the "farmer." Second Man was
formed by God to have a Soul (mind, will, emotions).
There was no evolutionary process, it was instant and it
was planned. God took Second Man into the most fertile
area on earth, and there God taught him how to "till the
ground," how to "farm." Rivers had now formed and God
used one to water "Eden," the area of planet earth into
which had been taken Second Man.

10. Genesis 2:18 to 25 *And the LORD God said, [It is]
not good that the man should be alone; I will make him an
help meet for him. 19 And out of the ground the LORD
God formed every beast of the field, and every fowl of the
air; and brought [them] unto Adam to see what he would
call them: and whatsoever Adam called every living
creature, that [was] the name thereof. 20 And Adam gave
names to all cattle, and to the fowl of the air, and to every
beast of the field; but for Adam there was not found an help
meet for him. 21 And the LORD God caused a deep sleep
to fall upon Adam, and he slept: and he took one of his ribs,
and closed up the flesh instead thereof; 22 And the rib,
which the LORD God had taken from man, made he a
woman, and brought her unto the man. 23 And Adam said,
This [is] now bone of my bones, and flesh of my flesh: she
shall be called Woman, because she was taken out of Man.
24 Therefore shall a man leave his father and his mother,
and shall cleave unto his wife: and they shall be one flesh.
25 And they were both naked, the man and his wife, and
were not ashamed.*

God "formed" all the animals and birds that we know so well today. Some of these animals and birds were "formed" by God to become what we now know as "farm" animals. There was no evolutionary process. It was planned specifically by God. So that Second Man (with mind, will and emotions) would have his female equal (remember First Man did not have a Soul, only a Spirit), God provided him with a Woman.

This was the moment in our history that we call the birth of agriculture. It was the start of farming on planet earth.

11. Genesis 3:1 to 7 *Now the serpent was more subtil than any beast of the field which the LORD God had made. And he said unto the woman, Yea, hath God said, Ye shall not eat of every tree of the garden? 2 And the woman said unto the serpent, We may eat of the fruit of the trees of the garden: 3 But of the fruit of the tree which [is] in the midst of the garden, God hath said, Ye shall not eat of it, neither shall ye touch it, lest ye die. 4 And the serpent said unto the woman, Ye shall not surely die: 5 For God doth know that in the day ye eat thereof, then your eyes shall be opened, and ye shall be as gods, knowing good and evil. 6 And when the woman saw that the tree [was] good for food, and that it [was] pleasant to the eyes, and a tree to be desired to make [one] wise, she took of the fruit thereof, and did eat, and gave also unto her husband with her; and he did eat. 7 And the eyes of them both were opened, and they knew that they [were] naked; and they sewed fig leaves together, and made themselves aprons.*

This is the end of creation. These are the humankind I refer to as Third Man. This is the man and woman that you and I are descended from. Before this moment of some six or seven thousand years ago, humankind had no "knowledge." From the moment in our history when Adam and Eve ate of the fruit of the Tree of Knowledge, humankind had inbuilt "knowledge" of everything. Through our spirit we were then given "understanding." This understanding has allowed us to grow exponentially in every way possible. We did not evolve from Apes. We did not evolve from a two inch long worm. This earth and everything in it did not evolve from an explosion in space.

This earth and everything in it was created by Almighty God.

Genesis Chapters 1 to 5 - A Slightly Different Version

As we study the original Hebrew language translation of this wonderful and truthful account by Moses, it gives us a completely different view of our "creation" by God.

One of the greatest deceits of Satan was to ensure that for millennia we believed that "Adam" was just one man. This deception ensured that generation upon generation went to their death not knowing the truth, the **PURE TRUTH** from GOD. That deceit is now exposed, and again God gives us the free will to believe or not.

I am now going to offer to you a version of the first five chapters of Genesis with the Hebrew translation slightly differently to the original. No words have been added or taken away! I have merely translated certain words differently. Let me stress that I am not a Hebrew language expert, I did this only because God prompted me to check certain words to ensure that they lined up with the same translations and explanations given in the four preceding chapters. As I checked these words, I noticed that where my bible read "singular," the original Hebrew word was "plural" and vice versa. In addition, different translations of other words caused a completely different meaning.

Let me ask you a question. If ALL of the words "Adam" (first mentioned in Genesis 2:19) were intended to mean one man as an individual, then why wasn't "Eve" mentioned until long after God spoke about females or women? "Eve" was first named in Genesis 3:20 yet female, woman, she, her, wife, and mother were all mentioned on no fewer than TWENTY-FIVE times following first use of the word "Adam". I don't believe God is inconsistent. I believe very simply that over millenniums, Satan has deceived honest translators and it has led to the GREAT DECEPTION.

As I used these different translations, a new story of our creation appeared and much more important, it fitted perfectly with what God had revealed to me and what I shared with you in the previous four chapters.

Genesis 1:1 *In the beginning God created the heaven and the earth.*
2 And the earth was without form, and void; and darkness [was] upon the face of the MASS of WATER. And the Spirit of God moved upon the face of the waters.
3 And God said, Let there be light: and there was light.
4 And God saw the light, that [it was] good: and God divided the light from the darkness.
5 And God called the light Day, and the darkness he called Night. And the DUSK and the DAWN were the first SPACE OF TIME DEFINED BY OUR WORD "AGE".
6 And God said, Let there be a firmament in the midst of the waters, and let it divide the waters from the waters.
7 And God made the firmament, and divided the waters which [were] under the firmament from the waters which [were] above the firmament: and it was so.
8 And God called the firmament Heaven. And the DUSK and the DAWN were the second SPACE OF TIME DEFINED BY OUR WORD "AGE".
9 And God said, Let the waters under the heaven be gathered together unto one place, and let the dry [land] appear: and it was so.
10 And God called the dry [land] Earth; and the gathering together of the waters called he Seas: and God saw that [it was] good.

11 And God said, Let the earth bring forth grass, the herb yielding seed, [and] the fruit tree yielding fruit after his kind, whose seed [is] in itself, upon the earth: and it was so.

12 And the earth brought forth grass, [and] herb yielding seed after his kind, and the tree yielding fruit, whose seed [was] in itself, after his kind: and God saw that [it was] good.

13 And the DUSK and the DAWN were the third SPACE OF TIME DEFINED BY OUR WORD "AGE".

14 And God said, Let there be lights in the firmament of the heaven to divide the day from the night; and let them be for signs, and for seasons, and for days, and years:

15 And let them be for lights in the firmament of the heaven to give light upon the earth: and it was so.

16 And God made two great lights; the greater light to rule the day, and the lesser light to rule the night: [he made] the stars also.

17 And God set them in the firmament of the heaven to give light upon the earth,

18 And to rule over the day and over the night, and to divide the light from the darkness: and God saw that [it was] good.

19 And the DUSK and the DAWN were the fourth SPACE OF TIME DEFINED BY OUR WORD "AGE".

20 And God said, Let the waters bring forth abundantly A MASS OF MINUTE ANIMALS THAT WRIGGLE, CREEP AND SWARM ABUNDANTLY & that hath life, and fowl [that] HAVE WINGS NOT NECESSARILY COVERED WITH FEATHERS, FLYING CREATURES WITH FEATHERS AND BIRDS THAT may fly above the earth in the open firmament of heaven.

21 And God created great LAND AND SEA MONSTERS, SEA SERPENTS, DRAGONS and every living creature that moveth, which the waters brought forth abundantly, after

their kind, and every winged fowl after his kind: and God
saw that [it was] good.
22 And God blessed them, saying, Be fruitful, and multiply,
and fill the waters in the seas, and let fowl multiply in the
earth.
23 And the DUSK and the DAWN were the fifth SPACE OF
TIME DEFINED BY OUR WORD "AGE".
24 And God said, Let the earth bring forth ALL WILD
ANIMALS, BIRDS, REPTILES, FISHES, ETC of the earth
after his kind: and it was so.
25 And God made the WILD ANIMALS, BIRDS,
REPTILES, FISHES, ETC after his kind: and God saw that
[it was] good.
26 And God said, Let us make HUMAN BEINGS in our
image, after our likeness: and let them have dominion over
the fish of the sea, and over the fowl of the air, and over the
cattle, and over all the earth, and over every creeping thing
that creepeth upon the earth. (IMPORTANT- God uses the
word "earth", meaning the whole earth, our planet and
EVERY WILD LIVING CREATURE upon it)
27 So God created HUMAN BEINGS in his [own] image,
in the image of God created he him; male and female
created he them.
28 And God blessed them, and God said unto them, Be
fruitful, and multiply, and replenish the earth, and subdue
it: and have dominion over the fish of the sea, and over the
fowl of the air, and over every living thing that moveth upon
the earth.
29 And God said, Behold, I have given you every herb
bearing seed, which [is] upon the face of all the earth, and
every tree, in the which [is] the fruit of a tree yielding seed;
to you it shall be for meat.
30 And to every beast of the earth, and to every fowl of the
air, and to every thing that creepeth upon the earth,
wherein [there is] life, [I have given] every green herb for
meat: and it was so.

31 And God saw every thing that he had made, and, behold, [it was] very good. And the DUSK and the DAWN were the sixth SPACE OF TIME DEFINED BY OUR WORD "AGE".

Genesis 2:1 Thus the heavens and the earth were finished, and all the MASS of PERSONS of them.
2 And on the seventh SPACE OF TIME God ended his work which he had made; and he rested on the seventh SPACE OF TIME from all his work which he had made.
3 And God blessed the seventh SPACE OF TIME, and sanctified it: because that in it he had rested from all his work which God created and made.
4 THIS IS THE COMPLETE HISTORY of the BIRTH of ORIGINALLY CREATED HUMAN BEINGS and ALL LIVING CREATURES and of the heavens and of the earth when they were created, in the SPACE OF TIME that the LORD God made the earth and the heavens,
5 And every plant of the field before it was in the earth, and every herb of the field before it grew: for the LORD God had not caused it to rain upon the earth, and [there was] not a HUMAN BEING yet FORMED that would be able to DRESS AND FARM the ground.
6 But there went up a mist from the earth, and watered the whole face of the ground.
7 And the LORD God formed NEW MALE HUMAN BEINGS [of] the dust of the ground, and breathed into THEIR nostrils the breath of life; and THE NEW MALE HUMAN BEINGS became living SOULS.
8 And the LORD God planted a garden eastward in Eden; and there he put the NEW MALE HUMAN BEINGS whom he had FORMED OUT OF THE DUST OF THE GROUND USING HIS ORIGINAL CREATION.
9 And out of the ground made the LORD God to grow every tree that is pleasant to the sight, and good for food; the tree

of life also in the midst of the garden, and the tree of knowledge of good and evil.

10 And a river went out of Eden to water the garden; and from thence it was parted, and became into four heads.

11 The name of the first [is] Pison: that [is] it which compasseth the whole land of Havilah, where [there is] gold;

12 And the gold of that land [is] good: there [is] bdellium and the onyx stone.

13 And the name of the second river [is] Gihon: the same [is] it that compasseth the whole land of Ethiopia.

14 And the name of the third river [is] Hiddekel: that [is] it which goeth toward the east of Assyria. And the fourth river [is] Euphrates.

15 And the LORD God took the MALE HUMAN BEINGS, and put THEM into the garden of Eden to FARM it and to CULTIVATE it.

16 And the LORD God commanded the MALE HUMAN BEINGS, saying, Of every tree of the garden thou mayest freely eat:

17 But of the tree of the knowledge of good and evil, thou shalt not eat of it: for in the day that thou eatest thereof thou shalt surely die.

18 And the LORD God said, [It is] not good that the NEWLY FORMED MALE HUMAN BEINGS WITH A SOUL should be alone; I will make THEM an help meet for THEM.

19 And out of the ground the LORD God FORMED USING HIS ORIGINAL CREATION every beast of the field, (IMPORTANT- *God* uses the word "Field" meaning land, soil, flat area, field **NOT** earth!) *and every fowl of the air; and brought [them] unto THE MALE HUMAN BEINGS to see what THEY would call them: and whatsoever THE MALE HUMAN BEINGS called every living creature, that [was] the name thereof.* (At this moment the Lord God "formed" every domestic farm animal that we know today.)

20 And THE MALE HUMAN BEINGS gave names to all cattle, and to the fowl of the air, and to every beast of the field; (IMPORTANT-God again confirms to us that it was at this moment that He "Formed" ALL of our Domesticated, Farm animals. These were the "Beasts of the FIELD not EARTH! There was NO Darwinian EVOLUTION! Please refer to the chapter on Second Man for the Hebrew translations!). *but for THESE MALE HUMAN BEINGS there was not found an help meet for THEM.*

21 And the LORD God caused a deep sleep to fall upon THESE MALE HUMAN BEINGS and THEY slept: and he took one of his ribs, and closed up the flesh instead thereof;
22 And the rib, which the LORD God had taken from EACH ONE OF THE MALE HUMAN BEINGS, made he WOMEN WITH SOULS, and brought THEM unto the MALE HUMAN BEINGS .

23 And THE MALE HUMAN BEINGS said, This [is] now bone of my bones, and flesh of my flesh: she shall be called Woman, because she was taken out of A MAN.

24 Therefore shall EVERY MALE HUMAN BEING leave his father and his mother, and shall cleave unto his wife: and they shall be one flesh.

25 And they were ALL naked, ALL HUMANKIND and THEIR WIVES and were not ashamed.

Genesis 3:1 *Now the serpent was more subtil than any beast of the field (DOMESTIC FARM ANIMALS) which the LORD God had made. And he said unto ONE OF THE WOMEN, Yea, hath God said, Ye shall not eat of every tree of the garden?*

2 And the WOMAN said unto the serpent, We may eat of the fruit of the trees of the garden:

3 But of the fruit of the tree which [is] in the midst of the garden, God hath said, Ye shall not eat of it, neither shall ye touch it, lest ye die.

4 And the serpent said unto the WOMAN, Ye shall not surely die:

5 For God doth know that in the day ye eat thereof, then your eyes shall be opened, and ye shall be as gods, knowing good and evil.

6 And when the WOMAN saw that the tree [was] good for food, and that it [was] pleasant to the eyes, and a tree to be desired to make [one] wise, SHE took of the fruit thereof, and did eat, and gave also unto HER HUSBAND with HER; and he did eat.

7 And the eyes of them both were opened, and they "knew" (BECAUSE THEY NOW HAD KNOWLEDGE) that they [were] naked; and they sewed fig leaves together, and made themselves aprons.

8 And they heard the voice of the LORD God walking in the garden in the cool of the day: and Adam and his wife hid themselves from the presence of the LORD God amongst the trees of the garden.

9 And the LORD God called unto Adam (THE HUSBAND OF THE WOMAN), and said unto him, Where [art] thou?

10 And he said, I heard thy voice in the garden, and I was afraid, because I [was] naked; and I hid myself.

11 And he said, Who told thee that thou [wast] naked? Hast thou eaten of the tree, whereof I commanded thee that thou shouldest not eat?

12 And Adam said, The woman whom thou gavest [to be] with me, she gave me of the tree, and I did eat.

13 And the LORD God said unto the woman, What [is] this [that] thou hast done? And the woman said, The serpent beguiled me, and I did eat.

14 And the LORD God said unto the serpent, Because thou hast done this, thou [art] cursed above all cattle, and above every beast of the field; upon thy belly shalt thou go, and dust shalt thou eat all the days of thy life:

15 And I will put enmity between thee and the woman, and between thy seed and her seed; it shall bruise thy head, and thou shalt bruise his heel.

16 Unto the woman he said, I will greatly multiply thy sorrow and thy conception; in sorrow thou shalt bring forth children; and thy desire [shall be] to thy husband, and he shall rule over thee.

17 And unto Adam he said, Because thou hast hearkened unto the voice of thy wife, and hast eaten of the tree, of which I commanded thee, saying, Thou shalt not eat of it: cursed [is] the ground for thy sake; in sorrow shalt thou eat [of] it all the days of thy life;

18 Thorns also and thistles shall it bring forth to thee; and thou shalt eat the herb of the field;

19 In the sweat of thy face shalt thou eat bread, till thou return unto the ground; for out of it wast thou taken: for dust thou [art], and unto dust shalt thou return.

20 And Adam called his wife's name, Eve; because she was the mother of all living.

(This is the first mention of Eve. From this individual woman would come all humankind. Eve was the "Mother of ALL living").

21 Unto Adam also and to his wife did the LORD God make coats of skins, and clothed them.

22 And the LORD God said, Behold, the man is become as one of us, to know good and evil: and now, lest he put forth his hand, and take also of the tree of life, and eat, and live for ever:

23 Therefore the LORD God sent him forth from the garden of Eden, to FARM the ground from whence he was taken.
(This confirms that First Man was taken from another part of the earth and that God provided a "special" area called Eden for Second Man)

24 So he drove out the HUMAN BEINGS; and he placed at the east of the garden of Eden Cherubims, and a flaming sword which turned every way, to keep the way of the tree of life.

Genesis 4:1 *And Adam knew Eve his wife; and she conceived, and bare Cain, and said, I have gotten a man from the LORD.*
2 And she again bare his brother Abel. And Abel was a keeper of sheep, but Cain was a tiller of the ground.
3 And in process of time it came to pass, that Cain brought of the fruit of the ground an offering unto the LORD.
4 And Abel, he also brought of the firstlings of his flock and of the fat thereof. And the LORD had respect unto Abel and to his offering:
5 But unto Cain and to his offering he had not respect. And Cain was very wroth, and his countenance fell.
6 And the LORD said unto Cain, Why art thou wroth? and why is thy countenance fallen?
7 If thou doest well, shalt thou not be accepted? and if thou doest not well, sin lieth at the door. And unto thee [shall be] his desire, and thou shalt rule over him.
8 And Cain talked with Abel his brother: and it came to pass, when they were in the field, that Cain rose up against Abel his brother, and slew him.
9 And the LORD said unto Cain, Where [is] Abel thy brother? And he said, I know not: [Am] I my brother's keeper?
10 And he said, What hast thou done? the voice of thy brother's blood crieth unto me from the ground.
11 And now [art] thou cursed from the earth, which hath opened her mouth to receive thy brother's blood from thy hand;

12 When thou tillest the ground, it shall not henceforth yield unto thee her strength; a fugitive and a vagabond shalt thou be in the earth.

13 And Cain said unto the LORD, My punishment [is] greater than I can bear.

14 Behold, thou hast driven me out this day from the face of the earth; and from thy face shall I be hid; and I shall be a fugitive and a vagabond in the earth; and it shall come to pass, [that] every one that findeth me shall slay me.

15 And the LORD said unto him, Therefore whosoever slayeth Cain, vengeance shall be taken on him sevenfold. And the LORD set a mark upon Cain, lest any finding him should kill him.

16 And Cain went out from the presence of the LORD, and dwelt in the land of Nod, on the east of Eden.

17 And Cain knew his wife; and she conceived, and bare Enoch: and he builded a city, and called the name of the city, after the name of his son, Enoch.

18 And unto Enoch was born Irad: and Irad begat Mehujael: and Mehujael begat Methusael: and Methusael begat Lamech.

19 And Lamech took unto him two wives: the name of the one [was] Adah, and the name of the other Zillah.

20 And Adah bare Jabal: he was the father of such as dwell in tents, and [of such as have] cattle.

21 And his brother's name [was] Jubal: he was the father of all such as handle the harp and organ.

22 And Zillah, she also bare Tubalcain, an instructer of every artificer in brass and iron: and the sister of Tubalcain [was] Naamah.

23 And Lamech said unto his wives, Adah and Zillah, Hear my voice; ye wives of Lamech, hearken unto my speech: for I have slain a man to my wounding, and a young man to my hurt.

24 If Cain shall be avenged sevenfold, truly Lamech seventy and sevenfold.

25 And THE SAME MALE HUMAN BEING, ADAM, knew his wife again; and she bare a son, and called his name Seth: For God, [said she], hath appointed me another seed instead of Abel, whom Cain slew.
26 And to Seth, to him also there was born a son; and he called his name Enos: then began men to call upon the name of the LORD.

Genesis 5:1 *This [is] the book of the HISTORY OF THE GENEALOGY OF THE CREATED, FORMED and MADE HUMAN BEINGS. In the day that God created HUMAN BEINGS, in the likeness of God made he THEM, COMPLETE, HIS FINISHED WORK;*
2 Male and female created he them; and blessed them, and called their name HUMAN BEINGS, in the day when they were created. (**Ask yourself the question, would God use one mans name immediately after saying "male and female" created He them?**)
3 And ADAM lived an hundred and thirty years, and begat [a son] in his own likeness, after his image; and called his name Seth:
4 And the days of ADAM after he had begotten Seth were eight hundred years: and he begat sons and daughters:
5 And all the days that ADAM lived were nine hundred and thirty years: and he died.

As explained in the chapter A SUMMARY OF CREATION, there was a very clear sequence of events and time lines. Up to Genesis 1:23, we have what scientists might call "prehistoric" earth.
Why would I say this? Because God told me. Let's again look at the word of God.
In Genesis 1:20 we see the first use of the word "creature". The original Hebrew word is SHERETS (SHEH-RETS) which comes from SHARATS (SHAW-RATS). The

translation of these words is EXACTLY as I presented them. Mass of minute animals that wriggle, creep and swarm abundantly! Is it coincidence that scientists claim the first living thing on earth to be a worm that lives in sediment? It is to be hoped that by now you will say NO! It's simply a God-incidence and it's the truth, **THE PURE TRUTH**.

Every other original Hebrew translation of the word "creature" in Genesis is NEPHESH. Remember NEPHESH? It simply means "breathing creature, to breath". Every other time "creature" is mentioned it simply means a living thing that breathes.

Let's look at another word; Fowl first mentioned in verse 20. This word comes from the original Hebrew OWPH (OFE) together with UWPH (OOF). This means "to fly, covered with feathers, a bird". Is it coincidence that it also means "to fly with wings without feathers"? It's interesting that the prehistoric birds referred to by scientists could fly yet had no feathers. Is this coincidence? Or yet again, is it God-incidence!

Finally, before moving on to humankind, let's look at the word Whale first mentioned in Genesis chapter 1, verse 21. The original Hebrew word is TANNIYN (TAN-NEEN). When translated this word means EXACTLY as I translated it which is, "a marine or land monster, sea serpent, dragon or sea monster." Is it coincidence that scientists tell us about prehistoric creatures like the dinosaur? Or, is it yet again, God-incidence!
Why don't we contrast this with the word Whale mentioned in Matthew and the "great fish" mentioned in Jonah?

Matthew 12:40 *For as Jonas was three days and three nights in the whale's belly; so shall the Son of man be three days and three nights in the heart of the earth.*

The Greek word used here for Whale is KETOS (KAY-TOS), meaning huge fish or simply, Whale.

Jonah 1:17 *Now the LORD had prepared a great fish to swallow up Jonah. And Jonah was in the belly of the fish three days and three nights*

The Hebrew word used here for Great Fish is DAG (DAWG) meaning a fish that moves by the vibration action of it's tail!

I don't think it takes a rocket scientist to spot the difference between marine or land monster, sea serpent, dragon or sea monster or huge fish, or a fish that moves by the vibration of it's tail!

If creation ceased at Genesis Chapter 1, Verse 23, what would we have? Whether it is millions or billions of years ago, we would have prehistoric earth exactly as the scientists have discovered. The only difference is that it was God created! Did this just last for one "day"? The Hebrew word for "day" is YOWM (YOME) and translated this is, "from sunrise to sunset, or from sunset to the next, or a SPACE OF TIME DEFINED BY AN ASSOCIATED TERM (often used adjective "AGE"!).

Now, let me share with you what God shared with me about humankind and about you and me.

Where I have changed the word "man" for HUMAN BEINGS, is because the original Hebrew uses the word ADAM (AW-DAWM) meaning HUMAN BEINGS (plural) as a SPECIES; NOT just as INDIVIDUALS.

Where I have kept the word "MAN" as an INDIVIDUAL is in Chapter 2, Verses 23 and 24. In both of these verses the original Hebrew word is IYSH (EESH) (singular) meaning

AN INDIVIDUAL, and NOT HUMAN BEINGS as a
SPECIES. In addition, look at Genesis 4, Verse 23, the
same Hebrew word IYSH is used here and it's clear to see
that God is referring to INDIVIDUALS, not HUMAN
BEINGS as a SPECIES.

Let's now take a look at Genesis Chapter 5.

If anyone has a problem of my interpretation of verse one,
then consistency cannot be applied to verse two. God uses
the word "Adam" (HUMAN BEINGS) in verse one. God
also uses EXACTLY the same word in verse two, yet
clearly if God meant "Adam" to mean one man, God would
NEVER have said "Male and Female "created" He
"THEM," and blessed "THEM," and called "THEIR" name
Adam. Any fair minded person would have to agree that
God in both verses is referring to HUMAN BEINGS as a
SPECIES and not as INDIVIDUALS.

The Hebrew word for Eden is EDEN (AY-DEN).
Translated it means the "region of Adam's (HUMAN
BEINGS) home, pleasant, delightful. Eden was not the
home of one man. Eden was an area of land within what
we know today as the "Fertile Crescent". It was the most
fertile land on earth. This wasn't just one man's home, it
was "home" to a SPECIES of HUMAN BEINGS. As you
have read, Second Man or "Adam" if you like, was
HUMAN BEINGS in countless numbers who farmed and
who occupied a very large area of planet earth.
Regrettably, God did not share with me the timescale of
this occurrence, it might have been forty, fifty or one
hundred thousand years ago. What we do know, is that
Moses recorded the GENEALOGY of one of these
HUMAN BEINGS whom we all love to refer to as
"Adam." It is from this one HUMAN BEING that we are
all descended.

Now, let me leave you with some additional thoughts. Imagine that you were a bible translator one thousand years ago or even four hundred years ago, around the time of the King James translations. Your reputation is on the line because you are translating the words of God Almighty. Would it not be more plausible for you to write about one man and one woman, named Adam and Eve?

Also, humankind has only known about the existence of Dinosaurs for LESS THAN 200 YEARS. Are you going to risk ridicule of yourself and God Almighty, by writing about "Sea Monsters, Dragons, Flat Worms, Birds with wings but no feathers", etc? Might I suggest that no translator at that period in time would ever dare to translate exactly the words of Moses, because very simply as far as they were concerned those creatures did not exist!

In addition, you have just read that there were countless numbers of MALE HUMAN BEINGS farming in Eden. You also read that AFTER the MALE HUMAN BEINGS, came WOMEN WITH SOULS. These WOMEN WITH SOULS were made from the ribs of the MALE HUMAN BEINGS. Is it therefore coincidence, or God-Incidence, that genetic scientists agree with this completely? Research by Melissa Wilson Sayres of University of California, Berkeley, and Carlos Bustamante of Stanford University in California, confirms that:

All males in a global sample shared a single male ancestor in Africa roughly 125,000 to 156,000 years ago.

All women on planet earth can be traced back to a mitochondrial "Eve" who lived in Africa between 99,000 and 148,000 years ago.

The "Mother" of all women emerged from EAST AFRICA. In addition, Michael Hammer from the University of Arizona, confirmed that men shared a common ancestor between 180,000 and 200,000 years ago. Also, several men in Africa have unique, divergent Y chromosomes that trace back to a man who lived between 237,000 and 581,000 years ago.

Having just read the truthful, simplistic version of the first five chapters of Genesis, how can anyone disagree with the scientists?

This additional chapter may at first appear too simplistic. If it does I certainly do not apologize. Remember, I am not a writer, I am not a Hebrew scholar, all I am is a Christian. Combined with all the other revelation knowledge which God shared with me, and which I shared with you in the previous four chapters, I firmly believe this account to be the truth.

One final thing, although no longer in mainstream bibles, let's look at the book of 2nd Esdras from the Apocrypha. It was written by the scribe and prophet Ezra, whose writings in the bibles of today precede the book of Nehemiah. In this old book, Ezra gives us a short sequential version of Genesis 1 to 5. It is thought that the composition of Ezra's historic writings was originally done in AD 100-120, but regrettably Hebrew, Aramaic and Greek texts have been lost. Nevertheless, there are many other translations in Latin, English, etc, and all are of value. My interest in sharing this passage is simple, it mirrors exactly the **PURE TRUTH** of creation as told by our Lord God to Moses. I have added slightly different translation from the King James version, but with nothing added or taken away.

2nd Esdras 3:3 to 7 *And my spirit was sore moved, so that I began to speak words full of fear to the most High, and said,*
4 O Lord, who bearest rule, thou spakest at the beginning, when thou didst plant the earth, and that thyself alone (**God PLANTED THE EARTH**)*, and commandedst the*

people, (at the beginning of CREATION You alone Lord God commanded the ORIGINAL HUMAN BEINGS whom You had CREATED).

5 And gavest a body unto Adam without soul, (The First HUMAN BEINGS You CREATED did not have a soul, only a spirit and body) *which was the workmanship of thine hands, and didst breathe into him the breath of life, and he was made living before thee.* (The Second HUMAN BEINGS You FORMED from the ORIGINAL and You gave them a soul)

6 And thou leadest him into paradise, (You took the ORIGINAL HUNTER GATHERER HUMAN BEINGS from the earth into EDEN, the area of land which we now know to be in the Fertile Crescent) *which thy right hand had planted ,* (You Lord God now gave rain and planted the seed which Second Man could now farm.) *before ever the earth came forward.* (Before the earth was MADE, finished).

7 And unto him thou gavest commandment to love thy way: (You Lord God commanded the HUMAN BEINGS not to eat of the Tree of Knowledge) *which he transgressed,* (One HUMAN BEING name Eve transgressed and so did her husband Adam) *and immediately thou appointedst death in him and in his generations, of whom came nations, tribes, people, and kindreds, out of number.*

The earth and everything in it did not evolve from an explosion in space. Humankind did not evolve from a flat worm or an ape. The Almighty God created everything.

The Missing Link - A Challenge for Humankind

I wish I could say that the words for this chapter were given to me by God, regrettably they are all my own. I can only pray that the Lord God Almighty may have had a hand in leading me to them.

Many years ago, long before I was a Christian, or ever even thought about God, I was literally driven to find an old book. In the mid 1970s, I had read about a man named Arthur Koestler. So impressed was I by this man's writing that I set out to collect all of his books. Over many years, I searched in resale bookstores all over the world for one book in particular, a book titled Janus, A Summing Up. After collecting almost all of Koestler's other books, in the early 1990s, I eventually acquired a copy of Janus.

Like most young people, I was a "seeker after the truth", but the problem was I sought it in all the wrong places. After initially reading Bricks to Babel by Koestler, it became obvious to me that this man also searched for the "truth." It seemed to me that he came closest to it during the writing of Janus. As a non-Christian reading Janus, I became absolutely fascinated by and in awe of Koestler's mind and understanding of humanity.

It's truly hard to express to you the intensity of my desire to find this particular book. It was more than just wanting a book, it became almost obsessive. Today I believe I know the reason and I'll leave you to guess what that reason was. Throughout the history of humankind, God has spoken to us and revealed various hidden mysteries. These revelations and the timing of them have been simply perfect. God has a plan for this age of humankind and His

259

plan will be completed in His perfect time. In other words, God does not reveal everything to us in one go. God reveals just enough as is necessary at any particular moment in time.

What you have read previously in this book is the **PURE TRUTH** as God gave it to me, but I personally believe that there may be one more thing to add. I pray that this chapter will promote discussion and a further searching of the Holy Bible, so that at the perfect time God will provide someone with this final revelation.

Let me stress again, I am not a scientist or in any way well read or knowledgeable about that which I am about to write. In my heart however, I do believe that at some point in the future maybe when I am long gone, the **PURE TRUTH** of this chapter will be revealed by God to humankind.

As I read Janus in the early 1990s, it was fascinating. As I reread Janus as a Christian just a few years ago, a light came on in my head.

Koestler writes about the cortex and the neocortex.

The cerebral cortex is the neural tissue that surrounds our brain. It is very important for our memory, thought, language and consciousness. I hope a light came on in your brain at this moment, but let's continue.

It is known that all mammals, including human mammals, have a much larger cortex than other creatures. Along with the larger cortex, we also have the neocortex.

The neocortex (or "newer" cortex) is known to be a newer part of the brain which developed to help us with other more intelligent functions. The neocortex always relates in size to the intelligence of the creature. In other words, it is much larger in humans than in any other species. This increased "newer" capacity has enabled humankind to interllectually reach where we are today.

Has anyone yet started to think about Second Man "Farmer" cortex, or Third Man "us," neocortex?

Darwinians, and all the other scientists, theorize that there was an evolutionary process. They sometimes describe this using the picture of an evolutionary tree. Humankind is at the top of this tree closely followed by our "ancestors" the apes.

Let me now present to you my own hypothesis, which I believe to be the truth.

Second Man was "formed" out of the dust of the ground and given a soul plus a cortex, or a more developed cortex. Remember that the soul is our mind, will and emotions. To put it another way, our soul cannot be our soul without our cortex!

Third Man (us) ate from the tree of knowledge and he was given an increased understanding of this knowledge, so his cortex now evolved or grew to incorporate a neocortex.

If any of us exercise a muscle, whether in our arm, leg, or dare I say, brain, that muscle will change to accommodate whatever the exercise might be. As the increased understanding of knowledge was given to man, this exercised his neocortex. Our neocortex then grew to accommodate increased understanding. As this growth occurred, we were able to memorize more and think more. Our intelligence grew in exactly the way that God had planned.

It is not coincidence, but God-incidence, that our neocortex is bigger than any other creature!

I do not believe that any of us evolved from apes, I believe that Almighty God has a plan that He fulfills perfectly.

If we look at the very simple evolutionary graph of humankind, it fits perfectly with the above.

Every scientist acknowledges that our evolution flatlined until Second Man the "Farmer." After the "farmer" with a cortex, the line on the graph increased slightly.

After the arrival of Third Man with a cortex, plus an ever growing neocortex, the line increases upward dramatically. Why was this? I believe it was because he ate of the tree of knowledge and from that moment God, and regrettably Satan, started to give us an understanding of this knowledge. To advance in memory, thought, language and consciousness our neocortex grew. Might I suggest that there is a definite and distinctive correlation to all of these things and in God's words to us?

In addition, we know that our brains use up 25% of our energy and protein requirements. Was it coincidence, or God-Incidence, that at exactly the same time that God gave us our soul (mind, will, emotions), He also taught us to "farm"? In other words, humankind would have on-hand a dramatically increased supply of protein from all the farm animals and cultivated plants. An increased on-hand supply of protein that was now vital to sustain a much greater intellect or brain. A vital supply of on-hand protein that would not only sustain a greater brain, but help it to grow even more to accommodate our ability to accept all knowledge and then to understand it!

I truly believe this to be the final "missing link" and I believe that God, through His own words, will reveal the exact truth of the above to someone quite shortly.

God told us that at the end of this age, knowledge would increase. Has there ever been a time on earth when there were as many scientists, physicists, nuclear physicists, engineers, etc? I don't believe so! Also, is not knowledge of almost everything on earth available to everyone at the simple click of a mouse on a computer?

May the grace of our Lord Jesus Christ be with you all. Amen.

Come Lord Jesus.

End of the World?

Why should we be concerned with this question? Apart from the obvious, let me cast your minds back to an earlier warning. Jesus told us this.

Luke 12:16 to 20 *And he spake a parable unto them, saying, The ground of a certain rich man brought forth plentifully:*

17 And he thought within himself, saying, What shall I do, because I have no room where to bestow my fruits?

18 And he said, This will I do: I will pull down my barns, and build greater; and there will I bestow all my fruits and my goods.

19 And I will say to my soul, Soul, thou hast much goods laid up for many years; take thine ease, eat, drink, [and] be merry.

20 But God said unto him, [Thou] fool, this night thy soul shall be required of thee: then whose shall those things be, which thou hast provided?

None of us know when our soul will be required of us, but we all know that it will be. None of us know when the end of this world will be, but we all need to have in place the greatest insurance policy just in case. This is what Peter taught us about the end of this age.

2nd Peter 3:10/11 *But the day of the Lord will come as a thief in the night; in the which the heavens shall pass away with a great noise, and the elements shall melt with fervent heat, the earth also and the works that are therein shall be burned up.*

*11 Seeing then that all these things shall be dissolved, **what manner of persons ought ye to be** in all holy conversation and godliness,*

Peter asks very simply, when the earth and everything in it is burned up, "what manner of persons ought ye to be"? The answer to this question is given by the Apostle Paul to Christian believers in the church at Thessalonika.

1st Thessalonians 1:5 *For our **gospel** came not unto you in **word** only, but also in **power**, and in the **Holy Ghost**, and in **much assurance; as ye know what manner of men we were among you** for your sake.*

Very simply, make certain that you are a believer in Jesus Christ. Make certain that you are a Christian. Gospel means very simply "good news". The Good news doesn't come any better when the earth is burning up than having in place the greatest insurance policy ever known. To obtain this insurance policy requires no great expense. It requires no money at all. The greatest insurance policy ever written was written in blood, the blood of our Lord and Savior Jesus Christ. Jesus paid with His life so that you could live. If you are a non-Christian and you have reached this far in the book, again I pray that you have or will be convinced of its truthfulness. Again, remember this because not only is it "good news", it is also the **TRUTH.** Romans 1:16 *For I am not ashamed of the gospel of Christ: for it is the power of God unto salvation to every one that believeth; to the Jew first, and also to the Greek.*

The gospel (good news) of Christ is **THE POWER** of God unto salvation to every one that believeth. What you have read up to this point confirms the power of God. This earth and everything in it was created by Almighty God. The gospel of Jesus Christ contains that self-same power. It is a supernatural power that guarantees to give you everlasting life if you believe the truth that you have just read. All you have to do is to accept the "good news" and believe in Jesus Christ as your Lord and Savior.

God never shared with me when the end of this world would be, but He did tell me what signs to look for. God told me that very clear signs would be given to humankind to signal the advent of the end of this age. Let me share with you now what these signs will be and hopefully assist you to condition yourself to be able to spot them.

We are coming to the end of this world as we know it. Before this happens, evil will manifest itself more and more. There might appear to be bad things happening right now, but they will get infinitely worse in ways that we cannot even yet imagine.

In exactly the same way as God gave us signs, Jesus also gave us warnings of signs to look out for. I would now like to discuss these warnings in more detail. Hopefully, this will help you to adjust your "focus" and therefore be able to "see" more clearly.

The warnings that Jesus shared with us concern the signs that will tell us of the end of the world. It doesn't get any more important than this, the second coming of Jesus, and the end of the world!

Matthew 24:3 to 35   *And as he sat upon the mount of Olives, the disciples came unto him privately, saying, Tell us, when shall these things be? and what [shall be] the sign of thy coming, and of the end of the world?*
4 And Jesus answered and said unto them, Take heed that no man deceive you.
5 For many shall come in my name, saying, I am Christ; and shall deceive many.
6 And ye shall hear of wars and rumours of wars: see that ye be not troubled: for all [these things] must come to pass, but the end is not yet.

7 For nation shall rise against nation, and kingdom against kingdom: and there shall be **famines, and pestilences, and earthquakes, in divers places.**
8 All these [are] the beginning of sorrows.
9 Then shall they deliver you up to be afflicted, and shall kill you: and ye shall be hated of all nations for my name's sake.
10 And then shall many be offended, and shall betray one another, and shall hate one another.
11 And many false prophets shall rise, and shall deceive many.
12 And because **iniquity shall abound, the love of many shall wax cold.**
13 But he that shall endure unto the end, the same shall be saved.
14 And this **gospel of the kingdom shall be preached in all the world for a witness unto all nations; and then shall the end come.**
15 When ye therefore shall see the abomination of desolation, spoken of by Daniel the prophet, stand in the holy place, (whoso readeth, let him understand:)
16 Then let them which be in Judaea flee into the mountains:
17 Let him which is on the housetop not come down to take any thing out of his house:
18 Neither let him which is in the field return back to take his clothes.
19 And woe unto them that are with child, and to them that give suck in those days!
20 But pray ye that your flight be not in the winter, neither on the sabbath day:
21 For then shall be great tribulation, such as was not since the beginning of the world to this time, no, nor ever shall be.

*22 And except those **days should be shortened**, there should no flesh be saved: but for the elect's sake **those days shall be shortened**.*

23 Then if any man shall say unto you, Lo, here [is] Christ, or there; believe [it] not.

24 For there shall arise false Christs, and false prophets, and shall shew great signs and wonders; insomuch that, if [it were] possible, they shall deceive the very elect.

25 Behold, I have told you before.

26 Wherefore if they shall say unto you, Behold, he is in the desert; go not forth: behold, [he is] in the secret chambers; believe [it] not.

27 For as the lightning cometh out of the east, and shineth even unto the west; so shall also the coming of the Son of man be.

28 For wheresoever the carcase is, there will the eagles be gathered together.

29 Immediately after the tribulation of those days shall the sun be darkened, and the moon shall not give her light, and the stars shall fall from heaven, and the powers of the heavens shall be shaken:

30 And then shall appear the sign of the Son of man in heaven: and then shall all the tribes of the earth mourn, and they shall see the Son of man coming in the clouds of heaven with power and great glory.

31 And he shall send his angels with a great sound of a trumpet, and they shall gather together his elect from the four winds, from one end of heaven to the other.

32 Now learn a parable of the fig tree; When his branch is yet tender, and putteth forth leaves, ye know that summer [is] nigh:

33 So likewise ye, when ye shall see all these things, know that it is near, [even] at the doors.

34 Verily I say unto you, This generation shall not pass, till all these things be fulfilled.

35 Heaven and earth shall pass away, but my words shall not pass away.

First of all, I find it interesting that Jesus tells us that the "days shall be shortened." Exactly the same thing is confirmed to us by Mark:

Mark 13:20 *And except that the Lord had SHORTENED those days, no flesh should be saved: but for the elect's sake, whom he hath chosen, he hath SHORTENED the days.*

We now know that the earthquake in Sumatra shortened our day by 6.8 microseconds. We also know that the Chilean earthquake shortened our day by a further 1.26 microseconds. Additionally, the Japanese earthquake of 2011, shortened our day by a further 1.8 microseconds. I think any fair minded person would say, "Well, so what?" A few microseconds are not going to be noticed by anyone other than the scientists who study these things, but let me present you with this thought. Every day I hear people say, "I just don't have the time," or "years ago I had much more time than I do now." In addition, people say to me, "Last year just flew by, I don't know where it went, it went so fast." To every human, other than the time-focused scientists, our clocks and watches all still appear to move at the same rate. We appear to still have sixty-seconds in every minute and sixty minutes in every hour. We still have twenty-four hours in every day and seven days in every week, so why is everyone saying they have less time? Today, we have every modern "time saving" device and yet everybody complains of too little time. I cannot explain this phenomenon and God did not give me the answer. What I can say is that I am not an educated man, but I am also not a stupid one. My watch might still show sixty minutes before the passing of one hour, but my days are shorter and from the comments of everyone else, theirs are too!

Also, there seems to be a requirement for instant gratification. No longer are people patient. I find it interesting that change has even taken place at the very highest levels in the financial world. Years ago, venture capitalists would invest in "start up" businesses with a long term, programmed view of things. That changed and over the last couple of decades, finance would only be invested if over the medium term, the business would guarantee a return. Regrettably, today in Western advanced economies, venture capitalists will only invest if the return is immediate. This is causing seriously big problems because good, solid businesses cannot get access to capital to invest and grow. Personally, I don't just see this as an economic problem, I see it as a spiritual one.

I could mention famine, pestilence and earthquakes in "diverse places", but I'm not going to. Today, we have greater communication than ever before and so you all know from either the Internet or TV which areas of the world are being affected by these things. You will glean from your own understanding whether these are more frequent and greater or not. I want to get your minds thinking on a broader scale.

Jesus tells us that *iniquity shall abound, the love of many shall wax cold.* In other words, there will be more lawlessness and wickedness, and the effect of this will be to harden people's hearts. Is this something that you see on a daily basis in your lives? Do you witness more love and respect between peoples toward one another? Do you witness a lack of respect and more of "every man for himself" types of attitude?

Jesus tells us that *this gospel of the kingdom shall be preached in all the world for a witness unto all nations; and then shall the end come.* Due to advances in all forms of communication, there are now very few countries left on earth that have still to hear the gospel preached.

Jesus tells us *there shall arise false Christs, and false prophets, and shall shew great signs and wonders; insomuch that, if [it were] possible, they shall deceive the very elect.* Try not to think of this just in religious terms. Prophets are God's mouthpieces on earth. They are God's messengers to humankind. False prophets are people who pretend that they are godlike because they claim they can perform godlike miracles. Examples of this might be financiers who promise huge returns on investments only to then flee with huge amounts of your money! These people are so believable that they even "deceive the very elect!" They may also be very small time, low level thieves.

Again, let me ask you a question; do you witness in your daily lives more and more people trying to trick you out of your money? It doesn't have to be direct. It can be indirect. Companies or individuals offering to do things for free, only to find that once you have allowed them access to your home or car, they suddenly find problems that cost ten times more to fix than would be charged by anyone else! Do you witness tremendous "sign up" offers being made only to find after a few months that your direct debit has increased (without notification) by 50%? I could go on and on, but hopefully I don't need to. The simple question is, do you witness these things more now than at any other time in your life?

In addition, Jesus is referring to false preachers. On this I will say nothing, I don't believe it's necessary to even comment. Judgements can be made on this simply by watching TV, listening to radio or surfing the internet, and of course, going to church!

One final thing; Jesus's Father, God Himself, gave us very simple rules to live by. One of these rules was, "Don't commit adultery." If humankind had obeyed this simple rule, there would be no sexually transmitted diseases on earth! Don't just think of AIDS, Syphilis or Gonorrhea, think also of Hepatitis, Herpes, Chlamydia and countless numbers of others. If humankind had obeyed this one simple law, the healthcare cost savings alone could virtually wipe out most developed nations national debt! This is without even considering the cost of divorce. Not just in financial terms, but social also. The cost of rehousing one partner or both and very often at the governments expense. The cost of providing for children from broken homes due to complete financial abandonment by absent fathers. The cost of treating depression due to break up. The list goes on and on, but hopefully you will see the simplicity. If we had only obeyed the word of God, society would be infinitely better off in every way.

Besides Jesus, the Apostle Paul also gave us clear warning. This is what Paul said about the coming of the end of the world.

2nd Timothy 3:1 to 15   This know also, that in the last days perilous times shall come.

*2 For **men shall be lovers of their own selves**, **covetous**, boasters, proud, blasphemers, **disobedient to parents**, **unthankful**, unholy,*

*3 Without **natural affection**, **trucebreakers**, **false accusers**, **incontinent**, **fierce**, **despisers of those that are good**,*

*4 **Traitors**, heady, highminded, lovers of pleasures more than lovers of God;*

5 Having a form of godliness, but denying the power thereof: from such turn away.

6 For of this sort are they which creep into houses, and lead captive silly women laden with sins, led away with divers lusts,

7 Ever learning, and never able to come to the knowledge of the truth.

8 Now as Jannes and Jambres withstood Moses, so do these also resist the truth: men of corrupt minds, reprobate concerning the faith.

9 But they shall proceed no further: for their folly shall be manifest unto all [men], as theirs also was.

10 But thou hast fully known my doctrine, manner of life, purpose, faith, longsuffering, charity, patience,

11 Persecutions, afflictions, which came unto me at Antioch, at Iconium, at Lystra; what persecutions I endured: but out of [them] all the Lord delivered me.

12 Yea, and all that will live godly in Christ Jesus shall suffer persecution.

13 But evil men and seducers shall wax worse and worse, deceiving, and being deceived.

14 But continue thou in the things which thou hast learned and hast been assured of, knowing of whom thou hast learned [them];

15 And that from a child thou hast known the holy scriptures, which are able to make thee wise unto salvation through faith which is in Christ Jesus.

Hard to know where to start on this one! Let's try the beginning! Paul tells us that **men shall be lovers of their own selves**. In other words, "self" will be priority number one and humankind will become very "selfish." Individuals will be concerned only with themselves and not with anyone else! Is this something that you witness more in your daily lives?

Paul tells us that humankind will become **covetous**, the definition of which is "excessively desirous of the possessions of another, an extreme desire to acquire or possess." Is this something that you see more of? Do you witness humankind being prepared to do almost anything to get "stuff?" Do you witness humankind always wanting it "now" and wanting instant "gratification?" Do you witness these people being prepared to tell lies with abandon to get what they want?

Do you increasingly witness that honesty appears to almost get punished whereas criminality appears to get rewarded? Do you increasingly witness that vulnerable honest people are being exploited?

Paul tells us that children shall be more *disobedient to parents*. Do you think that children are as obedient to parents today as they were fifty years ago? Or do you witness children of today being even more disobedient than ever before?

Paul tells us that people will become *unthankful*. When shopping, do you hear more courteous "thank you's," or less? Do you witness children receiving presents and then having to be told to say "thank you," and the "thank you" that follows seems almost forced? Basically, do you witness less politeness today or more?

Paul tells us that people will lack *natural affection*. What Paul means by this, is that people will become more hard hearted and less loving toward other people. Do you see people less caring and more hard hearted? Or do you see them more loving and more caring?

Paul tells us that there will be more *trucebreakers*. Paul is referring here to people who break their word, people who promise you one thing, but do another.

An obvious comparison to look at would be of people in authority. Do you see politicians and leaders keeping their promises? Or do you see them promising anything and everything to get into the position, but then shamelessly ignoring completely their original promises to you?

Paul tells us that there will be more *false accusers*. He is referring to people who accuse others falsely. Do you see people wanting to take responsibility for their own actions? Or, do you see increasingly people doing everything they can to falsely accuse others and to lay the blame elsewhere?

Paul tells us that more and more people will become *incontinent*. No, Paul is not referring to restroom behavior! He is warning us to look out for less self-control in people. Do you see more people exercising normal behavior? Or do you see more people unable to control themselves either through drink, drugs or mental illness? Paul tells us that people will become more *fierce*. Do you witness people being more passive today? Or do you witness more aggressive behavior?

Paul tells us that more people will be ***despisers of those that are good.*** If you are a good person, do you see more and more people like yourself? Or do you feel that you are among the minority?

Paul tells us that there will be more ***Traitors***. In other words, people without any loyalty. People who will sell their own families to get what they want. Do you see more loyalty today and more steadfastness? Or do you increasingly see people prepared to tread upon anyone to get themselves higher?

Paul tells us that more and more people will ***Have a form of godliness, but deny the power.*** Paul is referring to people in positions of authority who pretend to be very honest and upright Christian people, but who in secret are worse than the worst of criminality. Do you still have faith in your leaders? Do you still respect and believe that they are honest and not self-seeking? Or do you witness time and time again that these leaders are being exposed as liars, cheats, fraudsters, serial adulterers having the sole aim of getting what they can out of their privileged position before being caught?

In addition, what were we told to expect concerning antichrist spirits?

1st John 2:18 *Little children, it is the last time: and as ye have heard that antichrist shall come, even now are there many antichrists; whereby we know that it is the last time.*

John is telling us that in the last days many antichrists will come. Antichrist is simply anyone who is "anti" Christ, or anyone who is against Christ. We know about the righteousness of Christ, we know that Christ is righteous, we know that Christ is right. Anyone who is against good and that which is right, is antichrist!

Consider today, how many people do you read about who have committed crimes and not only do they not get punished, but they get rewarded! Almost daily, I read of people behaving in the most terrible way and sometimes getting punished by law, but sometimes not. Then they employ a publicist and suddenly they become a "celebrity" and are rewarded by the media and the public! Do you not see more and more of this type of thing happening? Do you not see antichrist spirits being manifested more and more?

You have read about the importance our Lord Jesus places upon little children.

Matthew 19:14 *But Jesus said, Suffer little children, and forbid them not, to come unto me: for of such is the kingdom of heaven.*

The most important church ministry is that of children's Sunday school. Yet, very often pastors, vicars, priests etc allow almost anyone to administer it. Jesus warns us here of the vital importance of these little souls. "Forbid them not to come unto me, for of such is the kingdom of heaven". Notice that the words of our Lord, "of such", means that Jesus see's not what those children are, but what they have the potential to become **IF**, (I offer no excuse for emphasizing the **IF**) we adults raise them up in the ways of our dear Lord. We would live in Heaven on earth, **IF** all children had been raised in the ways of our Lord Jesus.

Consider also now the enormous increase in pedophilia. I think it fair to say that every human involved in this type of activity has an antichrist spirit. They are anti, or against everything that Lord Jesus teaches. Again, I'll leave you to decide. Do you see more of this type of thing, or do you see less?

This chapter has not been written as an in-depth, theological exposition. It has been written solely to help you to set your mind and to help you "focus".

Hopefully, having now helped to prepare your mind and adjust your eyesight, let me continue.
In this chapter, I'm not looking to convince you of anything, I merely want to open your eyes. If my words help you to see more clearly, then your own intellect will do the rest. Your "free will" given to you by God can now be brought into action. You can choose to acknowledge and accept the truth, or you can choose to deny it; that choice is yours! Old Moses, way back in the book of Deuteronomy, offered the nation of Israel a choice. In chapter 28, Moses made known to the people all the blessings of God and all the curses. In chapter 30, verse 19, he implored them to choose life and live.
Deuteronomy 30:19 *I call heaven and earth to record this day against you, that I have set before you life and death, blessing and cursing: therefore choose life, that both thou and thy seed may live*

My intent has been to simply tell the **PURE TRUTH** from God's own words. My priority is to do this so that souls may be saved. However badly you might have lived your life up to this moment; it's never too late to be saved. People very often say, "I can understand what you are saying and I believe it; let me just take some more time and

then I will make a decision." I don't have any problem
with this because I was exactly the same. The only danger
with this is as we read before; none of us know if we will
have "some more time." This is what Jesus said:

Luke 12:16 to 20 *And he spake a parable unto them,
saying, The ground of a certain rich man brought forth
plentifully:*

*17 And he thought within himself, saying, What shall I do,
because I have no room where to bestow my fruits?*

*18 And he said, This will I do: I will pull down my barns,
and build greater; and there will I bestow all my fruits and
my goods.*

*19 And I will say to my soul, Soul, thou hast much goods
laid up for many years; take thine ease, eat, drink, [and] be
merry.*

*20 But God said unto him, [Thou] fool, this night thy soul
shall be required of thee: then whose shall those things be,
which thou hast provided?*

"Thou fool, this night (NOT TOMORROW NIGHT but
THIS NIGHT!) thy soul shall be required of thee"!
Please, don't take the same gamble. None of us know
when our final hour is at hand.

Don't dismiss the Holy Bible, not at least until you have
read it! Which intelligent person with a problem would not
want to get all the facts about that problem before taking a
decision on how to solve it? Which person would not want
to speak to others who were more qualified than themselves
to first get their opinions? Which person would not want to
first do all the analysis before taking any decision?
Surprisingly, when it comes to the most important decision
in their lives, the one concerning everlasting life or death,
most people are ignorant. They choose without any
rational thought to ignore God. Without questioning,
debating or reading, they make a decision. Has no one ever

277

questioned in their own minds why they behave in this unique way?

It isn't a complicated thing. I always keep things very simple. No one ever made Christianity this simple to me. Men complicated Christianity to the point where I never even wanted to understand it. I pray that by God's grace and through His words, this book brings it back to where it should be; a simple Truth!

We are all seekers after the Truth, what you have read is the Truth, the **PURE TRUTH** from **GOD.**

This is what Jesus said.

John 17:17 *Sanctify them through thy truth:* ***thy word is truth****.*

If you believe what you have just read and you are not a Christian, then please don't do as I did years ago and gamble.

IF you now truly in your heart believe that Jesus is the Son of God, and you want to choose life and live, then pray this simple prayer.

"Heavenly Father, thank you Lord for bringing me a sinner to repentance, as I turn away from my old ways and face You, forgive me Lord please of all of my sins. Lord Jesus I believe you are the Son of God, born of a Virgin and that You took upon yourself all of my sins and that You were crucified upon a cross and died so that I might live. Lord Jesus, I believe that you arose again on the third day and that you now sit at the right hand of God. Jesus thank you for dying for me, thank you Lord for taking my place. Lord Jesus please come into my life and

into my heart right now and be my Lord and
Savior, give me eternal life and make me a child
of God.
Amen".

My Personal Prayer

The final words from God to me concerning the **PURE TRUTH** herein contained were:
"In exactly the same way as Jesus was betrayed by His own people, the Jews; so also must you know that it will be 'Christian" people, not non-believers, who will do everything possible to destroy that which I gave to you."
Regrettably, God is never wrong.

The Apostles spent more than three years in the presence of Jesus. They witnessed complete healing of every sickness including the dead being raised back to life. In their presence, Jesus cast out demons and performed countless numbers of miracles. By miraculous means, Jesus provided for their every need, including food, clothing, finances, etc. The Apostles even saw Jesus command and alter the forces of nature and they saw Him walk on water. They were more than three years under the greatest Bible teacher of all time. The Apostles told the world that Jesus was the Messiah because they believed it in their hearts.
Why then did they all desert Jesus in His greatest hour of need?
Why did they fail their Lord and Savior?
Why did they all scatter defeated, disbelieving and in total despair at His capture?
The answer to all of these questions is very simple. They scattered because they ALL chose to **Ignore Biblical Prophesy**.
For more than three years, Jesus personally taught them repeatedly about all the prophesies concerning His death and resurrection. They chose to **IGNORE** them all! I pray

that Christians do not make the same mistake again. This is what Jesus said.

Luke 24:25 *Then he said unto them, O fools, and slow of heart to believe all that the prophets have spoken:*

I pray that this book is read in every church in the world. My prayer is that this book will bring Christianity back into the classrooms in every school in the world. I pray that it will be taken into schools and used to teach children the truth of creation. The truth that God created this earth and everything in it. I pray and ask these things in the name and blood of Jesus Christ, my Lord and Savior, and I believe I receive, because I ask in the name and blood of Jesus Christ, my Lord and Savior. Amen.

Even if people choose not to believe that which is written, I hope that as a minimum it will stimulate Christians worldwide to search the scriptures.

As I have maintained throughout my life, if you want to see the future then look to the past. Solomon said that there is nothing new under the sun. God gave us every answer to every question in His words, in both the Old Testament and the New Testament. All we have to do is to read, believe and understand them.

As mentioned earlier, never did I want to be a Christian, but for me the "rubber hit the road" in 1987. I had no one to turn to, so I cried out to God. God answered and from that moment a truly miraculous sequence of events took place. Despite reading my Bible on a very regular basis from 1987 to 2004, I understood very little. I knew numerous things about the Bible, but I understood very little. If you are in the same position, these final words are for you.

From 1987 till 2003, I knew God, but I did not know Jesus. In 2003, I invited Jesus to be my Lord and Savior because I "believed" with all my heart that He is the Messiah.

I couldn't fight anymore. I offered myself as a living sacrifice. Every fabric of my being I offered to God to do with as He wished. From that very moment, a change took place. The Holy Spirit, the Spirit of Truth, came to dwell with me.

I didn't know anything about church because I had never been there. I had absolutely no idea how to pray, my genuine belief was all I needed.

God gave me everything I needed; he had to because I understood nothing. I say these things because I want to leave you with the prayer that God gave me to say. I don't pray this prayer today because God has given me others, but I will be forever grateful to God that I kept it. As I looked back upon these words, I was astounded. Every word that I needed to pray back in 2003, God gave to me, and maybe you might benefit from praying these same words today.

"Knowing every word in the bible is totally useless unless you understand them." I would like to give you the prayers that God gave to me; believe and receive. Years ago, when I first prayed these prayers, I had absolutely no idea why I was praying them. After a personal visitation from the Holy Spirit in 2005, I knew exactly why.

"My Father and my God who art in heaven, hallowed be thy name. Thy Kingdom come, thy will be done, on earth as it is in heaven. Heavenly Father, good morning and what a very good morning it is too. Lord, I am so grateful to be in Your presence this morning, able to see and hear and touch and smell and taste every single thing that You Lord have created. Heavenly Father, I cannot express enough my love for you and for every single thing that You have done for me, I am so very, very grateful. Heavenly Father, Lord this morning I come to you in the name and the blood of my Lord and Savior Jesus Christ in asking you to please have the Holy Spirit dwell within me, Father I pray that you will simply use me as a vessel on this earth in which the Holy Spirit may reside in order that Your will and purpose for me be fulfilled. Lord, I pray that You will have the Holy Spirit control every single cell in my body, Lord, I pray that the Holy Spirit will control my eyes, my ears, my smell, my touch, my taste, my fingers, my toes, my hand, my arms, my legs, every single cell in my body, but most importantly Heavenly Father, I pray that the Holy Spirit will control my tongue. Lord let every word that comes out of my mouth be of You, for the spreading of the Gospel according to my Lord and Savior Jesus Christ, to the fulfillment of Your will and purpose for me on this earth, and to the magnification of Your glorious, Holy and Almighty name, and Father also I pray that you will please give me the gift of wisdom. Lord, wisdom not only to be able to discern all knowledge, but Father wisdom to be able to apply that discerned knowledge in the very best, most effective way possible in order that I may spread the Gospel according to my Lord and Savior Jesus Christ, to the fulfillment of Your will and purpose for me on this earth and to magnify Your glorious, Holy and Almighty name. Lord, also I pray with all of my heart that you will indelibly imprint upon my memory every single word of yours that comes to me from whatever source. Lord, indelibly imprint those words upon my memory and then through the power of the Holy Spirit within me, allow me to reproduce those words at will, for the spreading of the Gospel according to my Lord and Savior Jesus Christ, to the fulfillment of Your will and purpose for me on this earth and to the magnification of Your glorious, Holy and Almighty name. Lord, also I pray that you will continue to teach me, continue to guide me and to help me to walk in the path of righteousness as laid down by my Lord and Savior Jesus Christ. Heavenly Father, your teaching, next to You, is THE most important thing in my life, the thing I value most highly and long may it continue, and continue apace.

Father please continue to teach me to be humble, teach me patience, tolerance and understanding. Teach me never to prejudge, but always to be aware of all of the facts before taking any decisions and most importantly of all, teach me never to be angry, but always to immediately forgive those who trespass against me, just as You Lord forgive me when I trespass. Lord know from my heart how very grateful I am for every single thing that You have ever done or continue to do for me, Father I am so very, very grateful."

I would then continue with thanks to the Lord for any answered prayer and to make specific requests.

"Father I want to thank You for",,,,,,,,,,,(then list whatever or whoever you want and ask the Lord whatever you want, whether it be a blessing for someone, healing, etc, and always try to be specific with names, places etc).
Always end your prayers with, "Father I pray and ask all of these things in the name and the blood of my Lord and Savior Jesus Christ, and I believe I receive because I ask in the name and blood of my Lord and Savior Jesus Christ. Lord once more, a million thank you's in Jesus Mighty name, Amen."

One of the main things that Satan uses to stop people coming to Jesus is honesty. This might sound like a ridiculous thing to say, but in my own personal experience it was true. I believed in God, I read my bible and I communicated with God, but I didn't need "church" and those "churchy" people. I thought they were all hypocrites, but there was something else, I was basically an honest person. No way could I become a "Christian" and then be like the rest. Say one thing on Sunday and behave totally differently all week. It sounded to me to be a very honorable and honest thing to do and Satan loved it!

Satan also used my honesty in another way, he told me that if I became a "Christian" I would have to stop doing certain things that I enjoyed. These things were "not that bad" and I did enjoy them, but I knew that if I was not to become hypocritical like all the rest, I would have to change, and basically, I didn't want to.

Satan then used another tactic. I started to think about coming to Jesus Christ and giving these things up, but Satan said "supposing you do that and then find it's all rubbish anyway"? "You will have left your old life and friends that you really enjoyed, and find that it was all for nothing". You see, my friends were not Christians, they thought Christianity was at best totally boring and at worst, self righteous people behaving in a hypocritical way. If I became a Christian, I was scared that I would lose my old friends as well as my old lifestyle. Satan had me in the perfect place, comfortable in my own private little world and the gospel according to me! It suited me perfectly and Satan knew it! Satan loves to sow the seeds of doubt, and that's all these things were and nothing else.

The reality is that Jesus Christ is alive and well. To believe on Him is a very small gamble to take, but the truth is it's no gamble at all. The wonders that await you are eternal and greater than you can ever imagine. Please don't risk EVERYTHING by listening to Satan. The only way to the Father, is through the Son. Accept Jesus Christ as your Lord and Savior.

If this was my experience, then I'm sure others who are reading this now are feeling the same. It is with this in mind that I want to share with you more **PURE TRUTH** from the Word of God.

It comes from the writings of Peter. Of all the disciples and apostles, Peter was the most coarse, the most outspoken, the roughest and first to want to fight, but his heart was more than that of a Lion, it was True! Time and time again Peter failed Jesus. Always Peter was doing or saying something wrong, but never ever with malice aforethought, only ever out of a pure heart. Jesus knew this, and that's why we have Christianity today.

1st Peter 4:1 to 19 *Forasmuch then as Christ hath suffered for us in the flesh, arm yourselves likewise with the same mind: for he that hath suffered in the flesh hath ceased from sin;*

2 That he no longer should live the rest of [his] time in the flesh to the lusts of men, but to the will of God.

3 For the time past of [our] life may suffice us to have wrought the will of the Gentiles, when we walked in lasciviousness, lusts, excess of wine, revellings, banquetings, and abominable idolatries:

4 Wherein they think it strange that ye run not with [them] to the same excess of riot, speaking evil of [you]:

5 Who shall give account to him that is ready to judge the quick and the dead.

6 For for this cause was the gospel preached also to them that are dead, that they might be judged according to men in the flesh, but live according to God in the spirit.

7 But the end of all things is at hand: be ye therefore sober, and watch unto prayer.

8 And above all things have fervent charity among yourselves: for charity shall cover the multitude of sins.

9 Use hospitality one to another without grudging.

10 As every man hath received the gift, [even so] minister the same one to another, as good stewards of the manifold grace of God.

11 If any man speak, [let him speak] as the oracles of God; if any man minister, [let him do it] as of the ability which God giveth: that God in all things may be glorified through Jesus Christ, to whom be praise and dominion for ever and ever. Amen.

12 Beloved, think it not strange concerning the fiery trial which is to try you, as though some strange thing happened unto you:

13 But rejoice, inasmuch as ye are partakers of Christ's sufferings; that, when his glory shall be revealed, ye may be glad also with exceeding joy.

14 If ye be reproached for the name of Christ, happy [are ye]; for the spirit of glory and of God resteth upon you: on their part he is evil spoken of, but on your part he is glorified.

15 But let none of you suffer as a murderer, or [as] a thief, or [as] an evildoer, or as a busybody in other men's matters.

16 Yet if [any man suffer] as a Christian, let him not be ashamed; but let him glorify God on this behalf.

17 For the time [is come] that judgment must begin at the house of God: and if [it] first [begin] at us, what shall the end [be] of them that obey not the gospel of God?

18 And if the righteous scarcely be saved, where shall the ungodly and the sinner appear?

19 Wherefore let them that suffer according to the will of God commit the keeping of their souls [to him] in well doing, as unto a faithful Creator.

To translate into simple language, Peter is saying don't expect to become a Christian and for it to be like a walk in the park! Christ suffered physically more than any man, and He did it for you! You have spent enough of your past life living in sin, drinking, fornicating etc. Now is the time to leave that behind, but be aware that all of your old "friends" will find it very strange. More than strange, they will encourage you to continue in your old ways. The surprising thing is, when you explain to them about your Christianity, they will probably laugh at and abuse you. It will be very hard to take and Satan knows this. Don't try to battle this alone because you will never succeed. Pray to God and ask Him for help and He will give it to you. You will move through this "suffering" period, but whilst you are there rejoice in it because what you are "suffering" for

Christ is nothing compared to what He suffered for you. Your "suffering" will not be as for a murderer or criminal, it will be as a Christian and as someone who bears the name of Christ and is not ashamed. Commit your soul to God and to Jesus because They created you and They will keep you.

Your reward will come and it will encompass a freedom and peace and assurance like that which you could only dream of. Not just now in this life, but forever in eternity.

One person CAN make a difference

One person **CAN** make a difference. Very often Christians suffer self-condemnation because they never preached, evangelized, taught, etc, etc. They were simply never given an opportunity. If this is you, then please don't worry. What's important to God is the intent of our heart. God makes it very clear that not all will have an opportunity to "go behind the pulpit", but their rewards will still be great. Great credit will be given by God to those who merely sympathized with the actions of other Christians. How can we be sure of this? Let's read what God says:

Matthew 20:6/7 *And about the eleventh hour he went out, and found others standing idle, and saith unto them, Why stand ye here all the day idle?*

7 They say unto him, Because no man hath hired us. He saith unto them, Go ye also into the vineyard; and whatsoever is right, that shall ye receive.

Matthew 10:41/42 *He that receiveth a prophet in the name of a prophet shall receive a prophet's reward; and he that receiveth a righteous man in the name of a righteous man shall receive a righteous man's reward.*

42 And whosoever shall give to drink unto one of these little ones a cup of cold water only in the name of a disciple, verily I say unto you, he shall in no wise lose his reward.

Be under no illusion, God always uses "nobodies". In the days of our Lord, shepherds were "nobodies", they were considered to be unclean. Even the sheep were allowed into the Holy Temple, but the shepherds were not and nothing has changed. Shepherds were not even allowed to testify in court, yet they were chosen to testify to the coming of our Lord Jesus.

Luke 2:8 to 14 *And there were in the same country shepherds abiding in the field, keeping watch over their flock by night.*

9 And, lo, the angel of the Lord came upon them, and the glory of the Lord shone round about them: and they were sore afraid.

10 And the angel said unto them, Fear not: for, behold, I bring you good tidings of great joy, which shall be to all people.

11 For unto you is born this day in the city of David a Saviour, which is Christ the Lord.

12 And this shall be a sign unto you; Ye shall find the babe wrapped in swaddling clothes, lying in a manger.

13 And suddenly there was with the angel a multitude of the heavenly host praising God, and saying,

14 Glory to God in the highest, and on earth peace, good will toward men.

If you are truly serious about your Christianity, you will know that yours is the only voice Jesus Christ has on this earth. If you believe the word of God as it is written in this book, then please be the voice of our Dear Lord Jesus and proclaim this "good news". Please use every breath in your body to share this book with others, act now and make that difference. Your action now WILL help to put Christianity back into every school on this earth. Please telephone, tweet, blog, Facebook, email or speak personally to a friend and encourage them to read this book. We are born and progress towards death. When we are "Born again" we progress towards life, life eternal. If you love someone who is a non-Christian, gift them this book. If you are an individual and you know a lost soul or souls, gift them this book, it will save their lives. If you are a church, gift every member of the congregation this book so that they may in turn gift it to the lost so that they will be found.

I truly believe that this is the very last universal opportunity that God will give to humankind for it's salvation. God needs just one person like yourself to recommend His book, Pure Truth from God. If you do this, it will save countless numbers of lives and put Christianity back into the classrooms and nations of this earth. Please don't delay, don't hold back. Be that person and make the difference, in Jesus name I pray.

Tony Cooper.

www.puretruthministry.com

Tony Cooper
P.O. Box 1307
Roseville
CA 95678
U.S.A.

PURE TRUTH from GOD

References

Scripture verses all come from King James Bible Online Authorized Version www.kingjamesbibleonline.org

All scripture translations come from Strongs Exhaustive Concordance of the Bible together with dictionaries of the Hebrew and Greek words of the original, with references to the English words by James Strong S.T.D., L.L.D. Riverside Book and Bible House, IOWA FALLS, IOWA 50126.

"Foundation Truths" by Cuthbert Layland Parker www.clparker.com

"The Land of Eden Located" 1964 by David. J. Gibson
www.nabataea.net

"Quantum Physics" dailymail.co.uk/sciencetech/article-2225190
www.dailymail.co.uk

Randall Niles "All about the Journey" www.allaboutthejourney.org

"Nutcracker Man" dailymail.co.uk/sciencetech/article-1382932
www.dailymail.co.uk

"DNA Research" dailymail.co.uk/sciencetech/article-2510219
www.dailymail.co.uk

"Gluten sensitive and Lactose Intolerant Genes" dailymail.co.uk/
sciencetech/article-2221906 www.dailymail.co.uk

"Stains of Dairy Products" dailymail.co.uk/sciencetech/article-2162176
www.dailymail.co.uk

"SYNTHIA" dailymail.co.uk/sciencetech/article-1279988
www.dailymail.co.uk

"Mitochondrial EVE" livescience article 38613 www.livescience.com

"JANUS A Summing Up" Arthur Koestler Hutchinson & Co (publishers) Ltd, 3 Fitzroy Square, London W1P 6JD

"Bricks to Babel" Arthur Koestler Random House, New York.

Teachings given to myself by Dr Stephen Russell and the late Dr Rev Roy Harthern and his wife Pauline.

Special reference given to the late Bill Turner. The most Spirit-Filled, Experiential Christian I was privileged and blessed to have known and be taught by. www.thesecretofeternallife.com

Made in the USA
San Bernardino, CA
20 August 2014